WONDER WORKER'S
COMPLETE
BOOK OF
CLEANING

BARTY PHILLIPS

WONDER WORKER'S
COMPLETE BOOK OF CLEANING

BARTY PHILLIPS

Illustrated by Pat Birrell of Le Mare Graphics

SIDGWICK & JACKSON
LONDON

First published in Great Britain by
Sidgwick and Jackson Limited in 1980

Copyright © 1980 by Barty Phillips

ISBN 0 283 98546 1

Phototypeset in 'Monophoto' Plantin by
Servis Filmsetting Limited, Manchester
Printed in Great Britain by
The Garden City Press Limited
of Letchworth, Hertfordshire
for Sidgwick and Jackson Limited
1 Tavistock Chambers, Bloomsbury Way
London WC1A 2SG

Contents

Introduction

Until a couple of generations ago household cleaning was hard work but uncomplicated.

Mothers taught their daughters how to wash with soap and much hard rubbing, how to remove stains with lemon juice, how to leave clothes out in the sunlight to bleach. Metals were rubbed clean with abrasive powders and there was no confusing care-labelling system.

Since then new chemical processes, new manufacturing processes, new fibres and new techniques have made cleaning a complicated skill. But the skill, as so often nowadays, is not so much in the actual cleaning techniques as in knowing where to find the information and how to use it.

I have tried in this book to gather together every sort of information on every sort of cleaning likely to be carried out by people at home. I have tried to set it out so it can easily be referred to.

Though you can simply refer to this book each time you need some information, it would be useful to learn some of the information by heart – for instance, the care-labelling codes. People are too quick to dismiss these as too complicated, too simple, undecipherable, and so on. But if you study them you will discover they are quite simple and extremely helpful. Since they deal with fibres and wash programmes used all over the world they have to be in a more or less universal language and that's why they are most often found in symbol form with few words. (Though some countries do insist on words.)

In Chapter 1 I have laid out the care code in full. You can keep this book next to your washing-machine, or cut out the pages and keep them there, but what I really advise is that you learn them – as I only recently did. It makes washing much, much easier.

I hope this book will make life easier for lots of people. Now that furniture is less ornate and cleaning products better, especially since the discovery of synthetic detergents, keeping a house clean has become much less time and energy consuming. On the whole, cleaning techniques are few and simple. There are thousands of cleaning products on the market but most of them are just variations of a few basic types.

One thing I do feel strongly about is that manufacturers of cleaning products should state on the carton, package or can what the product is made of. Why should we believe the manufacturer's claim for a product if he won't tell us what it's made of? Often a brand name does not mean the product is better than its generic type – but it is likely to be more expensive.

With cleaning, as with mending, a wipe in time saves nine. Many modern cleaning products are excellent for keeping clean homes clean. If you live in a home that gets dirty easily – if you burn solid fuel or live in a dirty town or in the country where children, dogs and visitors bring in mud every time they come in through the door – then you can't expect to have such a spotless home as someone living single in a small flat above the ground floor with smooth surfaces and few visitors.

If you can find the time to wipe surfaces clean before they become grubby so much the better.

Once a wall does have finger and grease marks and scuff marks, you will need to use something more drastic.

At least we can be grateful that if we *do* have to spring-clean it doesn't have to be anything like the complete upheaval of Victorian times when heavy furniture had to be moved, curtains taken down and carpets beaten.

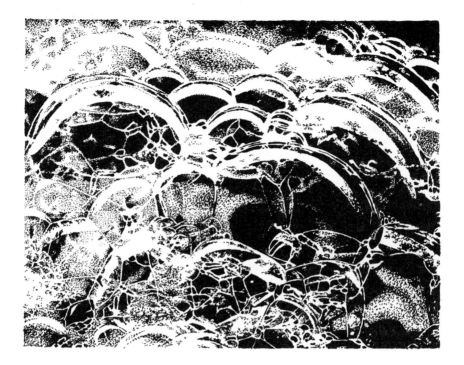

Chapter 1

A GOOD WASH

When I first got married we lived in Edinburgh for a few years and I discovered the Scottish phrase 'a good wash'. Unfortunately my wash was always the worst in the street. White clothes were grey and the babies' nappies greyer than grey. They were certainly 'clean' and didn't irritate the baby's skin but they did look awful hanging out on our little pocket-handkerchief garden.

I've since discovered that the greyness was partly caused by using too much detergent. Too much of the blue they put into it makes white things go grey. In fact, washing is not the simple process it used to be when a piece of soap and washboard and a lot of hard rubbing were what got things clean.

A lot of hard rubbing will wear away many modern fabrics. Some don't like heat, others don't like being spun. Some fabrics are made up of several different fibres, some of which like to be treated in one way and some in another.

The only way to be certain of getting a good wash nowadays is actually to read the labels on clothes, and the instructions on washing-machines and detergent packets and then follow them to the letter (or symbol). So first you have to understand the symbols. These symbols tell you what's washable in what way at what temperature; what can be spun or wrung or must be drip-dried; what may be ironed and what should be dry-cleaned and even sometimes in what sort of cleaning fluid.

To understand why all these instructions are necessary, consider what washing does to clothes.

HOW WASHING WORKS

To clean a garment, you have to remove the dirt from it. The dirt is particles lodged in the crevices of the fabric and on the hairs of fibres, or stuck to the fabric with grease. Sometimes it is a stain that has penetrated the surface of the fibres.

You can remove some dirt by shaking and brushing or rubbing. Shaking and rubbing work better if you put the garment in water because the water retains the dirt particles. Also, a lot of dirt dissolves in water.

Soap is a help in water because it breaks up grease and releases dirt held by greasy or oily deposits on fabric. Soap also enables water to penetrate crevices, and to take up smaller particles of dirt, because it reduces the water's surface tension – the natural resistance water has to having its surface layer of molecules disturbed.

The disadvantage of soap (whether in bars, flakes or powder) is that it reacts with minerals that are present in 'hard' tapwater to produce a scum that sticks to the clothes you are trying to clean. Soapless, or synthetic, detergents (powders or liquids) do not have this disadvantage.

Heating the water helps because the hotter water is the easier it is for dirt to dissolve in it. Unfortunately, many fabrics are harmed by heat, and many fabric dyes will dissolve in hot water and leave the cloth along with the dirt. The alternative to heating is just to give dirt more time to dissolve by leaving the garments to soak for some hours.

Some clothing fabrics are spoiled by immersion in water. Most of them can be 'washed' in a different fluid. This is misleadingly called - 'dry-cleaning'. It's not dry, it just doesn't use water.

One other way of dealing with dirt is to convert it chemically into a different substance that will easily dissolve in water. This is what a *bleach* does. Bleaches must be used with caution, otherwise they will convert both fabric and dirt.

CARE LABELS

Most garments, bedlinen and furnishing fabrics sold now have care labels, which tell you in detail how to clean them. Among objections that manufacturers had in the past to giving such instructions was lack of agreement on what terms like 'hot water' meant, and the difficulty of fitting instructions on to reasonably sized labels. These have been overcome by using an internationally agreed system of symbols. The following section gives the official explanation of the symbols as issued by the Home Laundering Consultative Council (H.L.C.C.).

THE INTERNATIONAL
CARE-LABELLING CODE

The code basically consists of these four symbols.

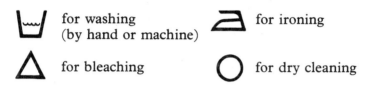

for washing   for ironing
(by hand or machine)

for bleaching   for dry cleaning

The symbols are always presented in the same sequence. In the U.K. they are mainly found arranged vertically; in other European countries they are more usually arranged horizontally.

Care labels may also include symbols recommending a particular drying method – see Drying, page 16.

See overleaf for list 'Summary of Washing Symbols'.

Summary of

Symbol	Washing Temperature Machine	Hand	Agitation	Rinse	Spin/ Wring
1 95	Very hot 95°C or boil	hand hot 50°C or boil	maximum	normal	normal
2 60	hot 60°C	hand hot 50°C	maximum	normal	normal
3 60	hot 60°C	hand hot 50°C	medium	cold	short spin or drip-dry
4 50	hand hot 50°C	hand hot 50°C	medium	cold	short spin or drip-dry
5 40	warm 40°C	warm 40°C	medium	normal	normal
6 40	warm 40°C	warm 40°C	minimum	cold	short spin
7 40	warm 40°C	warm 40°C	minimum do not rub	normal	normal spin do not hand wring
8 30	cool 30°C	cool 30°C	minimum	cold	short spin do not hand wring
9 95	very hot 95°C or boil	hand hot 50°C or boil	maximum	cold	drip-dry
	Do not machine wash				
	Do not wash				

Washing

100°C	Boil	Self-explanatory
95°C	Very hot	Water heated to near boiling temperature
60°C	Hot	Hotter than the hand can bear. The temperature of water coming from many domestic hot taps

Washing Symbols

Fabric	Benefits
White cotton and linen articles without special finishes	Ensures whiteness and stain removal
Cotton, linen or rayon articles without special finishes where colours are fast at 60°C	Maintains colour
White nylon; white polyester/cotton mixtures	Prolongs whiteness – minimizes creasing
Coloured nylon; polyester; cotton and rayon articles with special finishes; acrylic/cotton mixtures; coloured polyester/cotton mixtures	Safeguards colour and finish – minimizes creasing
Cotton, linen or rayon articles where colours are fast at 40°C, but not at 60°C	Safeguards the colour-fastness
Acrylics; acetate and triacetate, including mixtures with wool; polyester/wool blends	Preserves colour and shape – minimizes creasing
Wool, including blankets, and wool mixtures with cotton or rayon; silk	Keeps colour, size and handle
Silk and printed acetate fabrics with colours not fast at 40°C	Prevents colour loss
Cotton articles with special finishes capable of being boiled but requiring drip-drying	Prolongs whiteness, retains special crease-resistant finish

Temperatures

50°C	Hand hot	As hot as the hand can bear
40°C	Warm	Pleasantly warm to the hand
30°C	Cool	Feels cool to the touch

Washing

The number and the temperature shown in the tub symbol indicate a particular washing process.

Each washing process describes the best method of washing and rinsing a particular group of fabrics and recommends:

Maximum wash temperature.
The amount of agitation during the wash.
The method of water extraction.

Sorting and washing, using the numbered processes of the International Code, will give you the best results. Where a washing machine shows the wash tub symbols on the control panel, the complete process will have been provided for you, and all that is necessary is to match the number on the label to the machining programme. On other machines or when washing by hand, apply the label instructions to particular circumstances. To help, details of the processes are printed on all washing-powder packs.

When washing in launderettes, because of the simpler range of settings, it may be practical to combine loads and select the safest wash for all the articles in that load.

Warning: Any attempt to mix loads without selecting the mildest conditions may result in serious colour problems, loss of shape or shrinkage, and even permanent damage to the fabric.

Washing Processes

 1. This process is used for white cotton and linen articles without special finishes and provides the most vigorous washing condition. Wash temperature can be up to boiling (100°C), and agitation and spinning times are maximum. This ensures good whiteness and stain removal.

2. Process 2 is for cotton, linen or rayon articles without special finishes, where colours are fast at 60°C. It provides vigorous wash conditions but at a temperature which maintains fast colours.

3. Used for white nylon or white polyester/cotton mixtures, this process is less vigorous than either 1 or 2. The wash temperature (60°C) is high enough to prolong whiteness, and cold rinsing followed by short spinning minimizes creases.

4. This process is for coloured nylon; polyester; cotton and rayon articles with special finishes; acrylic/cotton mixtures; coloured polyester/cotton mixtures. In all respects except for washing temperature it is the same as Process 3. The lower temperature, hand hot (50°C), safeguards the colour and finish.

5. Suitable for cotton, linen or rayon articles where colours are fast at 40°C, but not at 60°C, this process has warm wash (40°C), medium agitation, normal spinning or wringing. The low wash temperature is essential to safeguard colour fastness.

6. This is for articles which require low-temperature washing (40°C), minimum agitation, a cold rinse and a short spin, e.g. acrylics; acetate and triacetate, including mixtures with wool; polyester/wool blends.

These conditions preserve colours and shape, and minimize creasing.

7. Similar to Process 6, this process is for wool, including blankets, and wool mixtures with cotton or rayon; silk which needs low-temperature washing (40°C) and minimum agitation but requires normal spinning. Washing in this way preserves colour, size and handle. These fabrics should not be subjected to hand wringing or rubbing.

8. Unlikely to appear on U.K.-produced goods, this is for silk and printed acetate fabrics, with colours which are not fast at 40°C, requiring to be washed at a very low temperature (30°C), with minimum agitation and spinning.

9. Again rarely to be found on U.K.-produced goods, this process is for cotton articles with special finishes which benefit from a high-temperature (95°C) wash but require drip-drying.

This symbol indicates those articles which must *not* be machine-washed.

Articles which must not be washed at all will bear this sign.

Bleaching

This symbol indicates that household (chlorine) bleach could be used. Care must be taken to follow the manufacturer's instructions.

When this symbol appears on a label, household bleach must *not* be used.

Ironing

The number of dots in the ironing symbol indicates the correct temperature setting – the fewer the dots, the cooler the iron setting.

Cool   Warm   Hot   Do not iron

Dry-cleaning

The letter in the circle refers to the solvent which may be used in the dry-cleaning process, and those using coin-operated dry-cleaning should check that the cleaning symbol shown on the label is the same as that in the instructions given on the front of the machine.

Ⓐ Goods normal for dry-cleaning in all solvents.

Ⓟ Goods normal for dry-cleaning in perchloroethylene, white spirit, Solvent 113 and Solvent 11.

  May be dry-cleaned professionally. Do not 'coin-op' clean.

Ⓕ Goods normal for dry-cleaning in white spirit or Solvent 113.

  Do not dry-clean.

Drying

Care labels may also include one or other of the following symbols recommending a particular drying method.

  Tumble-drying beneficial but not essential.

Line-dry.

  Drip-dry: for best results, hang while wet.

  Dry flat: do not hang to dry.

DRY-CLEAN ONLY LABELS

One of the most irritating things about the care-labelling system is when you're told 'Dry-clean only' when you can *see* the garment is washable cotton. In fact this is often because the lining or interlining is unsuitable for washing or because the embroidery, if there is any, will run or some other hidden but perfectly reasonable reason. Some fabrics, jersey for instance, stretch or go baggy with washing. So on the whole if the label says 'Dry-clean only' that is the wisest thing to do.

Some manufacturers, I suspect, do play over-safe and put dry-clean labels on perfectly washable garments. This is to safeguard themselves against people who shove everything into the hot wash and expect it to come out all right and make a fuss when garments are ruined. Unfortunately there are an awful lot of us who are careless like that, so I have some sympathy for manufacturers. If you cannot find any reason *not* to wash a dry-clean-only garment you can try very gently hand washing at low temperature using a mild detergent. Don't wash the belt, if there is one, and bear in mind that if washing doesn't work you have been warned.

WITHOUT A CARE LABEL

If you haven't got the manufacturer's recommendations about how to clean something then you have to work out what to do from a knowledge of what the article is made of. Since 12 January 1976, all textile products sold in the U.K. must, by law, be accompanied by a statement of fibre content.

(Fibres are short filaments that are spun together to make a long flexible filament called a yarn, which can be knitted or woven to make a cloth. With some materials, such as metal and some plastics, a yarn is formed directly from molten raw material, but the process of making the yarn is still called spinning, and such yarns are covered by the 'fibre' content regulations.)

Small items. such as watch straps, and second-hand goods do not have to have a fibre-content description. And, of course, clothes bought before 1976 may never have had one.

The A–Z of Fabrics and Fibres on pages 33–58 gives a brief description of the most common clothing materials and tells you how to clean them. Bear in mind that, whatever the material, the temperature at which you wash it depends on the colour-fastness of its dye, and that a special finish, e.g. to reduce flammability, may require special treatment.

GUIDE TO A GOOD WASH

Whether you have your own washing-machine or use a launderette, if you want your clothes to look their best you must deal with them carefully, thoroughly and correctly. Laundering, like almost anything else is a skill. You must understand the washing processes, whether washing by hand or by machine. At the end, your clothes should look like new: uncrumpled, clean and well stitched. Clothes can last twice as long and be twice as useful and satisfying to wear if you care for them correctly.

Preparing the clothes

Use any odd moment to prepare clothes for washing. Don't try to do it in a hurry. First you should mend, or at least tack together any tears or small holes in the fabric. Sew on loose buttons, or you will never see them again.

Empty all pockets. An old bus ticket can leave indelible coloured marks. I have more than once washed pound notes left in the pockets of a pair of jeans. They come out like blotting-paper. They are usually recognizable enough to be changed by a bank but it's not something I'd advise as a general rule. Used tissues in pockets make a terrible mess in a washing-machine and can block the drainage pipes. Old nails or toy cars can leave rust marks.

Brush off any loose dirt, especially mud. Close all zips, button up all buttons, hook up hooks and eyes and pop up snap fasteners. They may cause damage to other items (especially vests and tights) if you leave them open. Tie any loose ribbons, tapes or apron strings which will truss your whole wash up in knots otherwise. Tights should be put together in an old pillowcase tied at the top to prevent them being knotted together.

Sorting clothes

Sort all items into groups with the same wash code number (see pages 11–17 for details of the wash code and wash care labelling system). If any item is not labelled this way – and if you like old things and are a jumble-sale freak you may have a good many unlabelled items – but you know what the fibre is, you can refer to the table on your detergent packet or to my guide to fabrics and fibres. However, different garments using the same fibre may have different wash codes, depending on their colour-fastness and finish. So if you are in any doubt at all about which wash programme to use for coloured things, test first for colour-fastness, or wash alone or with similar coloured objects using a short gentle wash. Whites should always be washed separately.

Pre-wash treating for stains

Look over each garment carefully and treat for stains if necessary. There are various sprays on the market which will loosen many stains before washing. Spray the stuff on to the stain, leave for forty-five seconds or longer and then wash. This has worked well with several anonymous and faint stains on clothes of mine. Use it on collars and cuffs. These treatments contain a dry-cleaning solvent which is why they're so good for greasy stains. In my experience they have got rid of quite old stains and they are said to be able to deal with lipstick, sauce, wine, wax polishes, hair spray, medicines, egg, coffee, make-up, antiperspirant, beetroot juice, suntan lotion and similar things.

Pre-wash soaking

Pre-wash soaking can often produce a much cleaner garment, especially if you're dealing with really filthy overalls, dungarees, etc. However, some colours can't cope with being soaked and there may be other reasons why an article shouldn't be soaked, so where possible follow the manufacturer's instructions.

Sheets, cotton shirts, net curtains and, in fact, most white and colour-fast coloured items can be soaked perfectly safely.

Use a plastic bucket or bowl – it's best not to use the basin where someone will certainly want to wash hands and clean teeth before the soaking time is up. Don't use an enamel bath if it is chipped because it may stain your washing with rust marks. The bucket should be large enough to allow the clothes plenty of room. If there are protein stains, such as blood, egg, gravy, chocolate or milk, use warm water and a biological detergent. For other stains use hand-hot water and biological or other detergent.

Follow the instructions on the detergent packet and don't put in more than is recommended. Make sure the powder is thoroughly dissolved before putting the clothes in.

The clothes should be completely immersed and left to soak for several hours and, if very dirty, overnight.

Rinse the articles and then wash them as you would normally, according to fibre and colour.

Now you are ready to take your washing to the machine.

If you've washed something white in a coloured wash or left a white garment next to coloured while wet you can try getting rid of the colour by soaking the garment in hand-hot biological detergent solution for a few hours. (Follow the instructions on the packet. They are not all the same.) If that doesn't work rinse thoroughly then use Dygon Colour and Stain Remover as directed on the tin. Rinse and wash as usual. If you intend to wash various different types of fabric, select the wash programme suitable for the most delicate, i.e. if you are washing polyester and cotton together, wash as for polyester.

Bleaching

There are two types of bleach: oxidizing and reducing. But only oxidizing bleaches are used domestically. They remove stains by adding oxygen. They can be used safely on wool or silk. Most washing powders contain sodium perborate which is an oxidizing bleach. Others are hypochlorite (chlorine) bleaches which are the liquid household bleaches sold under various brand names. (*Reducing* bleaches work by taking oxygen away. These are used mainly by laundries and dry-cleaners.)

To bleach a whole article in chlorine bleach, use 15 ml of bleach to 12 litres of cold water ($\frac{1}{2}$ fluid ounce to $2\frac{1}{2}$ gallons). Immerse the article for ten to fifteen minutes. Rinse thoroughly before washing in the normal way.

To use hydrogen peroxide (from chemists) prepare a cold solution containing one part of hydrogen peroxide to eight parts water. Soak the garments in the solution for up to twelve hours. Rinse thoroughly before washing in the normal way.

Safety rules for bleach: never use undiluted hypochlorite (chlorine) bleach on any article. Always test for colour-fastness before starting treatment. Never use hypochlorite (chlorine) bleach on silk or wool or any article that has been given a stain-resistant finish. Always rinse thoroughly to remove all traces of the bleach.

In care labels a triangle containing the letters Cl (the chemists' symbol for chlorine) indicates that the article may be treated with chlorine bleach. If the triangle has a cross through it, this means that chlorine bleach must *not* be used. The symbol only refers to chlorine bleach. It doesn't apply to other bleaches.

Getting the temperature right

Set the temperature correctly for the group of clothes you are about to wash. This will be shown on the care label, inside the washtub symbol. If the garment has no care label, follow the instructions given in the A–Z of Fabrics and Fibres (p. 33). If the temperature is not right the detergent will not be able to work properly and you will get a poor, grey result. In some cases the wrong temperature may actually damage the fabric. Normally, machines can be set to six fixed temperatures, and the care-labelling code is keyed to these. When washing by hand you can recognize the temperatures as follows:

Boiling	100°C	212°F	Obvious
Very hot	95°C	203°F	Steaming but not boiling
Hot	60°C	140°F	Usually the highest temperature you'll get from your hot-water tap. Much too hot for the hands.
Hand-hot	50°C	122°F	The highest temperature you can put your hands into comfortably.
Warm	40°C	104°F	Slightly warm to the hands
Cool	30°C	86°F	Feels cool

If you have only a few of each type of fabric for washing, cottons, polyester/cottons and synthetics, you can do them in the machine together at the lowest of the recommended temperatures, but the results will probably not be quite as good as if you'd washed them at the right temperatures.

Wash for the fabric, never mind the shape. It is the fibre content which should decide what wash programme you choose, not the type of garment.

Wash all items at the right temperature every now and then before they get grey. Bleaches in washing powders are only really effective at high temperatures.

Getting the detergent right

Use the right washing powder for your kind of machine. If you have a front-loading automatic you must use a low-lathering soap powder or detergent otherwise soap bubbles will rise up and fill the bathroom. Suitable detergents are sold in supermarkets.

Use the right amount of powder. Types and sizes of wash are all so different that amounts recommended on detergent packets cannot be very accurate or precise. If you start with what they suggest, you can put in less or more as experience suggests. It is easy to use too much.

Dissolve the powder thoroughly before putting any articles into the solution. Some automatic machines are designed to dissolve the powder before it reaches the clothes. With those that don't, put the powder in, fill the machine with water and let it run for about a minute. When washing by hand, swish the water around good and hard until no detergent bits can be felt at the bottom. A quick stir is not enough.

Load the machine correctly

If you overload a washing-machine, the clothes will not move around freely and will not get so clean.

If washing by hand, squeeze the garments through your fingers, don't rub, twist or wring them, especially if they are synthetics or wool.

Rinsing

When you rinse clothes you are not just flushing out the dirt that was in them. It is just as important to rinse out the last traces of washing solution which will have all sorts of additives to make the wash look cleaner but which will leave it looking greyer if they're left in and may irritate the skin.

You will see from the programmer of any automatic washing-machine how much more time it devotes to rinsing than to the actual wash.

The number of rinses needed depends a lot on the size of the bowl or tub you use. One rinse in lots of water may well be enough. But you'll need two if the rinsing is being done in a spinner and even three or four if you use a bucket, bowl or small basin.

Rinsing temperatures are sometimes given on the care labels and wash codes. If no temperature is specified, use cold or cool water unless you know the fabric will take a hot rinse.

Detergents and the environment

If you are worried about the pollution you may be contributing to by using modern washing products, Jonathan Holliman in his book called *Consumers' Guide to the Protection of the Environment* (Pan/Ballantine in association with Friends of The Earth, 1974) gives some advice on 'how to reduce your contribution to the detergent problem'.

These include first finding ways of reducing the amounts of detergent you use and second finding the less polluting of the products available.

A group of fifty housewives in Hertfordshire undertook an extensive series of tests which showed that you need a quarter of the detergent recommended on a product to achieve a satisfactory wash.

Make up your mind how clean is clean and whether whiteness is really what you need. The 'optical brighteners' added to detergents merely absorb ultraviolet light and radiate it as visible white light. It's more a matter of aesthetics than actual cleanliness.

Don't buy enzyme detergents. If they disappeared tomorrow it would make no real difference. (It's the soaking that makes the difference apparently, not the enzymes.) In the U.S.A. Procter and Gamble and Lever Brothers have now stopped adding enzymes to all their detergent brands since sales have fallen off as American consumers have become worried about the harmful effects on health and the environment. Yet they will continue to be sold in British stores while customers are prepared to buy them.

If you live in a soft-water area you can switch directly to laundry soaps. If the water is hard, add a few tablespoons of washing-soda except for flame-resistant garments.

You can cut down on the amount of soap you use by installing a water softener. Some very dirty clothes can be left to soak overnight in water that has already been used to wash less dirty items.

Always use a washing-machine with a full load, if you can, to save on hot water and soap.

Fabric conditioners

Fabric conditioners are a mystery to many people. What are they supposed to do? Do they actually make any difference? They are supposed to be added to the final rinse water and do, in fact, leave clothes noticeably softer to touch. They are particularly good for babies' clothes and nappies, sweaters, towels and other soft garments, especially those worn or used next to the skin. They also make ironing easier by reducing the friction between the fabric and the iron and prevent static electricity which you often get with nylon and other man-made fibres. Static makes clothes cling and also attracts dirt so a fabric conditioner can be quite helpful and effective.

Keep the machine clean

When the wash is finished, wipe down the machine both inside and out, using a clean damp cloth. Disconnect the machine from the electricity supply first.

Drying

Spinning and wringing will remove enough water from clothes so that you can hang them up without them dripping. This means that I, for instance, am able to hang my clothes over the bannisters round the stair well and not over the bath. In a family of five, the bath would never be free for bathing otherwise.

There are various degrees of spinning. A spinner which does about 800 revolutions per minute gets clothes almost dry enough to iron and saves money on tumble-drying for those who use a tumble-drier. The efficiency of the spin may make the washing-machine more expensive but a good spinner is well worth it. The rest of the moisture must be got rid of by hanging the clothes up, by tumble-drying them in warm air, or by ironing. Sometimes, especially when spinning bulky items, the load is unbalanced and causes the machine to lurch about and travel all over the floor. You can prevent this by stopping the machine and redistributing the bulk of the fabric. Or put a couple of towels in as well if there's room.

Twisting, wringing or spinning synthetic fibres for too long can cause creases which are difficult to remove, especially when they are warm. Moreover, most synthetic fibres are non-absorbent and don't need a long spin. Don't overload the spin-drier and take the clothes out as soon as the spinning is completed.

If you can hang your clothes on an outside line they will have a marvellous fresh smell and a soft texture you don't get with clothes hung indoors. Outside drying is always worth the trouble if you have a garden or outdoor drying facilities and the atmosphere is not too polluted. Wipe the line before you hang out the clothes.

A ceiling rack on a pulley is the traditional way to dry clothes on wet days. Kitchens these days are not always tall enough to take one of these, which is a pity because they are convenient and not nearly as noticeable as the awful little racks that stand in a bath.

Heated drying-racks and drying-cabinets can be invaluable for people with never-ending washes such as nappies.

Tumble-drying is the most convenient and the most expensive way of drying clothes. The length of time the clothes are tumbled and the heat can both be controlled. Never tumble-dry acrylics at a high setting. Manufacturers' instructions (see the Care Labelling code, page 11) must be followed if you don't want things to matt, felt, shrink or crease. Never dry wool in a tumble-drier.

FINISHES

Starch

Starch does more than just stiffen limp fabrics. It also helps to keep out dirt, and most fabrics will wear better when starched. The soft gloss finish it gives to cottons holds down the fine surface hairs which collect dust and starch between the fibres keeps out dirt particles. It also strengthens weak fibres. Too much starch, however, may damage fabrics through dryness and cracking. So you must learn to get your starching right.

Most laundering starches are made from rice and maize. The granules penetrate the cloth and are then gelatinized by ironing. There are three main types: instant, powder and spray.

Instant starch is a powder, soluble in cold or warm water. It is quick because the granules have been pre-burst in the manufacturing process. You can add more or less powder to get varying degrees of stiffness. Dip the garment in the starch after the last rinse.

Powder starch needs to be made like mustard: first creamed with cold water and then mixed with boiling water to burst the granules and then diluted for dipping clothes. It's more of a bore to use than instant or spray and is best for articles which need to be very stiff. You can starch things in an automatic washing-machine but it's extravagant in water and not very practical unless you have an awful lot of things which need starching. Better to swish things around in the sink and then spin.

Spray starch is water soluble so you can use it even if the clothes are slightly damp. It is available in an aerosol can and is quick and easy to use for most clothes. Spray it on just before ironing.

Blueing

A white article will look yellowish unless it has some blue in it. Most white cottons and linens lose the blue with age and there are various types of laundry blue which will put it back. There are soluble blues, such as Prussian blue and aniline blue, which are usually a mixture of dyes. Ultramarine is insoluble and is the kind most used for laundry work, because it will not damage fabrics whereas other types will unless used with great care. Small bags and cubes of blue are available for hand-washing (but must not be used in machines). They should be put into the washing water before the clothes so the blue will dissolve properly and not leave blue spots.

Newer types of washing blue are called optical. They come from organic materials and give a strong blue-white glow under ultraviolet light. Commercial laundries use them as invisible inks to identify customers' articles. They can only make whites look whiter in daylight, not in artificial light. All detergent powders contain optical brighteners.

Some man-made fibres have a tendency to store static electricity which makes sparks fly and clothes cling to the body. It is quite harmless but annoying. Tumble-drying clothes often makes static worse. Ten minutes of cold tumble at the end of drying can reduce this effect. Fabric conditioners in the last rinse cut down on static too. Use them on tights and petticoats, and on dresses and skirts made of synthetic fibres. There are various antistatic sprays on the market. Try some on an unobtrusive area first to see if it leaves watermarks.

Re-texturing sprays

These give body to limp fabrics and make them look a lot better. Like antistatic sprays, you should try some on an unobtrusive area first to see if it leaves a watermark.

Creases

If you wash or spin or tumble man-made fibres at too high a temperature you will permanently damage the fibres and permanently crease the fabric. You could ask a dry-cleaner to press the garment, though this will probably only lessen the creasing rather than remove it and the creases will probably come back next time you wash the garment.

WASHING IN LAUNDERETTES

The choice of washing processes in launderettes is much more restricted than at home. Normally you will find 'hot wash' which should be used for colour-fast or white cotton goods (care label programmes 1 or 2) and 'warm wash' for fabrics made of man-made fibres (care label programmes 3, 4, 5 or 6).

Some launderettes have a wash-and-wear cycle which is particularly suited to items requiring a short or low-temperature wash. It should be used for clothes labelled for programme 6.

If garments are taken from the launderette while still damp they should be dried as soon as possible.

IRONING

Most fabrics are improved by ironing. The difference between something beautifully ironed and carelessly ironed is enormous. Set the ironing-board up near the radio or by the television or in the kitchen where you will have entertainment and/or companionship and you won't get bored. Make sure the ironing-board is at a comfortable height. Some people find it more convenient and less tiring to sit at the board on a tall stool or an adjustable typist's chair.

Modern irons have three temperature settings indicated by dots on the control knob. These are incorporated into the International Textile Care Labelling Code and will be shown as symbols on the care labels in clothes you buy.

	Hot (210°C)	Cotton, linen, rayon (viscose) or modified rayon (modal)
	Warm (160°C)	Polyesters, mixtures, wool
	Cool (120°C)	Acrylic, nylon, acetate, triacetate, polyester
	DO NOT IRON	This is only used in cases where ironing would spoil the fabric, not on easy-care fabrics where ironing is not necessary.

In fact on my iron I set the thermostat knob at lower than one dot for acrylics and have the iron only *just* warm. Remember it takes time for the iron to heat up or cool down. It's best to iron the cool-iron fabrics first and move up heat-wise. If you have a steam iron, the steam-heat setting is constant for all fabrics. If you have not got a steam iron, make sure the fabric is evenly damped. This is done by sprinkling water on it and rolling it up so the moisture is absorbed all through. Exceptions are 'wild' silks, and drip-dry fabrics which may be given a light pressing when dry. Alternatively you can dampen a clean tea-towel and iron the garment with the towel on it.

Experts advise not to dampen fabrics by sprinkling them with water just before ironing because the water will not be evenly spread and may cause marks. In fact it works very well on sturdy fabrics such as cotton but you should test first. I use one of those plastic jars with a spray attachment which you can buy in garden or D.I.Y. shops. A steam iron which also sprays will carry out the whole process for you. Never sprinkle water on man-made fabrics which have become too dry for ironing. Re-wet them and roll them up, which will spread the damp evenly.

There is a right way to iron a shirt and if you can iron a shirt you can iron practically anything. People have their own techniques. Mine is this:

Start with the *collar*, starting at the points and working towards the centre back; iron first on the wrong side and then on the right. Then do the *yoke*. Then the *cuffs*, wrong side and right. The *sleeves* come next. Iron along under-arm seams first. Run the point of the iron from the top of the sleeve down into the gathers at the cuff and up again towards the shoulder so you don't get ugly creases. Then iron the body of the garment starting at one front and working right round. Button the shirt, lay it front down, fold sleeves plus 50 mm (2 inches) of sides to back. Fold tail 75 mm (3 inches) and take up to collar.

Dresses can be ironed using this technique. When ironing tiered skirts start at the top tier and work down in layers. Run the point of the iron from some way down into the gathers, which will give soft folds and not hard creases.

Knitted wool should not really need ironing. If it is necessary, press lightly on the wrong side with a warm iron. Do not stretch.

Embroidery has to be ironed carefully. Fold a blanket three or four times and cover it with a clean cloth. Put the item face-down on the clean cloth. Put a thin dampened cloth at the back of the embroidery and then quickly apply a hot iron on the damp cloth until it is quite dry. The pattern of the embroidery will stand out.

Silk (except for tusser or wild silk) should be ironed with a warm iron when rather wetter than most fabrics. (Wild silk should be quite dry when being ironed.) An iron which is not hot enough will drag. But too hot an iron will scorch the silk. Test on a small piece of seam.

Cotton should be ironed when damp on the right side with a hot iron until quite dry.

Drip-dry cottons should not need ironing, but an occasional pressing with a cool iron helps to remove creases.

'Sheen' or 'glaze' cottons should be ironed when quite damp with a hot iron on the right side; *embossed* cotton on the wrong side. Don't slide the iron over the surface of embossed cottons or you'll flatten the pattern.

General rules for ironing *man-made fibres* where it is necessary: iron on the wrong side, taking care not to press any fasteners or buttons into the fabric – iron round them. Some irons have a button groove to make things easier. Use a cool iron. Even quite low heat can damage man-made fibres.

Press *heavy fabrics* under a damp cloth. A bit of old sheet will do, or a clean tea-towel.

SPECIAL CASES

Blankets   In most cases you will be advised to take large woollen items such as blankets to the cleaners. But you may like to try a traditional method of washing instead.

Make a paste with 250 ml (half a pint) of methylated spirit, 25 ml (one tablespoonful) of eucalyptus oil (from chemists) and as many soap-flakes as the mixture will absorb to make a thickish paste.

Wash the blankets in warm water by hand in the bath using the above mixture in place of washing powder. Do not rinse. Spin dry and hang up to finish drying. Though this recipe was given specifically for woollen blankets, I'm sure it would work on blankets made of other fibres too. Many blankets could be washed in a machine using a programme suitable for the fibre and the prescription as above.

Crêpe fabrics Some fabrics shrink after washing, especially crêpe materials. This shrinkage can be overcome by ironing the fabric while it is very damp. During the last stages of drying by ironing, the fabric will stretch considerably. Pull the fabric gently against the iron as you work.

Drip-dry clothes Drip-dry garments, such as shirts, are made from specially treated cotton or man-made fibres, or a mixture. The fabric is less absorbent and therefore dries more easily. If they are washed at too high a temperature the finish may be destroyed. It is unwise to use bleach on resin-finished cotton as this may combine with the finishing agent so that it cannot be rinsed out. The damage may not be immediately apparent but will eventually rot the fabric. The same advice applies to *crease-resistant garments* such as cricket trousers.

Duvets Duvets filled with synthetic fibre can be washed. If you can't fit them into your own washing-machine, the larger commercial machines in launderettes should take even a double one. But you can't wash duvets filled with feather and down – they should be dry-cleaned. Nor is this something you can do at home, nor will any old cleaner take them. Specialist firms will dry-clean duvets filled with down, feather and synthetic fibre. Some will collect and deliver locally and some provide a postal service for other parts of the country.

Feather pillows These may need to be washed if someone has been ill or spilled something. Immerse the pillow in a bath or tub of tepid water with 30 g (one ounce) of washing-soda. Rinse through by lifting up and allowing to drain and then immersing again. Do this two or three times in fresh water without soda. You can use soapsuds for the wash and if you do you should soften the first rinsing water with a little ammonia to ensure the removal of all soap.

Knitted clothes Wool should never be rubbed or moved around too much in water because of the scales on the fibre which will felt up and shrink the fabric. Although garments knitted with man-made fibres do not have this particular problem, the washing and drying treatment should be similar to that for wool outlined below because they can stretch grotesquely. Wool garments may stretch too. Once a garment has shrunk or stretched, there's very little you can do about it.

The technique for washing is to use warm water (or in the case of wool you could use one of the special cold-water wool detergents) and then gently squeeze the article in your hands. Do this only for as long as necessary to get it clean and don't lift it out of the water so it hangs heavily down. Let the water out of the sink, then squeeze the garment gently and roll it up in a towel to get out as much of the moisture as possible.

I have found it quite possible to spin knitted garments after a *cold* rinse for a *very short time*, but this is safer with wool than with man mades.

Dry all knitted garments flat on a towel on the floor. Once they are dry enough to keep their shape, you could finish them over something smooth and rounded, such as banisters, *not* over a clothes-line because it will leave a mark. Fasten buttons, zips, hooks, etc. and pull seams straight before drying. You can help prevent shrinkage by slightly stretching the garment during drying and pressing.

Lace shawls and any open knitted garment Should be hand-washed unless the manufacturer advises otherwise. Wash as for wool. You may have to lay two or three towels on the floor to dry a shawl on but they must be dried flat or they will not keep their shape.

Nappies Dirty nappies should be dealt with as soon as they are taken off. Scrape off faeces into the loo. Then soak the nappies overnight in a detergent solution. Rinse them thoroughly before washing them, specially if you have used an enzyme detergent. You can do this in the rinse cycle of a washing-machine. Nappies are best washed in the hottest wash in a machine. If you have to wash them by hand use water as hot as your hands can bear. Rubber gloves will make this easier.

If you do wash by hand, boil the nappies from time to time. Use a pan which has plenty of room for them (or do only a few at a time). Bring slowly to the boil and keep boiling for about ten minutes. Nappies should be rinsed thoroughly – until the water runs clear. This will mean three or four rinses in clean water. Spin them and then if possible tumble-dry them or hang them outside to dry. If you wash regularly by machine in a very hot wash, boiling is not essential.

Plastic pants or nylon pants Should be washed in hand-hot suds. Never boil them. Urine left on them will make them go hard and brittle. Throw them away then because they can be very uncomfortable for a baby to wear.

Pleated skirts are a real drag to keep looking their best. Some can be laundered. Others are not dealt with at all by certain local cleaners who do steam pressing. So it will almost certainly be worth having them dry-cleaned professionally by specialists. Their treatment will not be permanent but should last longer than ordinary steam pressing. It is very expensive though. Some cleaners also have a more permanent pleating service for fabric by the metre (i.e. before making it up into a skirt). How permanent this is depends on the fabric. The cleaner will, of course, advise.

Ties   Ties are an awful problem to clean. Because they're cut on the cross it's difficult to get them to keep their shape and they seldom keep that shiny and smart look they started off with. Local cleaners can't always be relied on to give ties back looking any better than when they were taken into the shop. Often the back seam has been pressed so it shows on the front as a shiny line. Even ties potentially washable are difficult to deal with, silk especially so, and the interlining often rucks up.

On the whole it is probably better not to try to deal with ties at home – though you could try specific spot removers as suggested in Chapter 4. Some cleaning firms have a special tie-cleaning service and it is worth sending or taking your ties to one of these.

Toys   Soft, washable toys should be washed fairly often in warm suds and rinsed thoroughly. Dark colours should be washed separately. You can wrap them in a towel to soak up excess moisture and hang them from the ears or feet to dry.

White woollen baby clothes   Always wash correctly as for wool and do not dry in direct sunlight or they will turn yellow.

CHAPTER 2

A to Z OF FABRICS AND FIBRES

This section is as up to date as I can make it but work is going on all the time to make man-made fibres more practical and more versatile. I have included brand names wherever possible. In each case I give the properties of the fibre or fabric as well as recommended methods for washing.

Acetate Man-made cellulose acetate fibre. It used to be made from the short unspinnable hairs of the cotton boll, but now usually comes from wood pulp. It is quite silk-like and is often made into taffetas, moirés, brocades, linings, curtain fabrics and velvety pile fabrics. Brand names include Dicel, Lancola, Lansil, Rhodia, Silene. The first cellulose acetate fibre was called acetate rayon but this is not now much used. 'Rayon', now usually called 'viscose', is made from simple cellulose. See also Triacetate.

TREATMENT Wash often in warm suds. Spin only if the care label says you can. Otherwise drip-dry or roll in a towel to mop up excess water and then hang up. Don't wring or tiny cracks will show in the fabric. Iron while still damp with a warm iron. Knitted garments should be given a cold rinse and a short spin. Acetate is soluble in acetone, acetic acid, alcohol and similar chemicals so don't use them for stain removal. May be bleached with hydrogen peroxide solution or sodium perborate.

Acrilan Brand name for an acrylic fibre. Acrilan SEF is a modacrylic.

Acrylic fibres These are by-products of oil refining. They are soft, warm and durable, and are mildew-resistant. Acrylic fibres are used to make easy-care fabrics which look and feel rather like wool, and which are used for underwear, jersey fabrics, curtains, men's suits, carpets, pleated garments, and fur fabrics. Easy to wash; quick to dry; won't shrink. Used alone or blended with other man-made fibres or natural fibres. Trade names include Acrilan, Courtelle, Crylor, Dralon, Orlon.
TREATMENT Wash in warm water. Rinse in cold water; short spin. (The cold-water rinse is to cool the fibre down so it will not crease while spinning.) Pleated garments should be rinsed in warm water, and drip-dried. Heavy knitwear should be pulled into shape and dried flat on a towel on the floor. Pile fabrics may be brushed lightly with a soft brush when dry. Some garments may need to be ironed lightly with a cool iron after the garment is dry. May be bleached with chlorine bleach.

Afghalaine Woven fabric originally made from wool fibres but now often from man-made fibres. Wash as for wool. Iron while still slightly damp. If too dry for ironing and you have no steam iron, roll it up in a damp tea towel for half an hour. Iron on the wrong side of the material if it's a dark colour, and don't press too hard on the seams.

Alpaca Wool of a South American animal of the camel family used for making cloth. The name is also used for cloth made from the hair of the Angora goat (mohair), which may have a cotton warp and Angora goat's hair weft. Wash as for wool.

Angola Woven fabric, similar to flannelette but lighter. Originally a blend of cotton and wool but now just as often rayon and wool. Mainly used for army shirts and not much else. Wash as for wool.

Angora This is fluffy, rabbit wool used for jumpers, hats, scarves, etc. It's very soft with characteristic white hairs dotted about on it. Nowadays it's sometimes mixed with nylon. Wash as for wool.

Antron   Brand name for a nylon.

Antung   Chinese wild silk, smooth woven fabric. Wash as for silk. Iron on the wrong side when quite dry with a warm iron.

Arnel   Brand name for a triacetate fibre.

Astrakhan   Originally the cured and dyed skin of certain lambs. The real skin is nowadays imitated in astrakhan cloth by using knitted and woven fabrics. Treat as sheepskin: dry-clean or shampoo or wash as for wool.

Ban-Lon   This is the name given to synthetic fabrics which have been 'Textralized'. This frightful word means crimped, or compressed into corrugations to form patterns. Wash according to the care label if there is one; if not, as appropriate for the fibre concerned (it is usually nylon). If you don't know what it is wash in a cool minimum wash, cool rinse, drip-dry.

Batiste   A woven fabric of silk, cotton, viscose, nylon or cotton/polyester, used in corsets and bras. Wash often in hot water and soap or detergent.

Bonded fibres   Off-white crush-resistant, porous, water-repellent and light. Used for interlinings. Brand names: Solena and Vilene.
TREATMENT   Wash or dry-clean. When washing try not to crease the fabric, use warm, detergenty water. Do not rub. Roll loosely in a towel to absorb as much water as possible. Do not spin or wring.

Bouclé   Yarn made of three strands, one of which is looped at intervals. Wash as appropriate for fibre used.

Braid   You should be able to clean silver lace braid or cord on a uniform if it's not too badly tarnished. Cover the braid with bicarbonate of soda and brush well in. Leave for an hour or two then brush it all out gently with a fine wire brush (a suede brush, for instance). You can make a paste of methylated spirit and French chalk to remove tarnish. Spread this on the braid, leave to dry then brush off with a stiff brush.
   Gold trimmings and gold braid and lace can be cleaned with a mixture of cream of tartar and dry bread rubbed up very fine, applied when dry and brushed lightly with a clean soft brush.

Brocade   A rich woven fabric with an all-over design of raised flowers or figures. Woven on a special loom. The background may be satin or twill. It's used for furnishings and dresses. May be acetate, cotton, silk, viscose or a mixture. All brocades should be dry-cleaned because they are so heavy to handle when wet.

Buckram   A stiff fabric, usually made of cotton, stiffened with lots of starch. Dry-clean only.

Calico   A medium-weight woven cotton. For some reason synthetics haven't wormed their way into this fabric. Wash as for cotton. Unbleached calico should have a splash of white spirit added to the water in the first wash to remove the starch and help whiten the fabric.

Cambric   A lightweight closely woven slightly starched fabric, originally made of linen but now often of cotton. Wash as for cotton; starch slightly.

Camel hair   Every home should have a coat made of this! It's expensive, soft and warm in lovely brown colours. Dry-clean only.

Candlewick   Originally a tufted cotton fabric but now may be made of nylon, polyester, rayon or triacetate. Used for bedspreads, dressing-gowns, bath mats and other things pertaining to bath, bed and dressing-rooms. Wash as for the fibre concerned.

Cantrell   Brand name for a nylon.

Cashmere   A wonderful soft, light wool from the Kashmir goat. It is scarce and expensive. Wash as for wool.

Cavalry twill   Tough, heavy woven fabric used for riding breeches, farmers' trousers, hacking jackets, etc. Made of wool, cotton or man-made fibres. Dry-clean unless the label says you can wash it.

Cellular   That famous underwear woven in a honeycomb structure with holes in it to trap the warmth. Blankets can be cellular too. If used for underwear it is usually cotton but may now be in viscose or a blend. If used for blankets it's usually wool or a blend of wool and synthetic. Wash as for the weakest fibre.

Celon   Brand name for a nylon made by Courtaulds.

Chenille   Yarn or fabric with a soft velvety pile, originally used for curtains and table-cloths, more recently for coats and jackets. May be cotton, rayon, wool or silk. Wash according to fibre. But if washing old chenille, wash with great care, gently and by hand or the whole thing may disintegrate into a blood-coloured liquid leaving a mound of what looks like cotton wool at the bottom. That's what happened when I washed my grandmother's curtains. The label in new garments may say dry-clean only.

Chiffon   Floaty, sheer fabric with a soft rippled finish. Originally made of silk, now nylon, rayon or other man-made fibres may be used. Used for party dresses, lingerie (if you're lucky), scarves, etc. Wash as for fibre concerned. Silk and rayon are the most difficult to deal with but can be washed if you are careful. Don't wring. When almost dry, iron gently with a cool iron, stretch the garment gently in all directions and then into its correct shape as you iron. Don't do it in a hurry.

Chintz (glazed chintz)   A woven printed cotton fabric, shiny on the right side. Used for curtains, bedspreads, etc. and now sometimes for skirts and dresses, usually with big flower prints. Should be dry-cleaned but if you *do* wash it, wash as for cotton and use starch or a plastic stiffener. These days chintz is usually permanently glazed in which case don't rub or twist or bleach it and you should not have to starch it.

Clarino   See Poromeric Material.

Clévyl T   Brand name for a P.V.C. material.

Cloqué   A heavy double-weave fabric in silk, acetate, triacetate or acrylic where the surface is blistered. Wash as for acetate and drip-dry.

Clydella   Brand name for cotton/wool mixture.

Corduroy (also needlecord, elephant cord)   A woven fabric with velvet ribs running along the cloth. Used for jeans, coats, dresses, children's clothes, upholstery. Made of cotton or cotton/rayon or cotton/polyester. Wash as for the more delicate fibre. Occasionally smooth the pile as it dries and shake it from time to time. You should not then have to iron it. If you do need to iron it, press gently while still damp on the wrong side with several thicknesses of material between the garment and the iron.

Corfam   See Poromeric Material.

Cotton   Natural fibre from the seed pod (the 'boll') of the cotton plant. Cotton fabrics are absorbent and tough and hang nicely. They are used for underwear, socks, blouses and shirts, dresses, trousers and jeans, sheets, towels, upholstery, nappies, babies' clothes, curtains, tablecloths, and many other items.
TREATMENT   White cotton should be washed in hot or boiling water (85°C (185°F) or more). Always test coloured cottons for colour-fastness, though it is safest to wash reds with reds, and so on, anyway. Coloured cottons should be washed at 60°C (140°F). For delicate cotton fabrics (voile, organdie, etc.) or cotton with special finishes (such as drip-dry or water- or stain-repellent) follow the care label instructions.

Courtelle   Brand name for acrylic fibre made by Courtaulds.

Crash   Originally a heavy linen, which is now often made of cotton or viscose. Wash as for the fibre concerned.

Crêpe   Any fabric with a wrinkled, crinkled surface. Wash in hand-hot water. Roll in a towel to absorb moisture and iron on the wrong side with a warm iron while still damp (or use a steam iron).

Crêpe de Chine   A lightweight crêpe of silk, polyester or viscose. Wash according to fibre. Real silk crêpe de Chine should be soaked in cool water before being washed for the first time. Roll it in a towel to absorb moisture and then iron straightaway. Use a warm iron on the wrong side of the material until it is quite dry.

Cretonne   This is like a cotton or rayon chintz but thinner. Wash in hand-hot water and detergent and rub dirty bits with a soft nail brush or spray with one of the new aerosol 'laundry stain removers'. If it hasn't got a special finish you should starch it. If cotton, iron with a hot iron while still damp. If rayon use a cool setting.

Crimplene   See Polyester.

Crylor   Brand name for an acrylic fibre.

Dacron   The brand name used in the U.S.A. by Du Pont for polyester.

Damask   A fabric with a woven, usually floral pattern often used for table-cloths. May be cotton, linen, wool or silk. Wash according to fibre.

Delaine   All-wool lightweight fabric, usually printed. Wash as for wool. Also now available in various man-made fibres.

Delustra   Brand name for a viscose fibre.

Denim   Heavy cotton, used for dungarees, jeans, upholstery, etc. Also available in rayon/cotton mixture. Wash as for weakest fibre. Denim will shrink slightly unless pre-shrunk.

Dicel   Brand name for an acetate yarn made by Courtaulds.

Diolen   Brand name for a West German polyester fibre.

Douppion   Silk slubbed material. Wash as for silk.

Dralon   Brand name for an acrylic fibre made by Bayer.

Drill   Twill fabric similar to denim. Treat as for cotton.

Duchesse satin   Heavy shiny fabric used for party dresses. Dry-clean only.

Dynel   Brand name for a modacrylic fibre.

Egyptian cotton   Very good quality, fine cotton grown in Egypt. Wash as for cotton.

Elastane   (Also known as elastomers, elastomeric fibres, elastofibres or spandex fibres). Synthetic fibres, mostly based on polyurethane, which have the elasticity of rubber. They stretch well and recover well, and resist many chemicals, including chlorine and perspiration, which degrade ordinary rubber. The yarn can be very fine. Used for foundation garments, leotards, swimwear, support stockings, tights, men's socks. Brand names: Lycra, Spanzelle, Vyrene. Helanca yarn has a similar elasticity but is a mixture of nylon and Terylene subjected to crimping during spinning.
TREATMENT   These fibres are always used with other fibres, so follow instructions for the weaker ones. Wash girdles, bras, etc., in hand-hot water or light machine wash; rinse; short spin; drip dry. Garments made from these materials (apart from Helanca) must not be ironed.

Enkalon   Brand name for a nylon.

Evlan   Brand name for a viscose fibre.

Faille   Fine ribbed fabric. Originally of silk or cotton, now often of man-made fibres. Treat as appropriate for fibre concerned.

Felt   Matted woollen material. Will shrink easily. Don't wash. Some dry-cleaners will not take responsibility for cleaning. To clean *felt hats*, make a paste with white spirit and French chalk. Rub well into the hat and let it dry. Then brush it off.

Flannel   Woven fabric made wholly or partly of wool. Heavy flannels should by dry-cleaned but you can often wash lightweight ones, as for wool. Used to make warm nighties and school trousers.

Flock fabric   Fabric with a pile pattern. Wash in hand-hot suds. Roll in a towel, don't spin or wring. Iron on the wrong side with a warm iron or drip-dry.

Foulard   Shiny woven fabric usually printed. Used to be silk now often acetate. Wash according to fibre.

Fur   It's best to get any good fur professionally cleaned once a year (see page 244). If you want to deal with an ancient old fur coat (or a fur fabric collar with no care label or a 'Do not dry-clean' label) then try a dry shampoo. Fuller's earth is the traditional medium used for this – you can still get it at chemists. Bran can be used in the same way. Brush the powder well into the fur, leave for an hour or two and then brush out carefully. This should get rid of grease and surface dirt. In fact, my silver fox fur hat, lost the musty smell it had acquired from being left in a damp cupboard, when I used fuller's earth on it. Talcum powder will do the job too.

Fur fabric   May be made of nylon, viscose, cotton, acrylic or polyester. Cotton and viscose should be dry-cleaned. Others may be washed according to fibre or care label instructions in the garment. If in doubt, wash as nylon. Alternatively you could lightly sponge fur fabric with warm detergent solution, sponge, rinse and dry with a towel.

Gabardine   A strong woven fabric, twilled with diagonal ribs, which is used for school raincoats. Made of cotton, worsted or blends of those and man-made fibres. Dry-clean.

Georgette Very delicate, sheer fabric a bit like crêpe. Made of wool, cotton, silk or man-made fibres. If of silk or wool get it professionally cleaned. Wash man-made fabrics according to the weakest fibre or follow the care label. Test for colour-fastness.

Gingham Striped or checked fabric used as cheap curtains and for summer frocks and some school uniforms. Originally cotton, now often in polyester/cotton. Test for colour-fastness. Wash in warm or hot suds, as for most delicate fibre.

Glass fibre Fine glass filaments. Used mostly for curtains. Care should be used when handling. Do not machine-wash or spin, wring, dry-clean or iron. Don't wash with other items. To wash, gently move fabric around in warm suds. Don't use bleach. Rinse in warm water. Drip-dry. Hang curtains over line – don't peg. Pull hem straight. Afterwards rinse out the sink well as bits of glass may come out. In fact it is sensible to wear rubber gloves while handling the stuff.

Grosgrain Strong, closely woven fabric available in various fibres and weights. Wash or dry-clean according to the weakest fibre or the care label if there is one.

Helanca Brand name for an elastomeric yarn made from a mixture of nylon and Terylene. The yarn is crimped so that it will stretch. It was invented before the polyurethane elastomeric fibres. See Elastane.

Habutai Fabric made of Japanese silk waste or cheaper fibres. Wash according to fibre.

Honan Wild silk cloth with a plain weave and high lustre. Wash as for silk. You can restore its sheen by spraying on white vinegar. Iron while still damp on the wrong side with a fairly hot iron. If the fabric has become very dry, roll it in a damp towel for half an hour (or use a steam/spray iron). (Also imitated in man-made fibres).

Hopsack Loosely woven cotton, linen or rayon fabric. Dry-clean. Also a woollen or worsted suiting fabric otherwise called hopsack serge.

Jersey Stretchy, knitted fabric in stockinette stitch, made of wool, silk, cotton, or nylon or other man-made fibres. It doesn't crease easily and packs well for travelling. Italian jerseys are especially fine.

Wash or dry-clean according to the care label. If there is none, wool or silk jerseys should be dry-cleaned.

Jute   Fibre from the bark of jute plants; used for sacks and carpet backing. Wash as for cotton or, if very stiff, scrub with detergenty water.

Kapok   A fine pale-brownish fibre which comes from the seed pods of the kapok tree. It is waterproof, light, fluffy and resilient. Used mainly for stuffing mattresses, and as quilting for life-jackets. It's liable to go lumpy in the wash and can be very uncomfortable once this has happened in a mattress or sleeping-bag.
TREATMENT   Dry-clean only.

Kid   Skin of a young goat used for gloves. White kid can be cleaned but must be handled carefully, by dipping cotton wool in dry-cleaning solvent and quickly rubbing the surface while the glove is on a hand. Use clean cotton wool with each rub. Dark kid gloves should be rubbed with a cloth dipped in Vaseline. Some grease-absorbent powder such as fuller's earth or French chalk should be used for unwashable leather or suede. Sprinkle the powder where it's needed then wrap the gloves in a towel and leave for an hour or two. Don't rush this. Then brush off gently. Non-washable leather and suede gloves can be put on the hands and 'washed' in a bowl of dry oatmeal, and then brushed. Other non-washable suede and leather items should be sprinkled with fuller's earth or oatmeal, left for an hour or two then brushed with a soft brush. *Hogskin* may be polished with white leather polish or furniture cream.

Lace   There are basically three sorts of lace: needle-point (when only one thread is used), bobbin and machine-made. Most lace is machine-made nowadays, though making bobbin lace is coming back into fashion as a craft and you can often find it at craft markets.
    Wash according to fibre: cotton, nylon, polyester or the weakest fibre in a blend. Use a washing powder or liquid that is specially formulated for delicate fabrics. You can starch cotton lace. Old or delicate lace should be put in a pillow case to be washed. Rinse in the same way. Curtain lace can be washed in hot suds and cotton curtain lace should be boiled from time to time. Pull into shape when hanging to dry. Use a hot iron on the wrong side. But lace made of man-made fibres shouldn't need ironing.
    Some lace tends to shrink but you should be able to prevent this by pulling it gently into shape as the lace is drying. Hang clothes on padded hangers to dry but make sure any colour on the padded fabric won't come out on the lace.

Old lace should be kept in a dry warm place and if you don't expect to use it for some time you should take it out and air it occasionally as black lace especially is susceptible to mould.

Delicate hand-made lace should not be dry-cleaned. It should be pinned to a linen-covered board with enough pins to keep the lace flat and dabbed gently with a soapy sponge. Then sponge with clean water, mopping up as much superfluous moisture as possible with a dry sponge. Leave it to dry on the board. The pins will keep it in shape. It is important to use pins which will not rust.

One person who specializes in washing old lace for a London shop gave me some advice from her own experience:

'There are different methods of dealing with old materials. I use borax quite a bit as it is a water softener, a whitener and a stiffener. I also use biological detergents for *short* soaks though lots of people would say I was wrong. But I prefer a fast soak than fiddling around with liquid detergents for days. You have to be very careful with biological detergent. Each make is different so you should watch the lace constantly and take it out as soon as it's looking clean. I also use bleach and acetone for difficult stains. Mildew is difficult. It forms a ring like a little horseshoe.

'When you're soaking very old lace the water should come out black because over the years it will have accumulated no end of dust and grime.

'Don't soak linens in ordinary plastic containers. The chemicals used are very strong even when diluted and the colour will come out of coloured plastics no matter what the manufacturers say. I eventually bought heavy hospital plastic bowls which sit in the bath. I haven't a boiler so I use water as hot as I can get it and keep the heat in by putting the bowls on top of one another.

'Use a wooden board to work on when treating specific stains. The chemicals may damage other surfaces. Household chlorine bleaches should be used with caution because they are so strong. I'd use a milder one more often.

'Never spin or tumble-dry lace and be careful to squeeze and not to wring. If you are not careful, rips will appear and existing tears will get bigger very quickly. My treatments are special treatments, to get the items clean after years of non-use. If you treated them like this more often you'd end up with an old rag.

'These things should be starched. I don't like that blue look which most people have in their linens. I think it's from powder starches. I use spray starches and each one is different so you have to experiment. Never mix different colours – oatmeal lace shouldn't be soaked with white for instance.'

Lamé   See Metallic Yarn.

Lancola, Lansil   Brand names for acetate fibres.

Lawn   Originally fine cotton but now may be made of polyester/cotton or viscose/cotton blends. Wash by hand or give the article a very short machine wash. Use hand-hot water, rinse thoroughly and wring or spin.

Leather
LEATHER SHOES   Wet leather shoes should be stuffed with newspaper and dried away from direct heat. A little castor oil rubbed into the uppers and soles, after they have dried, will soften them and recondition the leather. The shoes can then be polished.
WASHABLE LEATHER GLOVES   Wash the gloves while on your hands in warm water and soap-flakes. If they are pale gloves, wash them every time you wear them. Leave some soap in the gloves after washing. Gloves are best dried over a wooden or wire hand but I have dried mine over shampoo bottles quite successfully. When they are dry, rub the leather between your fingers to soften it.

Linen   Materials woven from the fibres of the flax plant. On the whole linen is very similar to cotton but has a better texture and longer life. It is used for good-quality table-cloths and sheets, glass- and tea-towels and some clothes.
TREATMENT   Remove stains before laundering. If very dirty, soak for fifteen minutes in detergent or soapy suds in warm water. Use a hot wash and rinse thoroughly. Spin and hang to dry. Iron with a hot iron while still damp unless you have an iron with spray steam for bad creases. Iron on the wrong side or the fabric will become shiny.

Lirelle Brand name for a polyester fibre.

Lurex Brand name for a metallic yarn.

Lycra A polyurethane fibre. See Elastane.

Marocain Crêpe fabric originally of silk. Acetate or viscose blends have been made but it's not much used now though you might pick up a marocain garment at a jumble sale. Wash in warm water, rinse. When nearly dry stretch it into shape. Roll up when not quite dry so the dampness is evenly spread for ironing. (This won't be necessary if you have a steam iron.)

Marquisette Openwork material usually used for curtains. Originally in silk, now in cotton, rayon or polyester. Wash according to the fibre.

Melton An old-fashioned heavy, felted fabric used for overcoats. The nap is teased out and cut short, leaving upright ends of wool fibre. Usually wool or wool and cotton. Dry-clean only.

Merino Ultra-fine, soft wool from pure-bred Merino sheep. (Merino used also to be a name for cotton and wool knitted underwear.) Merino wool in any of its forms tends to shrink when washed so special care should be taken not to rub, twist or wring it. While drying, the garment should be stretched first in one direction then the other. Soap makes felting worse so the garment should be rinsed very carefully.

Metallic yarns Basically aluminised polyester, non-tarnishable metallic threads. Brand names include Lurex, Metlon, Rexor. All types may be woven or knitted. Any fabric in which metallic yarn is mixed with yarn of other fibres is called lamé.
TREATMENT Dry-clean. Should not be steam pressed nor submitted to temperatures above 40°C (104°F).

Metlon Brand name for a metallic yarn.

Milium A fabric with a metallic finish which is a very good insulator. Used for ironing-board covers, sleeping-bags, curtain linings. Developed for space projects originally, so we're told. Dry-clean.

Mixtures When washing a fabric with a mixture of fibres, always use the method appropriate to the most delicate fibre in the mixture.

Modacrylic   This term means 'modified acrylic'. Modacrylic fibres are similar to acrylic but not as strong. They are suitable for flame-resistant fabrics. Brand names include Acrilan SEF, Dynel, Teklan and Verel. Used for children's nightwear, knitted and woven dresses, underwear, household textiles, fake fur, toys.
TREATMENT   Wash in warm water and detergent, rinse well. Drip-dry. If necessary iron with a cool iron.

Modal   Modified viscose fibres (including fibres which used to be known as polynosic). They are absorbent and retain their strength when wet. Usually blended with polyester or cotton to make household textiles and workwear and have various industrial uses. Brand names include Vincel.

Mohair   Soft, light long-fibred wool which is the hair of the Angora goat. It's a bit like the wool of the alpaca and is sometimes called alpaca but it is coarser. It is often used with cotton. Mohair wears well and shakes off rain and dust seemingly miraculously. Wash as for wool.

Moiré   Moirés are usually made of silk. If you hold a moiré fabric up to the light you will see the ripples or watermarks on it. These marks are made by impressing or embossing the markings on the cloth. Dry-clean.

Moquette   Heavy, coarse-pile upholstery fabric. Furniture early this century used to be upholstered in it and so did railway carriage seats. Can be wool, cotton or acrylic. The pile may be cut or uncut. Dry-clean all but acrylic moquettes which can be washed.

Movyl   Brand name for a P.V.C. material.

Moygashel   Trade name for certain Irish linens, cottons or spun rayons.

Mungo   Reclaimed wool, produced from old or new knitted fabrics or from milled cloths or felt. Worse quality than shoddy. Does not carry the 'Pure new wool' label. Feels coarser and less flexible than new wool. Wash as for wool.

Muslin   A thin loosely woven cotton material used for straining cheese (butter muslin) and now popular as shirt and dress fabric.

Wash in warm water, rinse well, iron while damp with warm iron. Starch.

Needlecord   See Corduroy.

Net   Material woven with a fine mesh and mainly used for curtains. Made of cotton, nylon, polyester, etc. Cotton net may shrink when washed for the first time. Net on dresses should be washed by hand in warm soap-flakes. Rinse, drip-dry and iron with a warm iron while still a bit damp.

All curtain nets should be washed often. Once the grime of the atmosphere has got a good hold it's almost impossible to get it out. Shake the curtains first, then rinse in cold water. Wash in hot water. Do not rub, twist or wring, just squeeze the suds gently through the fabric. Wash twice if necessary. Rinse thoroughly. Most curtain nets are made of man-made fibres nowadays and you should wash as for the fibre concerned. If the curtains have gone grey, wash in a proprietary curtain-whitener then try white nylon dyes. If these do not work, try soaking the curtains in biological detergent. But it is best to wash them before they go grey.

Ninon   Sheer fabric, rather like a smooth chiffon and often used for curtains. Originally in silk but may now be acetate, polyester or nylon. Treat as for the fibre concerned.

Noils   Short wool-combings, or silk from broken or defective cocoons. They are used to add softness to woollen fabrics.

Nun's veiling   Delicate fabric of silk or cotton. Wash as for wool.

Nylon   There are many types of nylon, but chemically they are all polyamides. Nylon is strong, elastic, doesn't lose its strength when wet, is lightweight, absorbs little moisture, is flame resistant, resistant to most oils and chemicals, moths and moulds. It can be textured easily. It's used for all sorts of garments including underwear and socks (though because it doesn't absorb moisture it isn't the best material for them on its own), shirts, dresses, overalls, etc. and for sheets (again not the best material on its own), parachutes, sleeping-bags, and tights and stockings, schoolwear and carpets. Brand names include Antron, Blue C Nylon, Bri-Nylon, Cantrell, Celon, Du Pont Nylon, Enkalon, Perlon, Timbrelle. See also Ban-Lon, Nylon Fur, and Paper Nylon.
TREATMENT   Nylon should not be boiled but washed in hand-hot water. Cold rinse and short spin, or drip-dry. Hang on plastic

hangers. Nylon dries quickly. Do not use bleach. Wash often. In its basic state nylon is grey so don't wash it in very hot water or boil it or the white pigment will come out. Don't expose it to direct heat or sunlight. You should never need to iron it. If it does need ironing, wait until almost dry and then use a warmish setting.

Delicate garments and pleated nylon should be washed every time you use them. Once dirt has wormed its way into the fabric, you'll never get it out without damaging the fabric. Squeeze as little as possible while washing, to avoid making creases. If the white has come out you can try a nylon whitener in the rinsing water, available from supermarkets.

Pleated garments should be dipped up and down in the water, rinsed in the same way and then dripped dry. Don't twist or wring. Pull into shape when nearly dry. Never iron pleated nylon. Never use bleach. Nylon shower curtains may get mildew at the bottom. You may sponge these with a weak solution of household bleach. A more drastic treatment is to use a fungicide available in plastic sachets from hardware shops. Curtains that have gone cloudy can be soaked in a bowl of warm water with a couple of tablespoons of water softener. Rinse well.

If sent for dry-cleaning, mark clearly 'Nylon'.

Nylon fur   Wash as for nylon. If the garment has an interlining or is stiffened, don't wash it at all but use a wet shampoo. Mix some liquid detergent in warm water to a lather and, using a sponge, gently rub the lather into the fur only. Treat a small patch at a time and don't let the backing and interlining get wet. Rinse with a clean, not-too-wet sponge and pat dry with a towel. Dry naturally and shake while drying from time to time. You can get upholstery cleaners which automatically ooze out the right amount of lather without getting too wet. They make the job easier but more expensive. Alternatively, use a dry shampoo, bran or fuller's earth as directed on page 40.

Organdie   Permanently stiffened delicate fabric which used to be used for party dresses for little girls. Used to be cotton, now often nylon. To wash cotton organdie, squeeze gently in hand-hot water and mild detergent, rinse well, wring and hang to dry. Iron on the right side while still damp with a medium-hot iron. If the fabric goes limp, rinse in a litre of warm water with 50 g of borax (one tablespoonful to a quart). Nylon organdie should be washed as for nylon.

Organza   This is a sort of stiffened chiffon, originally silk, now may be of various fibres. Wash according to fibre and handle with care.

Orlon   Brand name for a Du Pont acrylic fibre.

Osmalene   Brand name for a winceyette material. See Winceyette.

P.V.C.   (Polyvinylidene chloride and polyvinyl chloride or chloro-fibres.) Very strong man-made plastic material. Tough, water-repellent, flame-resistant. It is non-absorbent; soft. Used for night-wear, racing-drivers' overalls, rainwear. Brand names: Clévyl T, Movyl, Rhovyl, Saran.
TREATMENT   Hand-wash only, drip-dry only. Do not iron.

Paper nylon   Ordinary nylon which has been treated with a resin finish and is made into stiff petticoats. Always wash by hand and take care not to crack this finish. Fill a bath with hot suds, lay the garment full length. Dip up and down without squeezing or rubbing and scrub any dirty marks lightly with a soft nail-brush. Don't wring. Drip-dry. If you take care it should keep its stiffness but anyway a fifty per cent solution of plastic starch should help to stiffen it again. Press with a warm iron.

Peau d'ange   A dress fabric with a satin weave. Now often a mixture of acetate and silk. Follow the care label and treat as for the more delicate fibre.

Perlon   Brand name for a nylon.

Pique   A strong cotton or rayon fabric with fine cords running across it. It is usually white or light coloured and popular for collars and cuffs and tennis clothes. Wash according to fibre. (Pique embroidery is a form of white stitchery where the outlines are made by an overcast cord filled in with various stitches.)

Plisse   See Seersucker.

Plush   Similar to velvet but with bigger gaps between the fibres. Usually made of acrylic but may be found in silk, viscose, nylon, etc. Treat according to fibre.

Polyamide   See Nylon.

Polyester fibres   These are mainly made of by-products of petroleum refining. Very strong. High resistance to abrasion; sheer, lightweight, strong whether wet or dry. Won't shrink or stretch; resistant to moths and mildew. Can be durably pleated. Won't absorb much moisture. Often used mixed with cotton for shirts and sheets, which offer the best of both fibres – being absorbent and crease resistant. Brand names include Crimplene, Dacron, Diolen, Lirelle, Spinlene, Terlenka, Terylene, Trevira.
TREATMENT   Wash by hand or machine. Do not boil. Shake (no need to wring or spin) moisture off and hang in normal room temperature. Or you can give it a cold rinse and a short spin. You can safely tumble-dry it and should not need to iron it afterwards.
    Badly stained materials should be impregnated with concentrated detergent or soap. Leave for ten or fifteen minutes. This should loosen the stain after which you can wash as usual.
    Wash pleated garments by hand and hang to drip-dry straight away. You *can* give them a minimum machine wash without doing them a damage. (Check that the garment *is* polyester and not nylon though.) It's better not to iron polyester, but if you must, use a cool setting.
    Polyester/cotton sheets and pillowcases may become discoloured in the middle. You can try rubbing Stergene into the area and leave for an hour or two before rinsing. Or you could try a slightly hotter wash, though this may cause creases, and sheets may need ironing thereafter and may lose some colour too.

Polyethylene and polypropylene   These materials belong to a group of plastics known as polyolefins. They are the lightest of all fibres; very strong when wet or dry; resistant to abrasion, chemicals, damp and sunlight. Brand names: Courlene, Cournova, Polysoft. Used for backings for tufted carpets and for sacking, deckchair covers, awnings and rope.
TREATMENT   Wipe with a damp cloth.

Polyolefin See Polyethylene.

Polythene The common name for polyethylene (q.v.) (see above).

Polypropylene See Polyethylene.

Polyurethane Synthetic plastics of the polyurethane group are used to make elastomeric fibres (see Elastane). Polyurethanes are also used to make flexible foams for furniture and for carpet backings.

Polyvinyl chloride See P.V.C.

Poplin Originally a woven cotton fabric but may be of silk, wool or viscose. Treat according to fibre.

Poromeric material This is a plastic material used for shoes. Similar to leather even to the extent that it can 'breathe' and absorbs foot sweat. Resistant to fungus growth. Won't stain or fade. Expands and contracts with the foot but doesn't lose shape permanently. Brand names: Clarino, Corfam. Used for shoes, bags, wallets, sports equipment.
TREATMENT Wipe with a damp cloth, or wash. Polish with ordinary shoe polish.

Raycelon A twinned yarn of five parts viscose rayon to three parts Celon nylon.

Rayon Nearly all rayon is now made from viscose, and is known just as 'viscose' instead of 'viscose rayon'. See Viscose.

Rep Heavy woven fabric with a strong rib running across it. Usually used for furnishing. Originally cotton but may now be a mixture of cotton and man-made fibres. Wash as for weakest fibre.

Rexor Brand name for a metallic yarn.

Rhodia Brand name for an acetate fibre.

Rhovyl Brand name for a P.V.C. material.

Sailcloth Canvas cloth used to make sails, hammocks, deckchairs, etc. Made from linen, cotton, jute or man-made fibres, in several degrees of coarseness or heaviness. Wash as for the weakest fibre.

Samite   This biblical fabric which conjures up rich images is now mainly used for ecclesiastical robes. Mostly silk, in several colours and heavily embroidered. Dry-clean only.

Saran   Brand name for a P.V.C. material.

Sateen   Satin-like fabric used for curtains and linings. May be cotton or rayon. Treat as for weakest fibre.

Satin   Sexy, smooth, shiny material with a short nap which hides the thread structure completely. Originally of silk or cotton but now also found in polyester, nylon or acetate. Heavy furnishing satins should be dry-cleaned. Lighter ones may be washed, as for the fibre used. Iron silk satin while it is still slightly damp, using a fairly hot iron. Press on the wrong side until the material is completely dry. Acetate satin should be ironed on the wrong side with a cool iron while evenly damp. Don't sprinkle it with water or it may spot.

Sea Island cotton   A very high quality, fine cotton from a chain of islands just off the coast of Georgia. Makes beautiful shirts. Wash as for cotton.

Seersucker (also called plisse)   Crinkled, lightweight fabric, originally cotton and silk, now often found in nylon or polyester. Wash as appropriate for the fibre. Needs no ironing.

Serge   Durable suiting fabric in worsted or blends of wool and viscose or other fibres. Dry-clean or wash quickly in warm water, squeeze out water and dry away from direct heat. Iron under a damp cloth with a warm iron.

Shantung   Hardwearing Chinese silk fabric with slubs. Although originally made of wild silk from the tusser worm, now it may be acetate or nylon. Wash as appropriate for the fibre.

Sharkskin   Smooth woven or knitted fabric originally of cotton but now nearly always acetate. Wash as appropriate for fibre. Be warned, it may show watermarks if ironed over damp patches so dry evenly and don't iron until almost dry.

Sheepskin   Best to take it to a specialist cleaner. But if you do decide to clean it yourself, shampoo rather than wash. Use hand-hot water and soapflakes or mild detergent. Rinse with warm water. Squeeze out and dry away from direct heat.

Shoddy Cloth made from reclaimed knitted fabrics but of better quality than mungo. Wash as for wool.

Silene Brand name for an acetate fibre.

Silk This is a natural fibre, the product of the ugly little silkworm, which is the caterpillar of the silk moth, and other creatures. Silk does not conduct heat so keeps in the heat of the body. It is therefore warm. It is also strong, resilient and elastic, and therefore wrinkle resistant. Sunlight and perspiration can weaken it.

The mulberry silkworm is now completely domesticated – it does not exist in the wild. It produces the best silk. Silk from other creatures, notably the tusser worm, is called 'wild' silk. Silks are used for shirts, very occasionally sheets, dresses, evening coats, etc.

TREATMENT Silk taffetas and brocades should by dry-cleaned. So should silk ties. If the care label recommends dry-cleaning you'd be wise to follow that advice. Wash a garment every time you wear it. Perspiration stains may be impossible to get out and may weaken the fabric. Other stains should be removed professionally, but tell the cleaner what the stain is made of. Don't soak in biological detergent. Iron while still damp with a cool iron or with a steam iron. White silk may be bleached with a solution of hydrogen peroxide or sodium perborate type bleaches.

An old method of renovating silk was to sponge with a weak solution of household ammonia and iron on the wrong side.

Silk stockings will wear much longer if soaked in clean, cold water before being worn. They should be washed in lukewarm water and detergent. Squeeze gently, don't rub.

Coloured silks, if you wash them, need a special final treatment because the colours on silks are sometimes affected by traces of alkali or they may run or print off during drying. To prevent this add 10 ml of strong acetic acid to 3 litres of water (half a tablespoonful to a gallon). Strong acetic acid bought from chemists is about thirty per cent strength so the solution will be about 0.1 per cent, just sufficient to taste slightly sharp. After the final rinse, immerse the silk in this and leave it for a few minutes. Then dry without rinsing.

Silks must never be rubbed while they are wet, or the silk filaments break up and produce a white, chalky effect.

Slub A lump in a fabric where the yarn has been left untwisted to produce an ornamental finish.

Solena Brand name for a bonded fibre.

Spanzelle   Brand name for a polyurethane fibre. See Elastane.

Spinlene   Brand name for a polyester fibre.

Straw hats   Wipe with a cloth squeezed in detergenty water then bleach with 5 g of salt to 30 ml of lemon juice (one teaspoon of salt to one tablespoon of juice). Rinse in cold water and dry in the sun.

Stretch fabrics   See Elastane.

Surah   A fine twill, originally of silk but now usually acetate or triacetate. Usually printed (and known as foulard). Wash as appropriate for fibre.

Taffeta   A plain, shiny, closely woven fabric used for party dresses, linings, rainwear, etc. It may be of silk or wool, but nowadays is more likely to be acetate, viscose, polyester or nylon. Most taffetas should be dry-cleaned. Nylon may be washed.

Tarlatan   This is thin, transparent, stiffened muslin used for tutus and petticoats, etc. Dry-clean it or it will go limp. If it *has* gone limp use a plastic starch. Very stiff tarlatan may ladder your tights unless you cover the raw edge with bias binding.

Teklan   Brand name for a modacrylic fibre. It is flame-proof and so good for children's nightwear, soft toys, etc. Wash as for modacrylic.

Tergal   Brand name used in France for Terylene.

Terlenka   Brand name for a polyester fibre.

Terylene   Brand name for a polyester fibre.

Timbrelle   Brand name for a nylon.

Trevira   Brand name for a polyester fibre.

Triacetate   A development of cellulose acetate fibres. It's made from wood pulp and cotton. It can be embossed or permanently pleated, resists dirt and creasing, won't shrink or stretch, can be woven or knitted and dries quickly. It's often blended with other fibres for use in children's clothes, fillings for quilted materials and quilts, woven and knitted dresses, hand-knitting yarns. Brand names include Arnel, Tricel, Trilan.

TREATMENT Wash in warm water and detergent, swirl gently but don't squeeze. Drip-dry. If you machine wash do so in a short warm wash with a cold rinse and a short spin. Cool iron if necessary. Triacetate can be dry-cleaned but you should tell the cleaner what the fabric is because it should be cleaned in perchloroethylene and not trichlorethylene (in fact the care label should have a P symbol to tell you this). Triacetate is soluble in acetone, acetic acid and alcohol, so do not use them for stain removal.

Tricel Brand name for a triacetate fibre.

Tricelon A mixture of triacetate (Tricel) and nylon (Celon) made by Courtaulds. It has the softness of one with the strength of the other and should be treated as for triacetate.

Tricot French word for knitting, so a jersey fabric. Can be made of viscose, nylon or polyester. Wash as appropriate for fibre.

Trilan Brand name for a triacetate fibre.

Tulle A fine net of cotton, viscose, nylon or other fibres. Wash as appropriate for fibre. If the net becomes limp, dip cotton tulle in weak starch; dip nylon and rayon in a gum arabic solution.

Tusser (or tussore, or tussah) See Silk.

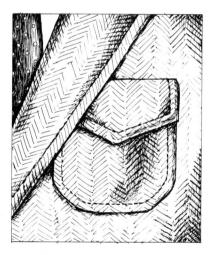

Tweed A heavy twilled woollen fabric, often made with two differently coloured yarns. Scotland is particularly famous for its tweeds. Dry-clean woollen tweeds. Tweeds are now made also in polyester or acrylic in which case you can wash according to which fibre you're dealing with.

Velour   A cotton, silk or man-made fibre material with a heavy pile. Usually now in acrylic. Usually better to dry-clean.

Velvet   A fabric of silk, cotton, wool, viscose, nylon, etc., with a rich pile. Many are uncrushable, spot-proof, and easily washed. Velvets differ a lot so be careful to find out which fibre you're dealing with and wash accordingly. If in doubt, dry-clean. To remove creases steam over a kettle spout.

Velveteen   Fabric like velvet except that the pile runs across the fabric instead of up and down. Used to be of cotton but now often of viscose. Wash as appropriate for fibre. Shake occasionally while drying and smooth the pile with a soft cloth or a velvet brush. Alternatively, dry-clean.

Verel   Brand name for a modacrylic fibre.

Vicuna   Very little of the cloth bearing this name comes from the soft and expensive hair of the vicuna, which is virtually extinct. It is a plain, dark cloth, finished in a characteristic manner – much worn by certain Prime Ministers. Dry-clean. (Import of genuine vicuna into the U.K. is now prohibited.)

Vilene   Brand name for a bonded fibre used for stiffening lapels, etc.

Viloft   Brand name for a viscose fibre.

Vincel   Brand name for a polynosic viscose fibre. See Modal.

Viscose   Viscous golden-brown liquid made from cellulose (usually from wood pulp). It is used for making rayon and many other fibres. The word viscose is now nearly always substituted for rayon. Modified forms include high-strength yarns in carpets and clothing. It can be made to look like silk, wool, linen, cotton, etc. but should not be treated as such. Brand names include Delustra, Evlan, Raycelon, Viloft.
TREATMENT   Wash often. Handle gently. Cool wash. Do not twist or wring or pull while washing, though you can squeeze gently to get the water out. If you do not have a steam iron, iron while still a bit damp with a medium hot iron. Shiny taffetas, satins, etc. should be ironed on the right side, matt crêpes etc. on the wrong side. Don't press over seams.

Viyella   Brand name for a woven cotton and wool fabric. Wash gently by hand in hot water. Use a warm iron on the wrong side of the fabric while it is still damp.

Voile   Sheer woven material originally of cotton but now also made in viscose, nylon or polyester. Wash as appropriate for fibre.

Vyrene   Brand name for a polyurethane fibre. See Elastane.

Whipcord   A closely woven heavy twill fabric originally of worsted wool or wool and cotton but now often viscose/cotton blends. Wash as appropriate for fibre.

Wincey   A lightweight flannel-type fabric, originally of wool and cotton but now often in wool mixtures. Hand wash. Use steam iron or iron on the wrong side while damp.

Winceyette   Similar to flannelette but lighter. Originally cotton or cotton and wool but now often in viscose blends. Wash as for wool or viscose.

Wool   Natural fibre from the coats of sheep, lambs and goats or camels. Special sorts of wool are made from the alpaca, llama, vicuna, camel, goat and rabbit. Wool has a coating of scales which will work against each other like a ratchet if the wool is rubbed while in water and this causes the wool to shrink and 'felt'. Wool also stretches when wet (but will never 'unfelt'). Most people find wool warm and comfortable. It absorbs moisture without making you feel cold. It is resilient, elastic and resists wrinkling.

TREATMENT   Because wool felts up so easily when wet it is essential only to squeeze the water gently through the garment. Never rub, twist or wring. Most experts recommend using a soapless detergent especially in hard-water areas. There are now special detergents for use with wool including Woolite and Adamite which can be used in cold water. I have found it quite safe to give woollen sweaters a short spin to get rid of the worst of excess moisture (wool should *never* be tumble-dried). The garment should then be laid flat on a towel on the floor and pulled gently into its correct shape and left to dry. When very nearly dry you could hasten its drying by hanging over a banister or chair back but as wool stretches when wet you can't do so until it's just damp to the touch. If it has dried out of shape it will stay like that until you next wash it.

New techniques have produced machine-washable wools. There are about twelve different ways of treating wool to make it machine-washable. But these techniques do make it feel different – a bit slithery. Some people don't like the feel of it and prefer to use old-fashioned wool and wash it by hand. If a garment is labelled 'machine-washable' you should follow the washing instructions to the letter. If there are none, give it a minimum wash at a low temperature.

It should not be necessary to soak wool before washing as it should release any normal grubbiness during gentle washing. Make sure any detergent is completely dissolved before adding the garment. I use a mild liquid detergent. Enzyme ('biological') detergents are not recommended for wool. Fabric softeners may be helpful.

If a garment loses colour in patches it's almost certainly because you've washed it badly. You've probably not let the detergent dissolve properly and direct contact with the undissolved powder has caused the colour loss. Water that is too hot causes colour loss in wool as in many other fabrics – depending on the dye used. Always dry woollens away from direct sunlight or direct heat. Never use chlorine bleaches. Wool garments should be allowed to 'rest' for twenty-four hours between wearings to let them get their shape back.

Yellowed white wool can be soaked in a solution of one part hydrogen peroxide to ten parts water. Then rinse in warm water. Never rub wool. Just squeeze it gently. Never use water hotter than lukewarm.

Oiled wool should be washed in warm (40°C, 104°F) water using thoroughly dissolved soapflakes (not detergent, which will remove the oil) or Woolite or Adamite. You can't re-oil wool, so treat it gently.

Worsted   Fine smooth yarn made from carded and combed wool which does not have the fluffiness and nap of ordinary woollen yarn.

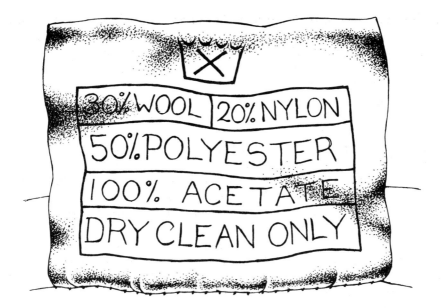

CHAPTER 3

DRY-CLEANING

Many fabrics can be washed but some, particularly wool, shrink and felt when washed in water and to avoid this they are washed instead in a special liquid or spirit. This is misleadingly called dry-cleaning. It's not at all dry, but it doesn't use water.

Dry-cleaning was discovered in France, which is why occasionally it is still called French cleaning. It was discovered by accident when paraffin was spilled over a cloth; when it dried out, where the paraffin had been, the cloth was clean.

Paraffin was found to leave traces of colour in the cloth so by degrees other agents were tried until benzine was found to give best results. The only equipment in those days was earthenware jars, white hair brushes and a scouring board. The garments had to be taken to pieces; the pieces were dipped in spirit, scoured on the board, re-dipped, to rinse away the loosened dirt, and dried in a warm room. Finally the garments were stitched together again and pressed.

The process is still called dry-cleaning because although fabrics are impregnated with spirit, this does not cause the fibres to swell and lose their shape as water does.

There have been many changes in dry-cleaning methods. Automatic cleaning machines, highly refined cleaning fluids, all shapes and varieties of steam presses have been introduced.

A garment is made mainly of one fabric, but it may have a lining of another and an interlining of yet another. It also may have buttons, trimmings, and zips held together by sewing thread, all of which may be made of different materials. If any of these bits and pieces are unsuitable for washing, you will either have to take off the unwashable bits or have the garment dry-cleaned. As explained in Chapter 1, most garments bought in Britain and in many other countries will have a care label indicating whether the article may be washed or dry-cleaned.

A wide and growing range of textiles can be both washed and dry-cleaned, and in some cases dry-cleaning is more satisfactory. Even if the label does not say so, lots of washable garments can be dry-cleaned. But if the label says dry-clean only then do not wash the garment. You may think the manufacturer is simply protecting himself from foolish people using the wrong wash programmes, but in fact there is often a good reason for the dry-clean-only label. It may be that the material will shrink or has a finish unsuitable for washing or that the colour will run.

Professional cleaners prefer that you should never try to dry-clean a garment or spot-clean anything yourself. They know too much about the difficulties and failures and have had too much experience of trying to put right the disasters caused by customers trying to clean stains at home. There are certainly some things which can be attempted at home if one knows enough. But if you have any doubt about the fabric or what the stain is or the right procedure to follow, or if the garment is a valuable one, don't play around with it yourself. Take it to a reputable dry-cleaner, tell him all you can about the stain and the fabric, and let him make the decisions and do the work. Get it there as soon as you can. Tell the cleaner what the fabric is made of and what was spilled on it. He will have a variety of chemicals to treat specific stains and, more important, the correct techniques for removing them. If you try to do it yourself you may 'fix' the stain, after which even a professional cleaner won't be able to get rid of it.

Dry-cleaning may seem expensive as the cost of labour is high. But it is good value for money compared with other services and it does help to prolong the life of clothes. People are curiously inconsistent. They will wash some clothes every few days, but wouldn't dream of having a suit cleaned more than once or twice a year.

Clothes should be cleaned after every fifteen wearings – or about once a month for a suit. Delicate silk shirts should be cleaned much oftener. Raincoats should be cleaned often. A dirty one will be permanently discoloured. Raincoats are supposed to be automatically reproofed by the cleaner.

I.C.I. were particularly helpful to me when I was researching this book. They make dry-cleaning fluids and have a testing laboratory at Runcorn in Cheshire. Martin Sherley who runs the laboratory said: 'If in doubt, don't fiddle with it. I'm always getting people who say "I have spilled egg on this sheepskin coat. I haven't touched it at all – just held it over the kettle for a bit"; so they've shrunk the leather and cooked the egg. If they'd taken it straight to a professional he would have got the coat back clean and wearable.'

However, dry-cleaning is not always perfect. Even if the stain is removed completely, the look of the garment may be spoiled. 'I tend to say, more and more, get a new skirt' said Martin Sherley. 'We can work on spot eradication for two days and remove the stain – the skirt's a mess and the work has cost £60 but we've done it!'

If a professional cleaner thinks he may ruin a garment by dry-cleaning it then he will tell you so. But you must make sure he knows what the garment is made of. Sometimes a dry-cleaner will not accept a garment even if it has a dry-clean label inside it. That is his right.

The dry-cleaning symbols you may find in care labels are listed on page 16.

HOW DRY-CLEANING WORKS

I used to imagine that dry-cleaning machines just tumbled the clothes round and round in some sort of nasty-smelling fluid and all that happened was that they came out just as dirty as ever with a horrible smell as a bonus. Happily this isn't the case.

Dry-cleaning does not really mean *dry* cleaning. All dry-cleaning machines use a solvent of some kind which dissolves greases, oils and waxes. In fact, a dry-cleaning machine does exactly the same things as a washing-machine but uses a dry-cleaning fluid, to dissolve and carry away dirt, instead of using water. Dry-cleaning machines should also remove water-soluble stains such as sweat and stains of food and drink, cooking splashes, mud, blood, oil and graphite (from trapping a coat in a car door for instance).

There are only four types of dry-cleaning solvents used by professionals. Carbon tetrachloride is not used now because it has been found to be extremely toxic. It should not be sold by chemists and you should not use it. If you have any in the house you should take it to a chemist and get him to dispose of it.

The four solvents now in use are trichloroethane; perchloroethylene; fluorocarbon and white spirit. The most common solvent now used is perchloroethylene which is entirely satisfactory for many garments, household furnishings and fabrics.

The fluorocarbon used in dry-cleaning is trichlorotrifluoroethane. It is a less powerful solvent than the more common perchloroethylene. It won't start to dissolve buttons and the finishes on some garments though it will remove grease from fingers. So it is strong enough but not too strong. It won't dissolve any bindings or interlinings whereas perchloroethylene may dissolve some. It has a low boiling point so it can be reclaimed after use by distillation.

Fluorocarbon is best for acrylics and other heat-sensitive garments because fluorocarbon boils at less than the temperature of a cup of hot tea and these machines don't pump any solvent out at the end of the process. Perchloroethylene machines do have to be vented out often through the roof. This means that fluorocarbon machines can be smaller and can be used almost anywhere. Another benefit of fluorocarbon is in suede and leather cleaning because it won't damage the colour and won't shrink the skin or crease or 'de-nature' it.

All these solvents are non-flammable. In fact they act as fire extinguishers. All solvents used in dry-cleaning at present are anaesthetics. Small amounts will give you a headache, make you giddy, even make you unconscious but won't, so they say, harm you permanently. Only a very few bad accidents have been caused by solvents and nearly always because people have put too many clothes in the machine.

Sweat and food stains and water-based stains generally will not come out with solvent alone. A small amount of water in the right form is also needed. Water and solvent don't mix, so the dry-cleaning detergent and water are mixed together in small amounts. This mixture will seek out soluble stains. So you have solvent, detergent, water and clothes sloshing around together in the machine (but for wool there must be no water).

Here is a description of what happens in the dry-cleaning machine. Solvent is put into the drum containing the correct weight of clothes. The drum rotates, tumbling the garments, and this forces the solvent between the fibres of the garments, dissolving out the greases, fats, oils and waxes, and releasing particles of grit, sand, dust, etc. After four to seven minutes the solvent is drained from the drum and the drum spins for about two to three minutes to get rid of as much dirty solvent as possible. The garments are rinsed in clean solvent for three minutes or so and then given another high-speed spin. Warm air is blown into the drum for fifteen to twenty minutes to dry the garments while they tumble. With perchloroethylene the drying temperature is around 60°C (140°F) but with fluorocarbon it need only reach 30°C (86°F).

Detergent is often added during the first part of the process to disperse the water evenly (if water is used at all) and to suspend the dust particles and prevent them from going back into the fabric.

DRY-CLEANING IN A LAUNDERETTE

In the more sophisticated machines which distil the solvent, clean solvent can go round many times. But coin-operated machines don't always distil the solvent. Many just filter out a fair amount of the dirt but this is not as effective as distillation. Such machines are useful as budget cleaning for curtains, coats and blankets and so on. They mostly use perchloroethylene, and delicate fabrics should not be cleaned in them.

In coin-operated machines, only the solvent cleaning process is carried out. All spots and stains may not be removed and usually you'll have to do the pressing at home. There may or may not be a rinse programme.

A usual load for a coin-operated machine is about 4.5 to 5.5 kg (10 to 12 lb). You must never overload a dry-cleaning machine and the clothes must always be completely dry before you take them out. People do use the machines the wrong way and may put 18 lb of clothes in a machine which is supposed to take only 10 lb. This is dangerous because the machine is designed to dry a certain weight of clothes in the time allotted to it. If you put too many clothes in, they will come out not quite dry. The residual vapour is toxic and may make you giddy or even unconscious. If you are using a coin-operated machine and the machine stops before it should or the clothes are still damp when you open the door, close the door again, look for the instructions, phone the manager and get him to come out and deal with the situation. Do not attempt to do it yourself. The horrid stories of people being overcome by fumes from damp dry-cleaned clothes in the back of the car are true.

You should never put soft toys in a dry-cleaning machine as they will take much longer to dry out and the fumes could be deadly dangerous to a child hugging his teddy in bed. Always read all the instructions carefully before using a dry-cleaning machine.

THE EXPERT

Usually when you take your clothes to the cleaner somebody whisks them into the back and that's the last you see of them until you collect them. Behind the scenes, pockets and trouser turn-ups should be searched for anything you might have left in them. If is common to find bank notes, coins and anything from lipsticks to valuable rings. Things which aren't worth much are usually returned with the cleaned garment but a good cleaner will let you know as soon as possible if anything valuable has been found.

Some cleaners will send the clothes to 'The Works'. Many of these are now divided into sections, or units, each carrying out the complete service of dry-cleaning and finishing for a small number of shops. The big works also deal with the bulky and more elaborate types of furnishings. Garment re-dyeing, furnishings and carpets are not done by small shops with their own small works at the back.

Unit shops consist of the shop itself with a small works combined. They can cope with most types of garments and soft furnishings. The introduction of fully automatic machines using non-flammable cleaning fluid has made these shops possible in busy High Streets. They provide a personal service where the customer should be able to get advice when necessary direct from the man at the machines.

A cleaner who can give you personal service may be more satisfactory than a chain-store cleaner where the man who does the cleaning may be very skilled but you never get a chance to talk to him, and the girl at the counter may not have a clue or may not pass your messages on.

There is no easy way to find a good cleaner. A good indication is the look of the shop. Choose one which is clean, bright and well kept, where the manager has time to discuss your cleaning.

All articles are sorted according to the type of fabric, the weight, the colour and how dirty they are. Delicate and frilly things, evening dresses, silks and light woollens, and man-made fibres, are all dealt with separately. Delicate items are put into net bags for cleaning. Very dirty overalls, gardening clothes, jodhpurs, etc., are kept separate from the time you hand them in, and all furnishings are kept separate from clothes.

Buttons are often covered with foil to protect them. After cleaning, the clothes are given any specialist finishing treatment necessary.

SPOTTING

'Spotting' is the removal of specific stains on a fabric. It has to be done by skilled people with a knowledge of fabrics, chemicals and what has caused the stain. Some stains come out in the normal cleaning process – any that still show are treated before pressing so they will not be set in. If it's an old stain it may be impossible to get it out. A good cleaner will tell you this. Unless there is a very simple stain on a robust fabric and you catch it at once, any stain is best left to the cleaner from the start.

Steam pressing and shaping also have to be done by skilled people who must know about modern fibres and fabrics. Information on new fabrics and special processes and temperatures suitable for their treatment is continually being issued to its members by the Fabric Care Research Association.

All sorts of different types of presses, steam finishes, specialized small appliances such as 'steam puffs' for shaped garments and hand irons may be used in the finishing departments of dry-cleaners.

A good deal of manual work is still done: pleats are set by hand, linings and underskirts and all elaborate clothes are ironed by hand. People usually specialize – in suit pressing, pleating or silk finishing, for instance.

SPECIAL SERVICES

Many dry-cleaners will do small repairs and alterations. Replacement of buttons may be included in the overall cleaning charge or there may be a small extra charge. Many cleaners will put new zips in, but beware! I have had four zips put in by one chain of cleaners – not one was satisfactory and the work took two weeks each time. On the other hand, a friend had three zips replaced for just over £1 in just under a week, so it pays to shop around.

Retexturing is a special service. It impregnates fabrics with a dressing which renews the set and the way they hang. It gives firmer pleats and is especially helpful for old exhausted-looking clothes.

Many clothes don't need retexturing, however. Retex fluid may be a crease-resistant (or crease-retaining) resin or a waterproofing agent. Never ask for it to be used on knitted materials, woollens, or lightweight fabrics.

Dry-cleaning is in itself one of the best methods of moth-proofing, but a special treatment can be applied which will give even more protection until the next cleaning.

Goods that need special treatment

Wool needs special attention, both in washing and dry-cleaning. The reason is that it has a coating of scales which will work against each other, in water, like a ratchet. This doesn't happen in solvent. The looser the loop in the knitting, the more the wool will move, the more the scales will rub against each other and the more the wool will shrink and felt. Once this has happened nothing will undo the damage.

It is important that the machine in which you are having any woollen garments dry-cleaned should have no water in the mixture. Most dry-cleaners are well aware of this but mistakes have been known to happen so you must make sure your cleaners know they are dealing with wool and not some man-made fibre.

Furnishings   Carpets, curtains, eiderdowns, duvets, pillows, cushions, loose covers, etc., can all be efficiently dealt with by a specialist cleaner.

Carpets and upholstery can be cleaned at home but cleaners sometimes prefer to clean carpets at their works where they can be treated more thoroughly.

Elaborate pelmets may have to be cleaned by hand and may even have to be unpicked and sewn up again afterwards. If you want pelmets re-dyed, they will certainly have to be unpicked.

Some cleaners will flame-proof curtains (especially necessary for schools, hotels, etc.) and stage wardrobes. This treatment will have to be repeated every time the items are cleaned.

Leather and suede   Leather and suede cleaning are highly specialized. Some cleaners specialize in all kinds of leather garments, including sheepskin, which go through a special cleaning process and are dried by special methods too. Suede and sheepskin are usually finished by spraying with oil to keep the skin supple. Dye may be added to the spray to revive faded colours. Many dry-cleaners subcontract the cleaning of suede and leather to the few specialists.

Experts say you should have suede and sheepskin cleaned as soon as dirt begins to show round collar and cuffs. If a garment is allowed to get very dirty the chances of a cleaner managing to get it really clean again are small.

Suede and leathers should be cleaned only in perchloroethylene or fluorocarbon. As an extra most cleaners will repair damaged cuffs, collars and pockets. Some will also touch up colours damaged during wear and many will match up buttons too. A good leather cleaner should have rows and rows of suede and leather dyes on his shelves.

Pigskin   Pigskin is difficult to handle. Modern skins are often made from pigs bred in Europe for food and the skins are often fatty. They are nevertheless dyed and made into coats and at the first cleaning half the fat drops out and they become harder, more wrinkled and generally less satisfactory.

If incorrect glues have been used the lining will shrink and the dye comes off in different panels in different ways. These coats are cheap compared with say, sheepskin, so they are tempting, but they're trouble.

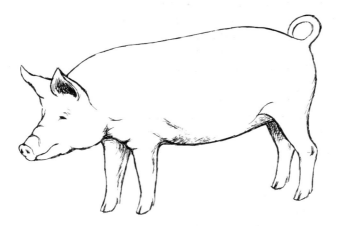

Velvets   Velvets dry-clean quite satisfactorily.

Acrylics   Acrylics must dry at a cool temperature.

WHAT TO DO IF THINGS GO WRONG

In normal circumstances, domestic laundry and dry-cleaning customers should have no cause to complain about the service they receive, says the Association of British Launderers and Cleaners in the foreword to its code of practice. And this is on the whole true, but not always. A friend of mine's clothes had obviously not been cleaned at all when he went to pick them up. When he tried to point this out he was greeted with a despairing cry by the girl behind the counter, 'Oh, no – not you too.'

As the A.B.L.C. points out, one of the main differences between buying a manufactured product and buying a service such as laundering and dry-cleaning is that subjective opinion plays a large part in judging a service whereas the acceptability of a manufactured product is in most cases a matter of fact and clear to the buyer. Here is what the A.B.L.C. says:

> In order to minimize the number of complaints and ensure that those that do arise are attended to speedily and effectively, members of the Association of British Launderers and Cleaners set themselves clear objectives in their customer relations policies, and apply practices, standards and procedures designed to achieve a level of service represented by the series of undertakings contained in the Code of Practice Statement. Many A.B.L.C. members will, as a matter of individual policy continue to provide levels of service and use trading conditions which in some respects exceed this standard code. The important thing from the customer's point of view is that all those who use the services provided by A.B.L.C. members can be assured of a fair deal.
>
> You can tell which laundry and dry-cleaning firms are A.B.L.C. members because they will be encouraged to display a sign or notice proclaiming their membership and will display a copy of the Code of Practice Statement. Laundry books will contain a reference to it too.
>
> The A.B.L.C.'s customer advisory service provides customers with an efficient and helpful procedure through which disputes which cannot be resolved between the member and the customer can normally be quickly settled.

The Code of Practice Statement reads thus:

> As a member of the Association of British Launderers and Cleaners Ltd, we undertake not to restrict our liability under the general law and shall so far as is reasonably practicable:
> 1. Handle all clothes, linens, furnishings and other items accepted by us for processing with proper and due care and attention.
> 2. Investigate any complaint promptly and, if requested, reprocess, free of charge, any article which is unsatisfactory due to fault on our part.

3. Train our staff to be competent, courteous and helpful at all times.
4. Keep our shops, vans, containers and premises clean and tidy.
5. Maintain the highest possible standard of quality and service consistent with the price charged.
6. Display in shop premises a list of prices for standard articles.
7. Have all orders ready or delivered at the time stated, unless prevented by exceptional circumstances.

The Association's address is: Lancaster Gate House, 319 Pinner Road, Harrow, Middlesex HA1 4HX.

The code of practice applies to all services, including repairing and dyeing, normally provided by domestic laundry and dry-cleaning members to customers who are private individuals, but does not apply to services provided by launderettes and coin-operated dry-cleaning establishments.

At common law, if a launderer or cleaner loses or destroys a customer's article through his negligence or that of his employees he is liable for the market value of the article at the time it is lost or destroyed, i.e. allowing for depreciation but reflecting to some extent the cost of replacement at current costs. If the article is only damaged and is capable of adequate repair the launderer/cleaner is only liable for the cost of that repair except that if this exceeds the market value of the article at that time the cleaner is only liable for the latter.

The liability of the cleaner is for negligence, that is to say, for breach of a duty or obligation, whether imposed by the common law or by an express or implied term in a contract to take reasonable care or exercise reasonable skill in relation to the articles left with him. In considering negligence it must be remembered that the launderer/cleaner holds himself out as possessing specialized knowledge and might be held to be negligent if he uses an unsuitable process or fails to realize that a particular article would be damaged, at any rate where such a risk would be generally recognized by others in the industry.

Among the possible causes of damage for which neither the common law nor common sense expects the cleaner to be responsible (unless he adds to the damage by his negligence) are: faulty manufacture (colours running or fabric stretching during manufacture, inadequate seaming or incorrect care labelling); previous misuse by the customer (e.g. drying of razor blades on towels, excessive use of bleach, spillage of acids etc.); and normal but unrecognized wear (e.g. weakening of curtains by exposure to light).

I have a home truth story about incorrect care labelling which stresses the importance of checking that the label does exist in the garment when you buy it.

A friend of mine bought an extremely beautiful and expensive pure wool sweater in a well known and expensive shop. She normally washes her woollen garments but decided, because this one was so special, she'd have it cleaned professionally. The cleaner cleaned it and returned it shrunk so that she hardly recognized it and certainly couldn't wear it again. The garment was clearly wool but had no textile label in it. The shop said the garment had been labelled when sold. The cleaner said it must have been washed and shrunk before he received it. He sent the garment to an independent laboratory who came back with the same answer. However, I saw the sweater just before it was taken to the cleaners and I know she hadn't touched it, so it's not always as easy to get compensation as it should be.

If a customer's article is lost or damaged by fire or burglary while in the cleaner's custody, the customer will expect compensation. At common law the customer is entitled to compensation only where the fire or burglary in question was caused by the cleaner's negligence. But to eliminate this potential source of dissatisfaction, A.B.L.C. members undertake to pay full compensation for loss or damage caused by fire or burglary – unless the customer is already covered by his own insurance – even though no negligence can be attributed to the cleaner.

The wide range of different articles offered to launderers and dry-cleaners for processing makes it impossible to prepare a printed price-list covering every type of article that might find its way to the cleaner. A.B.L.C. members display a list of prices covering garments most often brought to be cleaned. Prices for other standard articles or services will be quoted on request. Where articles are of exceptional value or of an unusual nature members reserve the right to charge a special price.

If your clothes come back shrunk so as to be unwearable, or dyed the wrong colour or irretrievably limp, for instance, it may be difficult to find out who is to blame:

The cleaner who could have used the wrong, or dirty, solvent.

The manufacturer who didn't label the clothes or made them badly.

You because you have previously washed the clothes and not got all the soap out or tried to remove a stain and did some damage in the process.

If you feel absolutely sure it was not your fault, be patient and keep trying. Keep all letters and communications.

If your cleaner is a member of the A.B.L.C. he can refer any dispute for arbitration by the Association's Customer Advisory Service (address above). Or you can approach your local Consumer Advice Centre, Citizens Advice Bureau or Trading Standards Department (look in yellow pages for address) who may be prepared to negotiate between you and the cleaner.

Any of these organizations or the cleaner himself may recommend an independent laboratory report if your cleaning is damaged. There are several laboratories who will test clothes for a small charge. You and the cleaner should agree to be bound by the laboratory's findings. You may have to put down between £5 and £25 as a deposit which you get back if the decision is in your favour. Or you can send the garments to a laboratory on your own initiative. If the laboratory can't say the cleaner was at fault it cannot always tell who was. But if it seems the manufacturer is at fault, take the garment back to the shop who should take it up with the manufacturer. (A fault in something the shop sold is legally the shop's responsibility.) The manufacturer may have his own laboratory. Sometimes the cleaner may be prepared to negotiate with the shop for you.

Provided you did tell the cleaner anything special about the garment when you took it in, you may be entitled to compensation for loss, damage or bad workmanship unless you accept the cleaner's offer to repair, reclean, repress or stretch the garment. The amount you get from a cleaner who accepts responsibility for the mishap is something you will have to negotiate. The amount should take into account: the original purchase price; an adjustment downwards to take account of length of time you have had the garment; an adjustment upwards to take account of inflation.

Generally if it was bought during the last two or three years you should expect to get about what you paid for it. Otherwise the cleaner should pay for someone else to do the repair.

If on the other hand the item was faulty when it was sold to you then the shop is bound to pay compensation. If it is really ruined the compensation will be the price you paid. If it is repairable, just the cost of the repair. When you think you know who was responsible and you have no luck by just dealing with the assistants, make a formal complaint to the manager or a director of the firm concerned. Keep a copy of the letter you send.

If you have been using a coin-operated machine and something goes wrong to damage the clothes, you should write or telephone the owner or manager. You should find his address pinned up in the premises. If the shop is a member of the National Association of the Launderette Industry (N.A.L.I.) write to The Secretary, N.A.L.I., 77 New Bond Street, London W1 and ask for their help.

Always keep all receipts. Complain as soon as you possibly can. The cleaner may sort things out quickly and simply – they often do.

On the other hand, it may all take ages. But do not give up hope. Keep all receipts, letters and so on. If you agree to an independent laboratory report, which may be inconclusive, ask to see the final report. As a last resort you could claim for compensation through the County Court. (The Consumers' Association have published a booklet called *How to Sue in the County Court* which tells you how to do this.) But, quite honestly, it's not usually worth while taking anything to those lengths unless you've lost something very valuable.

CHAPTER 4

STAIN REMOVING AT HOME

I said in the chapter on professional dry-cleaning that experts advise against trying to dry-clean stains at home. However, very few families are going to be able to take everything to a dry-cleaner, and stains do need to be dealt with as quickly as possible, so I shall try to tell you what you can safely do to what, and when you really must not.

The first part of this chapter gives instructions for the four basic techniques of spot removal. If you understand the reasons for the different techniques you can often work out for yourself how to treat a stain. I hope these first principles will help people to understand the main techniques, which are very simple. The second part of this chapter is in alphabetical order so that you can look up a specific stain/fabric and see what to do and (perhaps more importantly) what not to do with it.

BASIC RULES

Deal with a stain as soon as possible. Any stain you are not sure about or any stain on a garment whose fibre content you're not sure about (clothes bought in jumble sales, for instance, will probably have no label at all and labels they do have are likely to be unhelpful) should be taken to a professional dry-cleaner. Dress fabrics with special surfaces like taffeta, satin and velvet should always be cleaned professionally or you may remove the surface effect.

Before doing any cleaning, brush and shake clothes and get out all the loose dirt you can. Many stains can be removed by soaking the article in cold water, or water and detergent, and then washing or rinsing them out. Detergents containing enzymes are said to be useful for protein-based stains such as egg and blood.

When removing stains, always keep the stained side down so you are getting rid of it the way it came and not trying to push it through the fabric. The ironing-board is a good place to work. Start by dabbing with a damp clean white cloth in a circle outside the stained area. Keep a pad of clean material, or white tissue, or loo paper, underneath the stained area. Very often water is all that is necessary. It is possible now to get a plastic bottle with a squirter top which directs a very fine spray on to the fabric.

Make sure that you have the substances you may need so that you *can* actually deal with a stain immediately when you spill something.

Here's a list of things *not* to do.

1. Don't apply heat to the fabric in any form before tackling the stain. Many food stains contain albumen or similar protein which is fixed by heat. Don't, for instance, wash the garment in hot water. Heat may fix some stains so you'll never get them out, and may spread others.

    Do check the effect of whichever stain remover you're going to use on an inconspicuous piece of the garment – the inside hem, say, or an inside seam. Some treatments may harm one of the fibres in a mixture and some may make dyes run or fade.

2. Don't try to remove the last traces of very stubborn stains. It is often better to wear the thing with a bit of the stain still showing than risk ruining the fabric by application of too much solvent or by rubbing too much.

3. Don't tell lies! If you give up and then take the garment to a dry-cleaner do be honest about what you've done so far – don't say you haven't touched it.

BASIC TECHNIQUES

Here are the four basic techniques for getting stains out of clothes:

absorbing; washing in water; dry-cleaning in solvent; and bleaching.

Absorbing

This is used to deal with wet things spilled on fabric and also to get rid of greasy particles in fur and other fabrics that cannot be washed. There are various suitable absorbents: salt will absorb urine and fruit-juice stains from carpets, etc. Bran, fuller's earth, French chalk, talcum, will absorb grit and dirt from fur and other unwashable fabrics, in much the same way as a dry shampoo cleans hair. Shake the absorbent onto the fabric to be cleaned. Leave for twelve hours or so. Then brush out gently but thoroughly.

Washing in water

Don't underestimate the value of water for getting rid of stains. Any stain should be rinsed immediately with cold water – not hot because that may set the stain. You can then soak the whole garment in cold water and detergent (see chapters on laundering). But if the fabric can't be soaked because it's not suitable (wool for instance) you'll have to find some other way of getting rid of the stain. Don't use water on dyed wild silk or a moiré pattern which shows only on the right side of the fabric.

Bleaches

There are two kinds of bleach: one which oxidizes, removing the stain by adding oxygen to it. Hydrogen peroxide, which can be safely used on wool or silk and is available from hardware stores and chemists, is an oxidizing bleach. (Hydrogen peroxide is especially useful in restoring whiteness to wool that has gone yellow.) Chlorine bleaches (usually containing sodium hypochlorite) are liquid and are sold under various trade names. They are oxidizing bleaches. (*Reducing* bleaches such as sulphur dioxide, work by taking oxygen away. But they are mainly used by laundries and dry-cleaners.)

Before using any bleach always test a small piece of the fabric, where it can't be seen, for colour-fastness. The method for using hypochlorite liquid bleach (chlorine bleach) on small stains and spots is this:

1. Mix 10 ml of fourteen per cent bleach with 800 ml of cold water

($\frac{1}{2}$ fl oz to 2 pints). (Fourteen per cent is the usual concentration found in the brand-named bleaches you buy in supermarkets and stores.)

2. Put a clean cloth or a wad of tissue under the fabric below the spot and dab the stain with another cloth moistened with the diluted bleach solution.

3. Rinse the garment thoroughly and then wash or dry-clean in the normal way.

For larger areas of stain use 10 ml of bleach to 8 litres of cold water ($\frac{1}{2}$ fl oz to $2\frac{1}{2}$ gallons). Immerse the article for ten to fifteen minutes. Rinse thoroughly, and then wash or dry-clean as usual. This is obviously not suitable for articles that can't be washed.

If you're going to use hydrogen peroxide (from chemists):

1. Prepare a cold solution of one part hydrogen peroxide to four parts water.

2. Soak garments in the solution for up to twelve hours.

3. Rinse thoroughly before washing.

This again is obviously not suitable for dry-clean-only clothes.

Take care when using bleaches. They may damage fabrics or your skin.

Never use undiluted hypochlorite bleach; never use hypochlorite bleach at all on wool, silk or anything treated with a flame-resistant finish; always test for colour-fastness before treatment; always rinse thoroughly to get rid of every bit of bleach.

Dygon (made by Dylon International Ltd) will remove most tea, coffee, wine, fruit and other stains from white fabrics. Moisten the stain, sprinkle with a little Dygon powder. Rub with a soft nail-brush and rinse well. Stubborn stains may need a second treatment. Do not remove stains from coloured fabrics in this way unless they are guaranteed colour-fast.

Dygon will bleach greyed linens, cottons, towels, and so on. Wash and rinse the article first. Dissolve the contents of a Dygon tin in 9 litres (2 gallons) of warm water. Immerse the article for thirty minutes or more. Then wash and rinse as usual.

Solvents

Solvents are what professional dry-cleaners use (together with water and detergent if suitable) in their machines. A solvent is used to get rid of stains which are caused by grease or oil or have a greasy base. The most common (sold as spot remover under various trade names), is trichloroethane. Proprietary stain removers may be in liquid, aerosol or paste form. Other solvents you can use are white spirit (turps substitute), surgical spirit or acetone.

1. As always, if there's any solid matter (in other words if someone's been sick all down their shirtfront) get rid of as much of the thick stuff as you can without damaging the fabric. A blunt knife will get most of it off.

2. Put a white cloth or paper tissue under the stain to prevent it being transferred to another part of the garment.

3. Soak another cloth in solvent and dab in a circle starting outside the stain and working in towards the centre.

4. Rinse thoroughly and wash normally or, if the garment isn't washable, air it well.

Never use a solvent in a closed room – open all doors and windows. Never use near a naked flame; never use acetone on acetate fibres – it will remove the fabric as it does nail varnish. Always test for colour-fastness and always rinse or air after treatment.

Other useful substances for removing stains using these techniques are:

Acetic acid: white vinegar – it must be white – the malt or wine variety will stain. Use it straight from the bottle.

Lemon juice or a 5 per cent solution of citric or tartaric acid.

Fat (margarine or butter) used to soften tar and oil.

Household ammonia, an alkali. Use it straight from the bottle but with caution.

Always follow the manufacturer's instructions where these exist.
Many solvents are flammable and/or poisonous, so use them with care and common sense.

TESTING FOR COLOUR-FASTNESS

Test all fabrics for colour-fastness before trying to remove stains.

Some dyes only remain fixed for a limited number of washes or other treatments. So even when you've tested a fabric you should do it every time you have to treat the garment, especially if you think it will spend some time in contact with the stain-removal agent or washing solution. This is how to test:

1. Make up the washing solution, dilute bleach or solvent in the proportion in which you intend to use it.

2. Apply it to a piece of the garment which won't be seen. The inside hem or an inside seam, for instance.

3. Put the treated area between two pieces of clean old white sheet and press with a warm iron.

4. If any colour has been transferred to the sheet, the fabric is not colour-fast and should be dealt with by a professional.

WORK ON THE WRONG SIDE

Many stains, specially if you catch them quickly are worse on the face of the fabric, so the great thing is to try to draw them out rather than drive them through. If you can get them to come out the same way they went in then you have a better chance of getting rid of the mark completely.

The first step is to get rid of as much as possible of any solid or semi-solid matter. Work from the edges towards the centre so you don't spread the stain. A small bone spatula is recommended by experts but should you not happen to have one, a blunt, round-edged table knife will do perfectly well. Hold it at a low angle to the fabric so it lifts off whatever you've spilled. Don't press too hard and don't scrape. (If the solid matter has hardened you may have to soften it first with water or a suitable solvent.) It will help to pat it with a small, short-bristled brush held vertically. Don't use a brushing action.

When you've got rid of the solids, the idea is to try to dissolve the stain that's left in a suitable fluid which will carry the stain with it when flushed out with water or solvent.

If you can't get at the wrong side of the fabric – if it's on upholstery or a carpet for instance – you will have to sponge it, over and over again. Take great care not to let the liquid get into any padding or backing where it may do irreparable damage.

If you can, however, it's best to work on the wrong side, laying the fabric face down on an absorbent pad of paper tissue – or use a big blob of cotton wool covered by a light, white lint-free cloth such as an old sheet or a piece of butter muslin, or a paper kitchen tissue. Or use several thicknesses of old white towel. The ironing-board is a good place to work and you will need a good light to see what's going on. The absorbent pad helps to draw out the stain.

When you've dissolved the stain, start flushing with water or solvent from well outside the stained area, moving round and working towards the centre. You won't spread the stain any further that way. A plastic bottle with a fine-spray nozzle is useful for this. You can get them in hardware or gardening shops.

If the fabric or the stain has required treatment with a dry-clean solvent, blot up any left-over solvent with a clean, dry cloth or sponge and drive off any remaining solvent with a stream of warm air using a circular motion as you did when cleaning. Start well outside the area you've just worked and work round it, towards the centre. This will help to prevent those awful rings of cleaner-than-clean on an otherwise normally clean garment. A hair drier is the best thing for drying solvent.

If the stain was treated with wet-clean substances like water, or water and detergent, finish by rinsing thoroughly and washing the garment as you normally would.

FINAL TREATMENT

Sometimes powdery particles stay trapped between the fibres after the rest of the stain has dissolved and flushed away. Don't scrape away at these with a finger-nail just before rushing out to work. You can deal with them by applying neat liquid detergent and gently working the fabric between your fingers. The particles become suspended in the detergent which can be washed away with water, taking them with it. You must rinse the article three or four times to get rid of all the detergent. If you don't rinse thoroughly, dirt may stick to the remnants of detergent which will make that whole patch of garment get dirty more quickly than the rest. This job does need patience.

Don't use methylated spirit on rayon or tricel. Don't use dry-cleaning solvent on rain-proofed fabrics. With combination fabrics remember to treat as appropriate for the weaker fabric.

A to Z OF STAINS

N.B. Read through the Basic Rules beginning on p. 73 before applying any of the following methods for stain-removing.

Acids Remove at once with running cold water. Acids do not necessarily stain fabrics but they are quite likely to destroy them. Even a weak acid will affect fibres, especially of cotton, linen, nylon or a blend containing cellulose fibres (viscose), and on coloured materials may damage the colour. Nothing can be done to put such damage right so rush to the tap and rinse thoroughly with cold water. To neutralize any acid there may be left, sponge with household ammonia (diluted as directed on the bottle) or with bicarbonate of soda (baking-soda) dissolved in a little water, and rinse well.

Alcohol Not just drinks, but medicines, skin lotions and perfumes. Alcohol dissolves many finishes so when you do spill something treat it immediately. Wipe up what you've spilled and rub the spot with the palm of your hand. For individual types of alcohol stain, see under the various headings: beer, spirits, perfume, etc. I once spilled red wine on a new silk shirt and took it to the cleaners the following day. Already the alcohol had damaged the colour. I should have torn the shirt off my back then and there and run it under the cold tap.

Adhesives There are many, many different kinds of adhesives soluble in all sorts of different things.

Glue, if it is a water-soluble kind (animal and fish glues) usually comes out in cold water. If not, wet the stain with cold water, treat with household ammonia and rinse. If the stain is still there, wet it again, apply biological detergent and rinse.

For *cellulose-based* (household) adhesives, use non-oily nail-varnish remover or acetone, but *not* on acetate fibres.

Cyanoacrylates are the glues packaged in small tubes, which are very runny, colourless and 'bond in seconds'. There has been a certain amount of worry because cyanoacrylate glue *is* so runny and liable to get out of hand, and people have managed to stick their fingers and even eyelids together. In fact this glue is activated by moisture (which is why it works so well on fingers and eyelids) and moisture will also be its undoing. So if you get it on skin do not panic. It is not dangerous. Hold a damp cloth over the spot until it comes unstuck. Fingers can be unstuck by rolling a pencil gently between them. Even eyelids will unstick eventually if you hold a damp cotton-wool pad over the eye. It may be a bit painful but will do no permanent damage. Soothing words and lots of damp will cure the condition.

Epoxy adhesives consist of a glue and a hardener mixed together just before use, and they can be removed with methylated spirit *before they set*. Once they have hardened they cannot be removed.

For *model aircraft cement*, you can use acetone on any materials *not* made of acetate. Chemically pure amyl acetate will not damage such fabrics, but if the cement has acetone in it they will have been ·damaged anyway. Some manufacturers make a solvent for their cements. Test before using.

Polyvinyl acetate (P.V.A. and filled P.V.A.) can be cleaned off with methylated spirits.

There are many types of *synthetic rubber (contact) adhesive*. Many respond to amyl acetate, non-oily nail-varnish remover or acetone, which should subsequently be flushed with a dry-cleaning solvent. Remember, acetone and nail-varnish remover shouldn't be used on fabrics made of acetate fibre.

Some manufacturers of *rubber-based adhesives* have their own solvent which you can write up for. They will send it free. My advice is to get the solvent before you need it. Otherwise you can use a paintbrush cleaner. Do not use paint strippers which are too savage.

To remove *sticky labels and tape*, soak or leave covered with a wet cloth. Rub with methylated or white spirit.

Alkali (such as washing-soda, baking-soda, caustic soda). Wash immediately, as for acid, or permanent damage may be done to the fabric, especially if it is polyester or a polyester mixture. After rinsing in cold water, neutralize any last traces with white vinegar and rinse again.

Antiperspirants Treat with dry-cleaning solvent, then household ammonia, then rinse.

Aperitifs Rinse with cold water. Treat with liquid detergent and rinse.

Ball-point pen Not the disaster it's often thought to be. Most ball-point inks are completely soluble in methylated spirit and can be

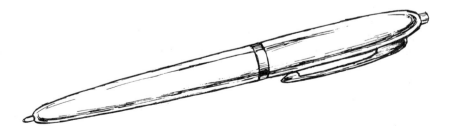

removed if you flush repeatedly with meths. Then air or rinse the garment thoroughly. On suede, try rubbing with an abrasive paper. On walls, try using a soft nail brush or old toothbrush.

Beetroot Sponge as soon as possible with cold water. Or soak in cold water overnight if necessary. Work undiluted liquid detergent into the stain and rinse. When dealing with wool *do not* rub the stain, just let the water run through the fabric. A sprinkling of borax on the dampened stain with boiling water poured over may help.

Beers and stout Treat with white vinegar and rinse. If necessary treat with biological detergent and rinse. If the stain persists, treat with hydrogen peroxide (test fabric first) and rinse. If the fabric is washable, wash at high temperature.

Bird droppings Soak washable articles in warm biological detergent following the directions on the packet. Treat non-washables with 60 ml household ammonia to 2 litres of water (one tablespoon to $3\frac{1}{2}$ pints), then with white vinegar and rinse. Or use an aerosol stain remover.

Blood The stain will usually wash out in cold salt water if you have caught it while it is still wet. Don't use warm water. When dealing with wool *do not* rub the stain, just let the water run through the fabric. If the stain has hardened brush off as much as you can, and soak in a warm solution of biological washing powder, following the instructions on the packet. Then wash or clean according to the fabric. Dried stains may respond to soaking in hydrogen peroxide solution.

Blue-black ink See Ink.

Butter Scrape off as much as you can. If the fabric is suitable, wash at high temperature. If not, treat with a solvent then dry with a hair drier or wash according to the fabric.

Candle wax Get off as much as you can. This will be easier if you can freeze the article in the freezer for an hour or so. Then you can crack the frozen pieces off. Small fragments can be removed by sandwiching the fabric between sheets of clean blotting-paper and then melting with a warm iron. Use the lowest setting and don't melt the fabric. Any wax left over should be dissolved and flushed away with a dry-cleaning solvent. Any colour left from the wax should be treated with methylated spirit and rinsed.

Car polish and wax   Treat with a dry-cleaning solvent, then liquid detergent and rinse.

Caramel   Rinse with cold water, treat with liquid detergent and rinse. If necessary treat with hydrogen peroxide diluted with an equal quantity of water, and rinse.

Carbon paper   Treat with undiluted liquid detergent and rinse well. If the stain resists that, treat with a few drops of household ammonia and then with detergent again. You may have to repeat this several times. On non-washable fabrics, dab with methylated spirit. On acetate and triacetate, use an aerosol stain remover.

Chewing-gum   Pick off as much as possible. If you freeze it first for an hour or so it will break off quite easily. Treat what's left with methylated spirit or white spirit. You may have to repeat this two or three times. There is a special product called Holloway's Chewing-Gum Remover, available from Holloway's Laboratories, Kingsley Works, Grange Road, London NW10. It's a spray that works by lowering the temperature of the gum so it hardens and can be cracked off. Use it with care. It can cause freeze burns if it touches the skin. The ice-cube method or using your freezer is cheaper. Solvent for cleaning decorators' paintbrushes also seems to melt chewing-gum. A friend of mine used it successfully on her daughter's hair.

Chocolate   Scrape off with a blunt knife; rinse with cold water, treat with biological detergent from the back of the stain, using a pad of tissue to mop up the detergent and the stain, then rinse. You can try a stain-removing solvent if a slight stain remains.

Coca-Cola and Pepsi-Cola   Rinse with cold water, treat from the back with liquid detergent, and rinse. If necessary treat with methylated spirit containing a little white vinegar, and rinse.

Cocoa   As for Chocolate.

Cod-liver oil   Fresh stains are easily removed (after you've spooned up as much as possible) by sponging on solvent from the back of the stain; then rinse. Old stains of cod-liver oil are practically impossible to get rid of, even with bleach. On carpets use a dry foam carpet shampoo. On baby clothes sponge with a strong solution of mild detergent and wash as usual.

Coffee   A fresh stain will probably respond to soaking in hand-hot washing-detergent solution followed by a good rinse. Or, if you prefer to use cold water as I do, rinse with cold water, treat with liquid detergent and rinse. If it still won't come out, let it dry and try methylated spirit. Hydrogen peroxide diluted half and half with water may be used for any slight stain left over. For milky coffee, soak in warm biological washing solution, then wash according to fabric. On carpets squirt the stain with a soda siphon then follow with a carpet shampoo.

Cough mixture   See Medicines.

Crayon   Dab the affected area with a solvent and flush any residual colour with methylated spirit. You shouldn't do more than this at home even if you haven't got all the stain out because the chances are you'll remove the original colour as well. On walls use a household cleaner. On wallpapers you may have to patch the piece.

Cream   Rinse in cold water, treat with biological detergent and rinse. On carpets, blot up excess or scrape it off. Use a little dry-cleaning solvent and then a dry foam carpet shampoo.

Crude oil   This is the sort of oil you get on your shoes and clothes when it's washed up on beaches. I remember my mother on a beach in Morayshire trying to clean up the birds who were stranded on the sand all clogged with oil. It was a hopeless thing to try and always made us depressed and disappointed. The oil problem is much worse now but you can at least get it off skin and clothes.

   Soften with white spirit to enable as much as possible of the solid matter to be gently scraped away. Then flush with a dry-cleaning solvent. Many seaside shops now sell a special product which is a solvent and detergent together and seems to work.

Discoloration   Any stain not quite removed by your previous treatments may be difficult to get rid of. On white fabrics, bleaching is simple, but on others you may remove the fabric's own colour and the article may have to be redyed. If in doubt take it to a professional dry-cleaner.

   For bleaching *linen and cotton*, soak the garment in white spirit to which a few drops of household ammonia have been added (five drops of ammonia to one eggcupful of spirit is a recommended amount). *Ammonia can be dangerous* so follow the manufacturer's recommended instructions.

For *silk and wool*, use diluted hydrogen peroxide (one part hydrogen peroxide to six parts water). Sponge the stain or soak for five to fiteeen minutes then rinse thoroughly and wash as usual.

For *polyester, rayon and nylon*, diluted liquid bleach solution can be used but never soak any object for more than 15 minutes. Rinse thoroughly. Always follow the instructions on the bottle. Dilute hydrogen peroxide with six parts water.

Dyes As dyes are designed to colour permanently it's hardly surprising that it's difficult to get them out. There are many different types. All need to be treated immediately with cold water. Don't use hot water because this will fix many dyes. Unfortunately, when removing dyes which are not meant to be on a garment, you may be removing the colours in the garment which *are* meant to be there. Wipe up any splashed or spilled dye immediately with tissues. Non-washable items should be professionally dry-cleaned at once.

After rinsing in cold water, treat with liquid detergent (washing-up liquid will do) and rinse. It may be necessary to treat again with liquid detergent followed by household ammonia and rinse again. Then treat with methylated spirit or amyl acetate (but don't use these on acetate or triacetate).

Egg Rinse with cold water, treat with biological detergent following the instructions on the packet and rinse. If necessary let it dry and then treat with dry-cleaning solvent. Very stubborn stains may be removed by soaking the garment in a pint of hydrogen peroxide solution (see p. 76) to which five drops of ammonia have been added. Rinse well. But I shouldn't try that on anything other than white.

Engine oil This is often very difficult to remove as you will have found out if you've ever had to tamper with the engine of your car. You can treat it with liquid detergent and then flush it with a dry-cleaning solvent. You may have to repeat the process several times.

Eye make-up You can often remove eye shadow by wetting the fabric then treating it with liquid detergent and rinsing. If this doesn't work, let the fabric dry and then treat it with a dry-cleaning solvent followed by methylated spirit and rinse.

Eyebrow pencil can be removed with solvent. Then dab it with a few drops of household ammonia with a clean cloth or cotton wool. Rinse in clean water.

Fat, Cold   Treat as for butter. If you spilled dripping which has bits of gravy in it, scrape off the fat then soak or sponge or spray with cold water or enzyme detergent, following the instructions on the packet. Treat any remaining stain with dry cleaning solvent.

Fat, Hot   When you are deep frying over a hot stove, fat can splatter around a good deal. If your clothing has man-made fibres, the splashes may be at temperatures higher than the melting point of the fibres, which then melt and fuse together. Dry-cleaning solvent should *not* be used in this case, as it may remove the colour and leave white spots. Just treat the stain with liquid detergent and rinse. You may have to do this more than once.

Felt-tip pen ink   Lubricate the stain with household soap or glycerine and wash as usual. Sponge any residual stain, or non-washable material, with methylated spirit. Ask the manufacturer for advice if all else fails.

Flower stains   Treat with dry-cleaning solvent, amyl acetate or methylated spirit. The fabric should then be saturated with water, treated with liquid detergent while wet, and rinsed. Flower-stained vases can be soaked in diluted household bleach for half an hour and then rinsed. Or use a proprietary stain remover.

Foundation cream   This usually comes out if you wet the fabric and then treat with washing-up liquid or liquid detergent and rinse. If necessary you can try a dry-cleaning solvent – that is, if the foundation is a very greasy one. Otherwise try an absorbing technique: rub fuller's earth or talcum powder into light-coloured fabrics, leave for two hours and then brush out.

French polish (Shellac)   Treat with methylated spirit and go on treating until all traces have vanished. Then rinse.

Fruit   Rinse with cold water, treat with liquid detergent and rinse. If you haven't quite got the stain out, treat with household ammonia followed by diluted hydrogen peroxide (six parts water) and then rinse again. If the fabric is suitable (for instance, white cotton or linen) you can try washing it at a high temperature. Alternatively, if the stain is wet, rub it with salt. This won't remove the stain but may make it easier to wash.

Fruit juices   As for Fruit.

Furniture polish   Treat with a dry-cleaning solvent.

Glue   See Adhesives.

Grass and other leafy stains   Treat with methylated spirit. The fabric should be dried and treated with liquid detergent and rinsed. Or use an aerosol stain remover. Washable clothes may be soaked in a biological detergent following the instructions on the packet and then washed according to fabric.

Gravy   Soak or sponge or spray with cold water or detergent, following the instructions on the packet. Treat any remaining stain with dry-cleaning solvent. On carpets follow with a carpet shampoo.

Grease   Scrape off as much as possible, treat with a dry-cleaning solvent, then dry with a hair drier or in the fresh air.
   Soap and solvents are expensive and it is often possible to remove grease with an alkali, which is cheaper. Sodium carbonate (washing-soda) is a water softener. It also emulsifies grease and so releases dirt. Don't use too much or you will remove the natural oils of the skin, shrink woollens and spoil the colour of printed fabrics. It also damages some metals, removes the surface of tinned articles, blackens aluminium and in time destroys metal. However, if you dissolve a few crystals in water in a bowl or the sink it should be effective in removing grease from white cotton or linen articles.
   Borax removes grease and softens water. It can be used for delicate fabrics and even for hair washing. You can get it at chemists. Dissolve the powder in water before you put any clothes or hair in it.
   Household ammonia (ammonium hydroxide) will remove grease

and soften water. It is irritating and attacks skin and eyes, so use it carefully according to instructions.

Paraffin oil dissolves grease and if hot water is added in a wash boiler it will clean machine oil off dungarees. It's flammable so don't use near a naked flame.

Petrol, though an excellent grease remover, is really very dangerous. As soon as it is exposed to the atmosphere it disperses large quantities of vapour, which can ignite instantly. You should not use petrol in the house at all. Never use it for dry-cleaning.

Benzine is also very flammable and should not be used.

Fuller's earth or French chalk will remove greasy marks from wool and silk by absorbing the grease. Mix it to a paste with water, dollop some on the stain and brush out gently when dry.

If the fabric is suitable you can try washing it at high temperature. You can remove some grease spots and candle wax (q.v.) by placing a piece of blotting-paper above and below the fabric and pressing with a cool iron. Some fabrics will scorch if the iron is too hot even if the paper doesn't. For acrylic fabrics the iron should be at the very lowest setting.

Hair dye   Vegetable hair dyes such as henna may be treated like this: rinse with cold water, treat with liquid detergent and rinse. If necessary you can treat again with liquid detergent, followed by household ammonia and rinse; then if necessary treat with methylated spirit or amyl acetate then treat with hydrogen peroxide (one part hydrogen peroxide to six parts water) and rinse.

However, most hair dyes will not respond if they have been left too long. When fresh they can be treated with liquid detergent then with white vinegar and then again with liquid detergent. Then the article should be washed as usual.

Hair lacquer   Sometimes clothes become slightly marked by the aerosol spray. These marks can usually be removed with liquid detergent. A 'blob' can be treated with amyl acetate which in turn is flushed away with methylated spirit or white spirit.

Hand cream   Wet the fabric and treat with liquid detergent (washing-up liquid will do) and rinse. If that isn't enough, treat with a dry-cleaning solvent.

Honey   Rinse with cold water, treat with liquid detergent and rinse again. If you need to do more, treat with hydrogen peroxide and rinse.

Ice-cream   Remove as much as you can with a spoon or a blunt knife. Then soak in a warm washing solution. If there's still a greasy stain when the fabric has dried, treat with solvent.

Ink, blue-black   Catch ink stains while wet if you possibly can. If allowed to dry there will still be a stain even after the blue colour has gone. Flush with cold water immediately, then treat with liquid detergent from the back of the stain and rinse. Repeat until no more colour comes out. The stain left after that should be treated with lemon juice, rinsed with diluted household ammonia and rinsed again.

Dried ink needs an acid to get rid of it. Salts of lemon (potassium quadroxalate) or oxalic acid are best but they are *deadly poisonous*. Pour boiling water through the stain and then apply the salts as dry powder. Use a matchstick to spread it around. Pour boiling water through again. You must rinse the fabric quickly and thoroughly to prevent the acid from rotting it. If the stain is on a coloured fabric dissolve the acid in water and dip the fabric in the solution and then into cold water so the acid won't affect the colour. Or use a chlorine preparation. Test fabric first.

Ball-point ink   See under Ball-point pen.

Coloured writing ink is usually soluble in water. Treat with liquid detergent (e.g. washing-up liquid) and rinse. Do this two or three times then treat with liquid detergent containing a few drops of household ammonia and rinse again. If necessary treat with hydrogen peroxide and rinse again.

Duplicating ink should be flushed with white spirit. The stain left after that should be treated with washing-up liquid or other liquid detergent and rinsed. You will probably have to do this two or three times.

Don't get *duplicating powder* wet at all. It will brush out completely with a soft brush. But if you try a solvent you really will make a mess.

Felt-tip ink   See under Felt-tip pen.

Indelible pencil is not easy to remove, as the name implies. Flush two or three times with a dry-cleaning solvent and then with methylated spirit. The stain left after that should be treated with liquid detergent (washing-up liquid for instance) containing a little household ammonia and then rinsed. If the stain still persists, treat with hydrogen peroxide and a final rinse.

Indian ink should be treated with a dry-cleaning solvent and then methylated spirit followed by liquid detergent and a rinse. If necessary, biological detergent can be used on the wet fabric and then rinsed.

Marking ink must be treated at once, otherwise it becomes almost impossible to remove, as indeed it should. Use a dry-cleaning solvent and repeat several times. If you can't get it out, you can console yourself with the thought that the things you *have* marked on purpose will stay marked for good.

Printing ink should be flushed with methylated spirit. Treat the left-over stain with washing-up liquid and rinse. You will probably have to do this two or three times.

Typewriter ribbon   Flush through two or three times with a dry-cleaning solvent then with methylated spirit. The stain should then be treated with liquid detergent containing a little ammonia and rinsed. If there's still a trace of stain, treat with hydrogen peroxide and then rinse again.

Iodine   Iodine makes a browny mark on most materials and deep blue-black on starched materials. Treat the stain immediately. One method is to moisten it with water and place it in the sun or on a warm radiator or in the steam from a kettle. For non-washable fabrics, flush with methylated spirit and rinse. You may have to do this more than once. If the stain is on acetate fabric, dilute the spirit with two parts of water.

Another method is to place a pad of cotton wool soaked with alcohol on the stain and leave it there, keeping it wet with alcohol for several hours.

Iron mould   Cover the stain with salt, then squeeze lemon juice over the salt and leave for an hour. Rinse well. Repeat the treatment several times if you have to. Proprietary rust removers can be used on white fabrics.

Iron mould is very difficult to remove from woollens and silks. Get specialist treatment from a local laundry or dry-cleaner and don't attempt to deal with the stain at home.

Jam   Rinse with cold water. Treat with liquid detergent and rinse. If necessary follow with a treatment of hydrogen peroxide (diluted in the same amount of water) and rinse again.

Ketchup   Rinse with cold water, treat with liquid detergent and rinse. If necessary follow that with a treatment of methylated spirit when dry, then rinse. If the stain persists, treat with biological detergent and rinse.

Lacquer   Treat with amyl acetate several times and then flush with a dry-cleaning solvent.

Leather   Stains are sometimes caused by leather rubbing against a fabric. These are usually difficult to get rid of because the dye will probably contain tannin. Try applying neat liquid detergent (washing-up liquid will do) to the stain. Then rub in well. (If the garment is of wool or other unwashable fabric, don't rub but flush the detergent through.) Repeat if necessary and rinse well. Final traces of colour can be bleached with hydrogen peroxide diluted with water half-and-half.

Lipstick Treat with dry-cleaning solvent or methylated spirit two or three times, then with liquid detergent followed if necessary by an ammonia solution. Then rinse thoroughly. If on walls, use an aerosol stain remover.

Liqueurs Rinse with cold water, treat with liquid detergent and rinse.

Mascara Treat with liquid detergent followed by household ammonia and then rinse. If necessary you can treat the stain with dry-cleaning solvent as well.

Meat juices Rinse with cold water, treat with biological detergent and rinse. If necessary allow to dry and then treat with dry-cleaning solvent.

Medicines Medicines can be made from so many different sub-stances there's no good advice to give which will cover them all. But cough medicines are so much the part of a young household, I give a suggested treatment for them.

Cough medicines are usually in a base of sugar syrup and can usually be washed out with detergent and water or flushed through (for non-washables) from the wrong side. If any stain is left because of any colouring in the mixture, treat with diluted household ammonia. Then treat with methylated spirit or amyl acetate.

Some cough medicines containing tar-like gummy ingredients can be treated as for tar. Soften first with Vaseline, lard or white spirit. Then treat with dry-cleaning solvent or wash.

Metal polish Saturate with water, treat with liquid detergent and rinse. If necessary treat with methylated spirit and rinse again.

Mildew Prevention is better than cure. Mildew is caused by fungus spores which are wafting about in the air all the time. In a damp, warm atmosphere they will grow on all sorts of things, such as wood, paper, leather and, of course, fabrics. They smell horrid and flourish for instance, on laundry that has been washed and left lying in wet heaps and not hung out straight away. Even man-made fabrics, which are supposed to be resistant, may get mildewy if allowed to lie in damp piles.

If you keep your clothes in slightly damp cupboards it could be worth your while to get a chemical moisture absorber. These are available from chemists and department stores. They are placed in cloth bags and hung in the cupboard or sprinkled between clothes in chests of drawers. The granules should be dried out from time to time, after which they will be ready to absorb more damp.

You can get water-repellent sprays for use on curtains, loose covers, upholstery, mattresses, shower curtains, etc. Some have special mildew-resistant finishes. Don't use these sprays on clothes unless the can specifically says you may. Don't breathe in the vapour and be careful not to let it spray on to plastic tiles.

Books and papers showing mildew should be wiped with a clean soft cloth. Stains can sometimes be bleached out with ink eradicator, but colours will be bleached too of course.

For fabrics, flush through from the wrong side with diluted bleach. Mildewed leather should be wiped over with undiluted antiseptic mouthwash. Wipe and rub dry with a soft cloth. Then polish.

Milk Rinse with cold water. Treat with biological detergent following the instructions on the packet and rinse.

Mineral oil Treat with dry-cleaning solvent and rinse. Then saturate fabric with water, treat with lemon juice while wet and rinse again.

Mud Allow it to dry because you will then find you can brush most of it off. Any stain that remains should be treated with a dry-cleaning solvent, then with methylated spirit followed by liquid detergent and rinsed.

Mustard Rinse with cold water, treat with liquid detergent and rinse.

Nail varnish Treat with amyl acetate or acetone not oily nail varnish removers. Flush out with white spirit. Don't use acetone on acetate.

Ointment Treat with a dry-cleaning solvent then rinse with cold water, treat with liquid detergent and then rinse.

Paint All paint spills should be dealt with immediately. Once paint has dried it's almost impossible to remove.

Blot *acrylic paint* with tissues and wash out with detergent and water. Then use a stain-removing solvent or methylated spirit. Test synthetics first.

Cellulose paints (such as those used on model aircraft) must be treated with cellulose thinners. Do not use on viscose fabrics (rayon) and take care when washing brushes.

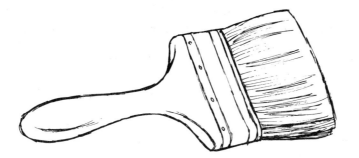

Emulsion paint, being water-based should be easy to remove, I know, but it's not, specially if you let it get dry. If you catch it while it's still wet you can wash it out easily in cold water. If it has hardened it will need treatment with methylated spirit not just once but over and over again. You may damage the fabric in the process.

You have to catch *enamel paint* quickly while still wet. It should be treated with methylated spirit or a proprietary paint remover.

Sponge *oil paint* with white spirit or dry-cleaning solvent and rinse. Like all paints, oil paint shouldn't be allowed to dry. If it has, though, you should treat it with a proprietary paint remover. Rinse thoroughly afterwards.

Perfume   Treat with household ammonia straight from the bottle. Then treat with liquid detergent and rinse well.

Perspiration   If the stain won't come out in the normal wash, wet the fabric and treat with household ammonia straight from the bottle and rinse thoroughly. *Or* try soaking in a biological detergent following the directions on the packet. If the stain still persists, wet the fabric again and treat with hydrogen peroxide and rinse.

If anti-perspirant deodorant is combined with the stain, treat with a dry-cleaning solvent, then use household ammonia as described above. If dye is combined with the stain and it has been allowed to set (that is, if you didn't deal with it at once), treatment with white vinegar is sometimes useful. Or you can treat white *linen* and *cotton* by soaking in methylated spirit to which household ammonia has been added (five drops of ammonia to an eggcupful of spirit). For *silk* and *wool* use diluted hydrogen peroxide (diluted by half). Sponge the stain or soak for five to fifteen minutes then rinse thoroughly and wash normally. For *viscose, nylon* and *polyesters,* dilute liquid bleach solution can be used but you should never soak the garment for more than fifteen minutes. Always follow the instructions on the bottle and rinse thoroughly.

Plastic   Sometimes heat or mothproofing agents can soften plastic hangers and buttons enough to cause stains on the cloth hanging on them or buttoned by them. Use dry-cleaning solvent or amyl acetate to remove the stains. Test coloured fabrics first. If this doesn't remove the plastic, cover the stain with a solvent soaked pad until the plastic has been softened. Then keep sponging with a fresh solventy pad until the stain has gone.

Putty   Pick off as much as possible, then treat with a dry-cleaning solvent. The stain left after that should be treated with liquid detergent and rinsed.

Resin   Treat with dry-cleaning solvent or turpentine or white spirit, from the wrong side if possible. Dilute the spirit with two parts of water if you intend to use it on acetate fabric. Test coloured fabrics first. Rinse by flushing with cold water.

Rouge   Treat with dry-cleaning solvent or methylated spirit two or three times, then with liquid detergent followed by household ammonia and then rinse.

Rust (See also Iron Mould.)   Treat with lemon juices and rinse. Proprietary rust removers can be used on white fabrics.

Sauce   Rinse with cold water, treat with liquid detergent (washing-up liquid will do) for the grease; then, when dry, with methylated spirit, then rinse. If there's still a stain, treat with biological detergent following the instructions on the packet and rinse.

Scorch marks   Dampen the scorched area in one part glycerine to two parts water, rubbing in solution with your finger tips. Then soak in a solution of 50 g of borax to 500 ml of warm water (one tablespoon to a pint). Leave it for fifteen minutes. Rinse well. Really bad scorch marks are impossible to remove because the fibres themselves become damaged.

Shine Shiny patches often occur on suits, and sometimes on black cotton jeans or other black cloths – dark colours show up the shine more. Some cleaners offer a de-shining service.

Alternatively you could try very gently rubbing the shiny parts with very fine-grade glass-paper. Don't rub for too long or too hard or there will be no seat left.

An old recipe for curing shiny clothes (presumably tweeds and twills) is: 'Well wash some ivy leaves in cold water and put them in a saucepan with enough cold water to cover well; boil slowly until the leaves are tender. Strain off the liquid and use for sponging the shiny places having first thoroughly brushed the garment.' Black clothes can be successfully cleaned by brushing all over with distilled water containing a few drops of liquid ammonia. This restores the colour.

Shoe polish This can be dreadfully difficult to remove. Treat with a dry-cleaning solvent then a liquid detergent (e.g. washing-up liquid) into which you've put a very little household ammonia, and rinse. If this isn't enough try treating with methylated spirit and then rinse.

Soft drinks Rinse with cold water, treat with liquid detergent and rinse. If necessary treat with methylated spirit to which you have added a little white vinegar and then rinse.

Spirits If the stain does not wash out in cold water, treat with methylated spirit and rinse. If you still can't get rid of it, treat with hydrogen peroxide diluted by half and rinse.

Stove polish Use salt to absorb as much as possible. Sprinkle on and work into the fabric, then brush out with a soft brush and keep doing this until most of the stain has gone. Then treat with dry-cleaning solvent from the wrong side.

Tar, Bitumen, Pitch (See also Crude Oil.)   This is bad news. Tar is very difficult to clean up completely. The simplest advice is to rub with grease, such as lard. Then both tar and grease should be washed out. But stains are often more complicated so perhaps the following advice will be more helpful for bad stains.

All the stains should be softened with white spirit so that you can gently scrape away as much of the solid stuff as you can. Or you can use Vaseline or lard. Then you should flush the stain with a dry-cleaning solvent. Often a grey residual stain will be left behind which you can sometimes get rid of by treating with white spirit. Another remedy is to soften the tar with margarine or butter and wipe away with a clean rag. Then use the dry-cleaning solvent to get rid of the mixture.

Tarnish   Stains caused by tarnished metal, such as brass, copper, tin, silver and so on, can be dissolved by flushing through from the wrong side with white vinegar or lemon juice. Rinse well. If the acid changes the colour of the dye of a fabric then sponge with diluted household ammonia or diluted solution of bicarbonate of soda. Do not use bleach, which may damage the fabric.

Tea   The treatment is much the same as for coffee. If wet, wash out with boiling water to which a little borax has been added (1 oz. borax to 1 pint water). If dry, steep in washing-soda dissolved in boiling water (1 oz. soda to 1 pint water). For milky tea, soak in warm washing solution using a biological detergent and following the directions on the packet.

If necessary, wet the fabric and then treat with a biological detergent and rinse. If the stain still persists let it dry and try methylated spirit. Hydrogen peroxide diluted half and half with water is useful for removing any residual stain.

If the garment is washable a fresh stain may come out if you soak it in hand-hot detergent and water. If the stain is set and the fabric is suitable, soak first, then wash at a high temperature.

Tobacco   Rinse in cold water, treat with white vinegar and rinse again. If you need to, treat with liquid detergent containing a little methylated spirit, then rinse. Or treat with hydrogen peroxide diluted half and half and rinse.

Toothpaste and dentifrice   Water will remove both these quite easily.

Treacle   Rinse with cold water, treat with biological detergent and rinse.

Turmeric   This spice, used in curry powder, pickles and mustard, leaves a bright yellow stain which is very difficult to get rid of, especially from cotton. If washable, soak in diluted household ammonia or white spirit. If not, treat from the wrong side, if possible, with ammonia or white spirit. If this doesn't work you'll have to use a bleach. Test the fabric first.

Typewriter ribbon   See under Ink.

Unidentified stains   You may not know what every stain is caused by. It's quite easy to come back from a good meal and not realize you spilled anything down your front, let alone what it is. Also, second-hand clothes may already have stains which, of course, you won't be able to identify.

If the garment is washable you could try rinsing it in cold water and then wash as you would normally. But on the whole I'd advise you to take it to a local dry-cleaner or launderer who is willing to carry out stain removal.

Urine   Rinse with cold water, treat with household ammonia straight from the bottle and then white vinegar. Then, if necessary, rinse with cold water, treat with hydrogen peroxide diluted by half and rinse.

Vaseline   New stains (for instance on babies' nappies) can be removed by sponging with a dry-cleaning solvent before washing. Old stains should be soaked in a solvent overnight, rinsed and then washed.

Vegetable oil (For example, cooking oil, castor oil, linseed oil.)   Treat with a dry-cleaning solvent which you may have to apply several times. Then saturate the fabric with water and treat with methylated spirit to which you have added a little white vinegar. Then rinse.

Verdigris   See Tarnish.

Walnut   The outsides of walnuts cause a dark brown stain which is practically impossible to get rid of. Very fresh stains can be removed if the fabric can be boiled in hot water and detergent. Old stains will leave a grey colour which may be got rid of with a strong chlorine or hydrogen peroxide bleach. Non-washable fabrics can't be treated at home and your only hope is a dry-cleaner.

Water-colour paint   Rinse in cold water. If that doesn't get all the colour out, wet the fabric and treat with household ammonia used straight from the bottle. Rinse very thoroughly. Or wet the fabric and treat with hydrogen peroxide diluted half and half and rinse.

Wax polish   Treat with dry-cleaning solvent and then with liquid detergent and rinse.

Wine   Treat with liquid detergent and rinse. Apply white vinegar and rinse. Hydrogen peroxide (diluted half and half with water) is useful for removing any slight stains left over.

Xerox powder   Do not use solvent. Brush out the powder immediately. As long as it doesn't get wet you should be able to remove it completely.

Zinc and castor oil   Dampen the stained area. Apply white spirit. Leave for a few minutes then rinse in warm water.

SPECIAL FABRICS AND GARMENTS

If you want to know how to clean spots from certain kinds of fabric here are some of the more common ones.

For *wools and silks* use only lukewarm water.

Velvet, chenille and corduroy should only be washed if guaranteed washable and then only in lukewarm water.

Always use lukewarm water for *synthetics*.

Triacetate and acetate must be at room temperature before you use a dry-cleaning solvent. Never use methylated spirit.

Always test *viscose* for reaction first. Handle gently when wet particularly with older rayons. Modern rayons have much more strength when wet, but it still does no harm to take care.

Dralon velvet can be cleaned using a dry-foam shampoo.

Raincoats   Methylated or white spirit will often get rid of odd stains. Proofed coats can be sponged lightly with dry-cleaning solvent but don't get them too damp. Showerproof coats can often be washed. Check the label. You must rinse thoroughly or the coat will no longer be proof against showers.

Sometimes raincoats come back from the cleaners seemingly minus their showerproofness. This may be because you didn't specify you wanted the coat reproofed. You can try to reproof at home, though this is difficult. Reproofing and stain-repellent aerosols are available from department stores. Spray the garment all over thoroughly, going twice over places where the rain will fall most heavily, i.e. the shoulders. If you want the coat professionally cleaned by a specialist cleaner, write to the Association of British Launderers and Dry Cleaners, address on page 69. Do not use dry-cleaning solvent on waterproof materials.

Never use a grease (dry-cleaning) solvent on rubberized raincoats. Use a paste of French chalk and water, and leave it on overnight. Or use soap-flakes and water on a sponge or nail-brush. Do not press or iron. Don't use grease solvents on plastic raincoats either. Just sponge with soapy water and rinse well. Dry away from heat.

You can add extra rainproofing where it's wearing off by rubbing with beeswax then covering with brown paper and ironing it. The paper will absorb any excess wax leaving enough to give protection from the rain. Don't use newspaper, it will leave ink marks on the garment.

Suede Collars of suede jackets often get a bit greasy and eventually dirt clings to the grease leaving a great dark stain. For regular overall cleaning you should always take suede to a professional, but you can try getting a greasy collar clean by using a proprietary suede-cleaning cloth, which you can buy inexpensively at most department stores. If you wear a scarf or high collar under the jacket you'll avoid this problem.

Spilled drink and food marks down the front of a jacket will probably need professional cleaning but you may be able to prevent even those to some extent, and also marking from rain, by spraying on a proprietary stain-repellent. This should be used on new or newly cleaned suede, not on an already grubby one.

CHAPTER 5

DYEING

Sometimes an article has become stained or the colour faded to such an extent that dyeing seems the only possible solution. This section will deal with basic dyeing of fabrics but will not discuss creative dyeing such as wax resist, tie-dyeing and so on.

If you want more advice on dyeing, Dylon have a Consumer Advice Bureau which is always willing to help. See addresses, page 242.

BASIC TECHNIQUE

There are several different kinds of dye on the market: hot-water dyes (powder or liquid), cold dyes, instant dyes, suede dyes, leather dyes and carpet dyes.

Make sure you choose the dye most suitable for the job you want to do and read all the instructions before you begin the actual dyeing. See that you have all the necessary materials and then follow the instructions through as you dye.

Check that the article you want to dye actually *can* be dyed at home. Acrylics (such as Orlon and Courtelle), for instance, will not take dye. Nor can fabrics with special finishes, such as drip-dry or water-proofed fabrics. Before deciding to dye an article check with this guide whether it will take the dye or not.

Acetate	Good result with hot-water dye
Acrylic	Don't dye
Cotton	Good results with all dyes
Elastane	Quite good results with hot-water dyes only. (Cannot be dyed with cold dyes.)
Glass fibre	Don't dye
Linen	Good results with hot- and cold-water dyes
Modal	Good results with hot- and cold-water dyes
Nylon	Good results with hot-water dye
Nylon/polyester	Quite good results with hot-water dyes only
Polyester	Reduced shades with hot-water dyes Don't use cold-water dyes
Polyester/cotton mixture	Reduced shades only with hot- and cold-water dyes
Polyester/wool mixture	Do not dye
Silk	Good results with hot-water dyes, reduced shades with cold-water dyes
Triacetate	Reduced shades with hot-water dyes – special instructions are included with Dylon dyes
Viscose	Good results with hot- or cold-water dyes
Wool	Good results with hot-water dyes, quite good with cold

Polyesters can only be dyed to very pale colours. Use three times the normal quantity of dye. Do not dye polyester/wool mixtures because the fibres need different treatments and the fabric will not, therefore, dye evenly. Polyester/cotton mixtures can be dyed: the more cotton there is in the fabric the deeper the colour you'll be able to get.

Weigh your fabric before buying the dye. Each bottle or tin of dye will only cope with a certain amount of dry fabric and you may have to buy several packages if you are dyeing a sheet or several articles together.

Wash new articles before dyeing them to take out any dressings such as starch. Dye cannot get through such dressings, nor can it penetrate waterproofed fabrics or drip-dry fabrics.

If you are dyeing old clothes, wash them first and remove stains.

Before dyeing a garment you should ideally let down all the turn-ups and open out all seams. Then if you need any extra fabric (for mending, say) it will all be dyed evenly. With socks or stockings it is a good idea to dye darning wool at the same time.

Do not attempt to dye any fabric that has faded unevenly without first using a colour remover. Do not try to cover scorch marks, bleach marks, stains, etc. with dye. The stain affects the way the fabric reacts to the dye and may be even more obvious in the long run. Do not try to use the same dye solution twice. Do not dye wool garments in automatic washing-machines. They will shrink. You should treat wool, as far as possible, as you would when washing it (see p. 57).

Patterns will not be obliterated by dyeing, though they may look more subtle!

Make sure your washing-machine, boiler or sink is large enough to hold what you want to dye with enough room for the water to cover the fabric completely and allow it to be stirred round easily: the clothes being dyed must be moved around continually.

When using a machine do not dye more than half the machine's maximum wash load or the articles won't have room to move freely.

Word of warning: if you use a commercial launderette machine for dyeing *do* put the machine through a wash cycle with detergent or bleach afterwards or the person coming after you will be very displeased. A friend not only failed to do that, but came back along the street half an hour later to see an old lady gazing in astonishment at her bright pink washing.

Wet the fabric thoroughly before putting it into the dye solution unless you are using a product which washes and dyes at the same time. Heavy woollen jumpers, dresses, coats, etc., should be steeped in cold water for about twenty minutes before being plunged into the dye bath, otherwise there may be some dry patches and the result will be uneven.

Rinse thoroughly after dyeing. Wash separately if you have used hot-water dyes. Always rinse in the tub of the machine, never in the spinner.

REMOVING ORIGINAL COLOUR

Dygon colour and stain remover will remove colour from nylon, cotton, wool, velvet, linen, candlewick, viscose and acetate rayons.

Do not use it on polyesters, triacetate or materials with special finishes. The contents of one Dygon tin or one capful from the bottle will treat 250 g (½ lb) dry weight of fabric. Colour removal can be done in a washing-machine or by hand.

When using Dygon, make sure the room is well ventilated, try not to breathe the fumes and keep it out of reach of children.

When removing colour from woollen articles you must handle the wool very gently. Allow it to cool before giving a lukewarm rinse, warm wash and final rinse.

When removing colour from woollens in a washing-machine, use the drum just as a container, don't agitate it but move the articles round gently with a wooden spoon for the recommended time or until the colour disappears. Then rinse or wash as for wool.

Nylon overalls and acetate rayon may be treated as above but don't raise the temperature above 60°C (140°F) at any stage. Before removing the colour from acetate, remember that though acetate can be dyed, the shade will be slightly reduced. Special instructions may be included with the dye.

In all cases follow the manufacturers' instructions carefully.

DYEING WITH MULTI-PURPOSE DYES

You can use these dyes in hot or warm water. They are bought in powder form in small tins. They are suitable for dyeing or tinting nylon, cotton, wool, linen, silk, velvet, polyesters, unpleated triacetate, elastane, acetate, and viscose rayons. *Do not use* on acrylic or materials with special finishes. Use one Dylon tin for each 250 g (½ lb) dry weight of fabric. If dyeing nylon black double the quantity of dye.

If you want to dye large quantities mix the dye to a smooth paste with 50 ml (two tablespoons) of cold water, then add 500 ml (one pint) of boiling water. For small amounts mix the dye as you would normally and use only as much as you need.

Don't use more than 7 litres (1½ gallons) of water to each tin of dye or the colour will not match the shade card.

If you are using a twin-tub or single-tub machine wash and rinse the article as usual before dyeing. Mask the inside of the washing-machine lid with kitchen foil or it will be very difficult to get clean again. Wipe away any spilled dye at once. Rub the machine afterwards with very hot water, washing powder and a cupful of bleach. Automatics should be put through a hot-wash cycle with washing powder and a cupful of bleach.

COLD DYES

This is a newish technique, introduced by Dylon. The dyes must be used with a special 'cold fix' preparation or with washing-soda. Cold dyes can be used on all natural fabrics, except those with special finishes and on viscose and silk. They are not suitable for nylon or other synthetics, cashmere, angora, mohair or fabrics with special finishes.

Wool (for which follow special instructions) and polyester/cotton and silk will only dye to pale shades with cold dyes.

If you get a patchy result, don't try to dye the article again. Get professional advice.

COMMON FAULTS IN HOME DYEING

Patchy colour

1. You did not leave enough room in the dye bath for the articles to move freely.
2. You did not stir the articles continually for the full ten or fifteen minutes.
3. The articles were not wet thoroughly before you put them in the dye.

The colour comes out too pale

1. In the case of hot-water dyes the water temperature may not have

been hot enough. You *must* allow the water to reach boiling point then simmer for the full dyeing time. (But do not treat polyesters at a temperature higher than 60°C, 140°F).
2. You have not used enough dye for the quantity of fabric. It really is worth weighing the fabric first.
3. In the case of cold dyes, you may not have put in the right quantities of salt and washing-soda or cold fix. These quantities are important. They are always given with the manufacturer's instructions.

Uneven absorption of the dye

Patchiness will be caused by insufficient movement or the dye vessel being too small. Otherwise, uneven take-up may be because you've tried to dye a fabric with a special dressing or special finish. These fabrics will not dye satisfactorily.

The result is too dark

You have used too much dye. You will not now be able to get the dye out unless you use a colour remover.

The dye has not taken at all or only just

1. The fabric chosen is unsuitable for dyeing. Always check the fabric first.
2. You have chosen the wrong sort of dye for the job.
3. A heavy finish on the fabric has prevented any dye getting through.

Wrong colour

1. The original colour was not a light even colour, stain-free and clean. You should wash the fabric and/or pre-treat with a colour remover. This is not recommended for polyesters.
2. The dye blended with the basic colour to produce a different colour.

SPECIAL ADVICE

Large articles, velvet curtains, candlewick bedspreads, etc.

Various types of fabrics are given the name velvet. You must know what the fibres in the fabric are before you attempt to dye it.

Cotton velvet can be dyed with any of the dyes mentioned here.

Nylon velvet should be dyed with hot-water dyes.

Dralon velvet is made of acrylic fibres and is unsuitable for any dyeing.

Faded areas, often found in curtains affected by sunlight, cannot be covered by over-dyeing and the curtains should be stripped down to a level colour base with colour remover. This will not work on fast-dyed fabrics and you should test a piece first.

Velvet is very heavy when wet so you'll have to find a very large vessel for the dye bath. A washing-machine would be ideal but you can't load one to more than half its normal capacity. If one curtain is more than half the wash load you should get the curtains profession-ally dyed.

If each curtain can be done at home but has to be dyed separately you *must* use fresh dye liquid for each one, and make sure that the amount of dye and the weight of fabric are always in the same proportion and that you follow the same process with the same temperature for the same fibre. Any variation of the dyeing process will result in different depths of colour.

Velvet should be drip-dried or very lightly spun and then allowed to dry naturally. Too much spinning will give the velvet bad creases. You should then steam-iron the velvet to raise the pile.

Blankets

Use a wash-and-dye product for best results. Blankets made of wool, nylon, cotton, viscose and mixtures of those fibres can all be dyed, but only to pale shades.

Do not dye blankets made from polyester or polyester mixtures, acrylics, etc.

The colour result will depend on the original colour of the blanket and the fibres in it. After dyeing them, you must always wash blankets separately – though no doubt you will do this anyway because of their size.

Stockings and tights

Use one tin of cold dye to three to five pairs of heavy nylons or tights. For four pairs of 15 denier tights use half the dye solution to $2\frac{1}{4}$ litres (4 pints) water.

Shoes

Shoes must be clean first. This may not be easy as the usual reason for dyeing them is that they are old and grubby. You can wash canvas shoes in hot water and detergent then stuff them with newspaper and allow them to dry in a warm place.

Dyes are usually available in shoe-menders. Follow the instructions on the bottle.

Satin shoes should be dyed with multi-purpose dye. Clean the shoes first and remove all stains as the dye will not hide bad blemishes. Pad the inside of the shoes with crumpled newspaper or white tissue paper or kitchen tissue.

Lightly damp the surfaces of the shoes with clean water. Dip a small, clean brush (an old toothbrush would be suitable) into the dye solution. Shake off the surplus liquid. Work the brush all over the shoes with a light circular movement. Allow the shoes to dry in a warm place but away from direct heat.

You may have to repeat the process, remembering that each application of dye deepens the colour.

Dyeing feathers with multi-purpose dye

Feathers are very fragile, specially old ones acquired in jumble sales or junk shops. The feathers should be washed in warm water and detergent, rinsed thoroughly and then immersed in the dye bath while still soaking wet.

Raise the temperature of the dye bath to 90°C (195°F) and maintain this temperature for ten minutes only, moving the feathers constantly but gently about. Rinse the feathers until the water runs clear. Dry standing up in a bottle in a warm place but away from direct heat.

HOME-MADE DYES

If you are using home-made vegetable dyes, strain the mixed dye through a clean cloth to remove any bits and pieces. To set the dye after rinsing lay the garment for a while in a solution of Epsom salts and water. For a shirt or other smallish light garment use 60g (two ounces) of salts in enough water to cover. Increase the strength and quantity of water according to size and weight of the garment.

If you want to dye lace curtains to an ecru colour, don't try dye – use cold tea. You can use tea to get a beige or old ivory shade when dyeing gloves or lace. The dye will be quite permanent and can be used for dyeing thread for darning.

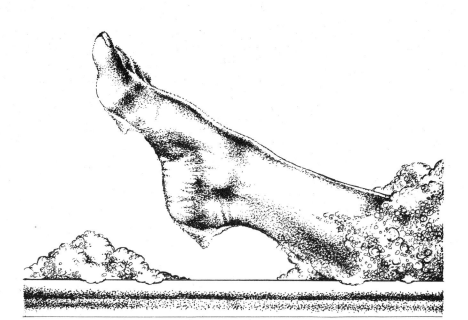

CHAPTER 6

BODY CARE

Cleanliness is as cleanliness does. We have to try to keep clean to ward off disease and to prevent ourselves from smelling unpleasant. But being too clean can cause problems. In the nineteenth century cleanliness became almost a religion and disinfectants were used to clean everything. I met an old lady once who actually used to pour Milton over her Sunday joint to kill the bacteria!

All of us have parasites. There are mites in our eyelashes, mites on our skin and lice in our hair. Too violent an attack on the friendly organisms that live on our skin may actually be bad for our health. The use of too many deodorant and cleansing sprays, especially in the more delicate and vulnerable parts of the body may well get rid of some of our bacteria but will certainly leave room for less beneficial ones to take their place.

Michael Andrew in his fascinating book, *The Life that Lives on Man*, says:

> The horrid truth is that each of us has about as many bacteria and yeasts on the surface of his or her skin as there are people on earth;

far from being 'clean' after a bath the number of organisms released from the surface actually goes up as they emerge from the nooks and crannies where they multiply. However hard we may wish to retreat from our animal origins we will not be able to escape our fellow travellers. But the huge majority, numerically are harmless or even beneficial.

So there's no point in being obsessive about cleanliness, though there is some point in knowing how to keep our bodies looking their best and operating well.

Experts have varying views about the best treatment for different parts of the body. The techniques I give here are not 'the right way' but they have been recommended by professionals and certainly won't do any harm.

SKIN

The skin is the largest area of your body. An average man has 1.6 square metres (seventeen square feet) of skin! It protects your vulnerable workings from the outside world. It is tough and resilient, protects tissues underneath and helps to regulate body temperature. It is one of the body's chief barriers against infection. Because it is dry and slightly acid and its surface is constantly being replaced, invaders rarely colonize the skin, but can be a cause of illness if they penetrate below the surface.

Skin stretches, contracts and renews itself constantly. It deserves and needs care and attention.

Heat dries it, cold chaps it, friction from clothes can irritate it; dirty air can pollute it. So do look after it.

Skin is made up of two layers, the outer covering called the epidermis and the actual skin, called the dermis. The outermost part of the epidermis is made up of flat, dead cells that are being shed all the time. The underlying part is made up of rapidly dividing cells which are constantly being pushed upwards to replace the dead cells above them. Tiny blood vessels and nerve endings are woven into the flexible connective tissue of the dermis, and sweat and oil glands are embedded in it.

Skin is thinnest on the lips and thickest on the scalp, palms and soles.

Skin should be protected from harsh chemicals or detergents and you should not over-expose your body to the sun. Never massage soap or lather into the skin and if you *do* use soap at all, wash it off thoroughly – using distilled water or tapwater.

Superficially the skin of face and body may seem the same but there are huge differences. The skin on the face has a looser cell structure. It has many minute hair follicles and sweat glands which make it easy to moisturize. There are also more sebaceous glands on the skin of the face, so there are more naturally secreted oils there too.

The face

The skin of the face is delicate and exposed to all weathers – to sun, to dust, and to wind. Most of us don't give it much thought at all until we get a pimple or lines begin to appear. Skin varies very much on the face, on various parts of the face, and also according to the seasons, and one's own health.

Some minor permanent changes occur eventually in every skin as it grows older. But the more serious skin problems caused by neglect and bad care need not happen.

Good preventive care means good protection for both layers of skin. Surprisingly it is specially important on the inner layer because that is the basic structure of the skin.

Sunlight is permanently damaging to the skin. Over a long period too much sunlight may lead to dark areas on the surface of the skin, dark red spots and even skin cancer. The supporting tissue, elastic fibres and blood vessels in the lower layer may also be permanently damaged. You may not notice any change for several years but once these changes occur you cannot undo them. You can protect yourself by staying indoors, or by wearing special make-up, or hats, or gloves, or by sunshades.

Use sun screens liberally and re-apply when you've been swimming or often if you perspire a lot. Start protecting your skin NOW. Don't forget, a sun lamp can do as much damage as the sun.

Other enemies of the skin are wind and dry, overheated rooms. Older people are always more susceptible because their skins can't retain moisture as they used to. Don't overheat your skin by bending over a hot cooker – stand away from the full blast of the heat – or by sitting too near a fire. Dirty air is another hazard. The best defence against polluted air is to use lots of moisturiser to keep out the dirt and to keep in the moisture.

Cleaning the skin

An average skin over an average day will collect a film of dirt, pollutants and chemicals as well as the cosmetics you used in the morning, if not the day before, scent, powders, eye make-up etc., decomposed cells, sweat and bacteria. All these things tend to accumulate and clog the pores.

Just below the surface are the dead cells of the outer layers, dry and shrivelled. These are what make your skin look coarse, rough, dry and full of tiny lines, and they show up the pores. A skin cleanser must remove all surface film, and then must itself be easily and completely removed. There are four types of skin cleansers: oils and greases; cold creams; soaps and lotions (or rinsable cleaners).

Oily cleaners and cold cream are non-irritating but not very good at removing the dirt; they are also difficult to remove themselves. The soaps and lotions do remove the dirt well and are easily rinsed off afterwards.

Soap is drying but will do the skin no harm if left on for as short a time as possible and rinsed off thoroughly. Normally people are not thorough enough about rinsing off the cleanser. Wiping off with a tissue is not good enough. You must rinse the cleanser off thoroughly. Rinsing with water alone will not take off an oily cleaner so use a skin toner for rinsing.

My own beautician advises using distilled water or rose or orange water for the rinsing. Keep wiping the skin with the water on a clean piece of cotton wool until the pad stays absolutely clean.

If you do use soap, use a little only, don't let it stay on the skin any longer than you can help and use the plainest, simplest soap you can get hold of. Smells and colourings often contain irritants.

Fresheners, toners and astringents are all basically for toning; closing the pores and bracing the skin after cleansing. They will also remove grease and any dirt left by mistake. The simplest type is just a nice smell dissolved in water, for soothing the skin and nothing else. Other fresheners have cleansing ingredients, sometimes alcohol and sometimes a soap-like substance. The alcohol also acts as a mild thinner. Alcohol has a drying effect so shouldn't be used on older skins.

Moisturizing

Every time you clean your skin you wash off some moisturizers and protectives. You must replace the natural ones with something else. No moisturizer actually sinks into the skin to make it moist. What it does is to cover the surface of the skin with a film and prevent the natural moisture from evaporating.

Moisturizers also protect the skin from outside pollutants and act as lubricants, making the skin smoother. Men ought, of course, to wear moisturizers too. Few do and you can tell as they grow older by their bad complexion – it's not always drink, you know.

There are dozens of moisturizers to choose from. Women should use heavier overnight ones and a lighter one during the day. This has the advantage of providing a smooth base for cosmetics which will spread more smoothly and look smoother too.

On the whole, greasy moisturizers are advised because they are excellent barriers. Water-based lotions feel good initially but the water will evaporate during the day, leaving the skin unprotected. The moisturizer you choose should be as free as possible of colour and scent. You should never wear pigments and powders next to your skin. They can often irritate sensitive skin, and powder will dry it up. There's nothing wrong with coloured foundations but always wear them over moisturizers.

Expensive moisturizers are probably no better than cheap ones. Greasy ones – Vaseline, cold creams and so on – are perfectly satisfactory. Moisturizers containing hormones act differently. They actually change the metabolism of the skin and are supposed to 'plump it up'. There is some controversy about whether it's wise to use them as skin treatment. Since many women take the pill quite freely it is difficult to see why hormone skin treatments should be frowned on.

Humectants are smooth substances like glycerine. Small amounts are often added to creams and lotions to help attract moisture from the air. Too much can make the skin dry, so avoid those which claim to include large percentages.

Thinning

Every now and then (but not too often) you should remove the dead cells from your skin. You can do this with a rough towel or a specially made abrasive. But don't be too rough, don't overdo it and don't do it too often.

A simple face routine

Here is a very simple routine for various skin types.

The face should be cleaned carefully every evening to get rid of old make-up and old skin. There are three parts to the cleaning procedure. You should first use a cleanser to take off all the top grime. Wipe it gently all over your face, brows, cheeks, under the eyes, over the eyelids, under the chin, behind the ears, etc. Then wipe off the cleanser. Since you will never entirely remove the residue with cotton wool, you next use what's called a 'toner' to remove any left-over grease and to close the pores. This can be a brand product or distilled water (of the kind you use in a steam iron) or what I prefer to anything else – rose or orange water, which you can get from chemists. Many people use lukewarm tap-water. What is important is to rinse off the cleanser absolutely.

Having got your skin thoroughly clean and toned, use an oil-based moisturizer to prevent the skin from becoming dry and cracked. The richer the moisture the fresher-looking and softer the complexion.

Movements recommended by Elizabeth Arden for cleansing, toning and nourishing:

1. Start from base of neck, moving up to jawline from left side of neck to right.
2. Next, go along left jawline from chin to ear, from chin to outer corner of eye, etc. overlapping strokes so as to cover entire cheek.
3. Repeat for right side of face.
4. Then move to left temple and sweep up towards forehead.
5. Stroke from brows into hairline.
6. Now sweep up from right temple to forehead.
7. Extra care must be taken for the eye area – gently glide from outer corner of eye along lower lid and then from inner corner of eye across lid.
8. Finally stroke down bridge of nose and across upper lip.

Treating your skin type

Normal skin should be cleaned with soap or cleansing lotion, rinsed thoroughly and moisturized every morning and night. You can thin once a week at bedtime.

Dry skin should be cleaned with a cleansing lotion, rinsed thoroughly and moisturized every morning and evening, and thinned once a week at bedtime.

Very dry skin should be moisturized and cleaned in the morning; cleaned with a lotion, rinsed thoroughly and moisturized at bedtime, and thinned very gently once a week.

Oily skin should be cleaned with soap, rinsed thoroughly and moisturized in the morning and at bedtime. If you possibly can, freshen and moisturize after lunch as well.

Very oily skin, especially young people's skin, should be washed with soap, rinsed thoroughly and moisturized every morning. Rinse and moisturize again after lunch. At bedtime, clean with soap again and rinse thoroughly. Use a medicated lotion at bedtime too if necessary.

Professional skin treatment

Professional skin treatments may seem unnecessary when you can treat your skin so well at home. In fact they probably are. But there is no doubt that a good professional will do the job more thoroughly, with more expertise. You will benefit from an hour's relaxation and cosseting. In fact any time I've been for a facial I have come out positively glowing. Such treatment need not be expensive. Compare the £7 or so spent on a facial with the money you spend on cigarettes every week or on a new shirt. As a part of the treatment, you can have blackheads, whiteheads and small cysts removed.

Specialist beauty firms will give you time and trouble. Beauticians working for themselves are often very good. Hairdressers may have someone doing beauty treatments. You can always ask about their training and find out what their treatments consist of before you commit yourself. Those working in big stores, for instance, have to work to a time and keep up a constant patter intended to sell the expensive branded products they are using.

An occasional professional treatment is useful in that you will be told exactly what type of skin you have and what to do for it. Try examining your own skin through a magnifier in a very strong light. It will be a shock but an edifying one.

Make-up

Having cleaned and moisturized and given yourself a beautiful skin, you should make the best of it with subtle make-up chosen to suit your colouring and personality.

Many busy women – especially those at home a lot of the time and those with young children, don't give themselves time to experiment with different make-ups – they may even feel guilty at spending money on lipsticks. This is a mistake. It's only by trying things out and experimenting and keeping on doing it that you will get it right. And the odd little bit of make-up bought now and then is not going to cause the children to starve. Even better is an occasional visit to a beautician who will point out, not *just* the fashionable way to wear make-up but how to recognize and emphasize your own good points as a permanent thing. If the expert seems to have an exaggerated idea of how much make-up you should wear, you can always go straight home and cleanse it off, but at least you'll have the basic rules and more confidence.

One or two hints may be useful here. During the day eyes should never look dark and heavy (though I know a girl who always outlines her eyes with charcoal because she says she doesn't care what the fashion is – men *like* it). Use eye-shadow thinly. You will find that make-up goes on far more smoothly over a fresh application of moisturizer. If moisturizer and make-up together make you look too shiny, use a little powder over the top. You don't need much.

It really is helpful to look in the glossies to see photographs of step-by-step make-up. Their colours may not suit you, but the techniques are useful and you don't have to emphasize it as strongly as they do.

During the day, make-up should be fresh and natural (or at least look it). But for evenings you can afford to be more daring. Heighten the cheek-bones with a slightly darker shade of make-up. Be bolder about the eyes.

The Neck

A scraggy neck is a sorry sight, very ageing and quite unnecessary. But you must start preventive treatment early. Hold your head well and proudly, then you won't encourage deep horizontal lines across your neck. Use a small pillow at night or, if you can bear it, none at all.

Give your neck as much care as your face and always include it in your daily skin care. The neck receives less oil from the sebaceous glands than the face. This makes it finer textured but more vulnerable. When applying cleansers and lotions always do so with an

upwards motion. Hold your chin up and start from the collar-bone.
Sweep up the left side of the neck with the right hand and vice versa.
Then with the back of the hands give little firm pats under the chin.

The Body

Body skin has regional variations in thickness. In some parts it may
be twenty-five cell layers deep. To a minor degree bodily wastes are
excreted through the skin, and the amount and composition of fluid
in the body is regulated by sweat. Those of us who bath a lot – every
day, say – are doing the body skin no good because bathing removes
much of the body oils we have.

The frequency with which you apply body and face oils and
moisturizers must depend on your own skin. To maintain a soft
supple body skin you should oil the body after every bath or shower.
Application daily will result in a better skin. And of course, bath oils
(not salts) help.

In spite of the differences between face and body skin, they both
need the same basic treatment: cleaning, toning and moisturizing.
After bathing or showering, a good rub with a Turkish towel or a
'scrub' with a special towel will get rid of old, dried-up skin cells and
get the blood circulating.

Pay special attention to your elbows which, since they are behind
you, are easy to forget about but can look like old chicken legs if you
neglect them. A loofah is useful for scrubbing off dead skin. Then
moisturize, and do it often.

Under the arms and between the thighs, where sweat is not free to
evaporate, bacteria will break down the oil in the sweat and cause
strong obnoxious body smells. Some people suffer more from sweaty
smells than others. For most people, daily washing in those parts will
be enough to prevent smells; others may need to take a bath or a
shower every day using lots of soap. If sweat dries on clothes it smells
strong and musty, so underwear and socks should be changed every
day and for people who sweat a lot, so should shirts.

Deodorants put on first thing in the morning and after bathing or
washing will prevent most people from being smelly.

'Feminine' products for using around the pubic and vaginal areas
can kill off friendly bacteria which normally stave off unfriendly
bacteria and should be used seldom, if at all.

TEETH

I once knew a courageous woman who had to have all her teeth removed when she was forty. She had them replaced immediately and went out to dinner the same night. There the man sitting next to her unknowingly and cruelly entertained her with jokes about false teeth. What's more she managed to laugh and he never found out. Most of us are afraid of our dentist but we should not allow our teeth to go bad. Tooth decay can be prevented to a certain extent if you understand what causes it.

There should be thirty-two teeth in a full adult set: eight incisors at the front for biting off food, four canines for tearing, eight premolars for slicing and twelve molars for grinding. Often the molars right at the back (wisdom teeth) don't appear at all. They may be present but not come through the gum, or they may not even have formed.

Tooth decay is caused by plaque, a sticky film which builds up on all tooth surfaces. It contains harmful bacteria and their products which cause tooth decay and gum disease.

The exposed part of each tooth is covered with enamel, a hard non-cellular substance. Dentine, which is hard with a honeycomb structure, forms the underlying part of the tooth from the crown to the root. Dentine is made of cells and can repair itself to a certain extent (which enamel cannot). Cement covers the roots of the teeth; it is like bone and anchors the tooth to the surrounding bone. The cement is full of nerves and if it is exposed because of receding gums it is very painful indeed.

Pulp fills the spaces in the dentine. If it is invaded by caries (decay) it becomes infected and dies. The infection may eventually pass out of the end of the root of the tooth and attack the surrounding bone, creating an abcess. Then you'll need antibiotics and probably the tooth will have to be taken out.

We do, of course, eat far too many soft and sugary foods. These encourage plaque bacteria which act on the food particles, turning them into acids which seep into the tooth and attack the enamel just below the tooth surface. If you go to the dentist at this stage, treatment will be quick and fairly painless. If you don't, the decay will spread until the enamel surface collapses leaving the dentine open to attack. If you still don't get treatment, the decay will reach the pulp at the centre of the tooth where the nerves are. The nerve will die, an abcess will form and you'll probably lose the tooth.

Dental decay isn't the worst worry, however. Gum disease (periodontal disease) can be disastrous to the teeth too. In its early stages it's often quite painless and is easy to ignore.

Inflammation or bleeding of the gums (gingivitis) may be the first indication of gum disease. Healthy gums don't bleed. Older people are particularly susceptible to gingivitis. The gums eventually become swollen and inflamed and begin to draw away from the teeth.

It becomes painful to chew and pus may start to form around the teeth.

The bleeding is caused by the action of poisons produced by the old enemy plaque bacteria. If the inflammation goes unchecked the condition gets worse and the bone supporting the teeth will be attacked and will eventually disintegrate and your teeth will become loose and fall out or have to be pulled out. Poor diet may lead to gum disease. You should go to a dentist immediately you notice any signs of trouble.

As you can see, it is important to remove plaque from all tooth surfaces every day to maintain healthy teeth and gums.

Methods of cleaning teeth have changed a good deal since I was a little girl. There are various schools of thought and I offer you the advice my hygienist gives me, which has worked miraculously for my own teeth.

First choose your brush with care. There are many different types available but not all are effective at removing plaque. Bristle brushes are not now recommended because they have sharp edges which may scratch your teeth and gums. They also hold water and may become soggy. A wet soggy brush won't remove plaque.

What you want is a flat-trimmed, multi-tufted brush with fine round-ended flexible filaments. A soft or medium one is kinder than a hard one, which may damage teeth and gums and won't be flexible enough to get into the crannies.

Automatic toothbrushes may be useful for elderly and handicapped people. It is important to clean every surface of each tooth. There are several effective brushing techniques. Your dentist or hygienist will probably recommend one to you. The old 'scrubbing' method is not a good one.

One method is to place the brush head at an angle of $45°$ towards the gum where the gums meet the tooth with half the filaments on the gum and half on the tooth. Then roll the brush towards the biting surface with a twist of the wrist, applying firm pressure.

The top teeth should be brushed downwards and the bottom teeth upwards. Start at the back and clean only two teeth at a time using several strokes over the same surface.

To clean the backs of the front teeth use the brush lengthways. Remember to clean the backs and fronts and the biting surfaces of both upper and lower teeth. The biting surfaces should be cleaned last, using a backwards and forward motion.

Toothpaste should be applied to a dry brush and it is better to keep two toothbrushes for each person, one for the morning and one for the evening, so the brushes have a chance to get thoroughly dry between uses. Brushes should be renewed every two or three months.

Always use a mirror when cleaning your teeth.

Brushing will remove a good deal of the plaque on your teeth but will leave plaque between them. This should be removed once a day with dental floss. This is specially designed nylon thread which cleans between the teeth and under the gums. You can buy it at chemists.

Cut off about 250 mm (10 inches) of floss and tie the two ends together to make a loop. Place the loop over the middle (second) finger of each hand. Use the first fingers and thumbs to guide the floss gently between the teeth, keeping it against one tooth surface. One finger should be on either side of the tooth. You will feel the floss slip down. Then clean the side of each tooth with a gentle up and down motion, slipping the floss gently below the surface of the gums. Look in the mirror to see what you're doing.

You must have a demonstration of how to use floss and you will need to practise a bit before it comes easily. Your dentist or hygienist can show you what to do. It's worth the small extra effort to do this once a day, especially as you grow older, because gum troubles are common, extremely painful and do lead to loss of teeth.

Interdental brushes These are small, single-tufted brushes which can clean larger gaps between teeth and other places you can't get at with an ordinary brush.

Woodsticks Using toothpicks is an excellent continental habit. They shouldn't be used just as toothpicks, but for the regular removal of plaque. Woodsticks are a sophisticated, triangular wooden version of toothpicks and the flat surface is used towards the gum. The stick is passed gently between the teeth, cleaning the sides which the toothbrush cannot reach.

Disclosing agents Plaque is often difficult to see. Disclosing tablets look like bright red aspirin. They are made from a vegetable dye. You chew them; the dye stains the plaque on the teeth so you can see where it is. It also stains your tongue for several hours, making you look like something out of a horror movie. You should use these once or twice a week. The dye is also available as a liquid.

Toothpaste Toothpaste itself does not remove plaque. The techniques described above are much more important, though toothpaste which contains fluoride does help to strengthen the teeth and protect against decay. Too much toothpaste can actually make it more difficult to remove plaque. Smokers' toothpastes and powders are very abrasive and shouldn't be used more than once or twice a week at most.

Dentures

False teeth should be cleaned with soap and water, toothpaste or denture paste and a soft brush specially kept for this purpose. Clean them after each meal if you can (bits of spinach which you can't feel with your tongue look dreadful caught in the teeth); night and morning too.

Bleaching and scouring agents should never be used as they may damage the dentures. Always hold the teeth over a basin when cleaning them so they won't break if you drop them.

Babies and children

Teeth can start decaying as soon as they appear, so tooth cleaning should start with the first tooth. At first all you have to do is rub the baby's teeth with a cotton bud or a piece of gauze and fluoride toothpaste. As the baby gets used to it you can progress to using a soft nylon brush.

Children should be taught to clean their teeth as suggested by your own dentist or hygienist or as I described above. But they will need supervision and help for a time until they go through the whole process as a matter of course. In fact you should go on cleaning your child's teeth until he/she can do it as efficiently on his own, but allow the child to do some himself each time.

Do remember that diet is as important for teeth as for anything else. The worst foods for teeth are sticky sugars: sweets, cakes, biscuits, sweet drinks, and ices. They can glue carbohydrates to the teeth and encourage plaque to form much more quickly. The chemicals created by them generate lactic acid which attacks enamel.

If we were all to avoid sugars and sweet things and to brush our teeth correctly and regularly, few people would have decayed teeth. As it is, people are so careless of oral hygiene that in many areas fluoride has been added to the drinking water supply. This has reduced dental decay by about sixty per cent.

Even if you brush your teeth regularly and don't eat the wrong foods, you should still have your teeth examined by a dentist every six to nine months. Don't wait until you get inflamed gums or toothache.

HANDS

Our hands have a tough time. We subject them to hot water, cold water, detergents, cold winds and hot sun, dust and earth. On the whole you wash your hands about a dozen times a day. This is altogether too much cleaning for the poor old skin which will become red and rough and may even get a rash. The nails suffer as well.

Obviously it is sensible to wear rubber gloves for as many jobs as possible: washing-up, polishing, scrubbing, gardening, fiddling with the car, etc. It's also wise to use hand cream several times a day and especially after washing-up or hand-washing clothes.

However, gloves get dirty and sweaty inside and may make some hands worse. Always buy rubber gloves slightly too large so that they let a little air in. If your hands are in bad condition wear thin cotton gloves inside them for a while. You can buy rolls of dispensible plastic gloves which are a good idea but a bit expensive. Try not to let your hands get too hot when wearing rubber gloves. Keep them out of washing up water. Use long-handled brushes, for instance. Never wear this sort of glove for more than an hour at a time.

Replace the oils removed by constant washing with a good handcream used several times a day.

NAILS

Care of the nails is an important part of hand care.

A nail is made up of three layers of keratin, which are held together with a natural 'glue', a mixture of oil and moisture. When this 'glue' dries out, nails become weak, brittle and flaky. The longer you allow your nails to grow beyond the fingertip the thinner the glue becomes and the more likely your nail is to crack. A short, oval curved nail is stronger than a long, breakable claw.

The cuticle is the nail wall surrounding the nail. It is constantly

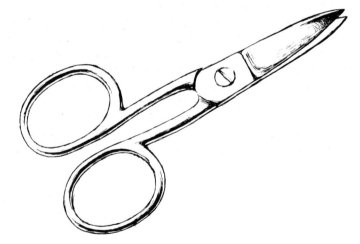

producing new cells and throwing off old dried ones. The cuticle acts as a protective seal to prevent dirt and infection getting into the living nail bed which is beneath the skin, beyond the half-moon. Unless the cuticle is kept smooth and healthy it sticks to the nail, covering the half-moon. If it becomes dry or stretched through moving up with the nail as it grows, the cuticle will split and break. It looks ugly and may well cause a hangnail, which is very painful.

The cuticle protects the matrix which is the living part of the nail producing the new nail cells. These new cells push the old dead cells forward so your nail is actually made up of dead cells. Damage to any part of the nail you can see will eventually grow out, but if you damage the matrix by a blow or by crushing it, you may damage the growth and shape of the nail for a long time – perhaps for good.

Detergents, soap and water, chemicals, etc., will all dry out the nails and cause the layers to separate and the nail to break. If you like long, hot baths, try to keep your hands out of the water as much as possible. Don't use your nails to open cans and prise off lids.

Dry your hands carefully each time they have been in water but don't get into the habit of pushing the cuticle back with the towel as this may crack it. Keep a hand cream by the sink and in the bathroom and use a little every time you dry your hands. Modern lotions are absorbed quickly and don't feel sticky. For dry, grubby jobs (sweeping, for instance) use a barrier cream which will bring the dirt off easily when you wash. Some people wear cotton gloves at night when the hands and nails are in bad shape, so the cream stays on longer and doesn't get rubbed off by the sheets.

Don't use a nail-brush too often as it will scrape little grooves in nails and cuticles. If your hands have got grubby – gardeners will understand what I mean – use the softest brush you can find and apply it very gently. A tiny bit of cotton wool, or cotton, damped and wrapped around an orange stick is the best way of getting dirt from underneath the nails, but don't jab or prod. If you don't wear nail varnish a chamois buffer will give them a natural shine.

Gently massaging the area above the half-moon with the thumb of the other hand will stimulate the circulation of the matrix and help the nails to grow. Horizontal and vertical ridges on the nails are usually a sign of recent illness and will eventually grow out.

If your nails are to look good all the time you should manicure them once a week. Many hairdressers have a manicurist who can do this while you're under the drier. But it's not a bad thing to make yourself take half an hour off one evening and do it yourself. No amount of nail varnish will make shabby nails look well groomed. The best time is after a bath or hair-washing session when the nails are slightly softened.

First remove the old varnish with tufts of cotton wool well soaked in an oily varnish remover. Don't use acetone on its own because it contains no oil and nails need oil. Modern varnishes are tough and long lasting so hold the pad over the nail for a few seconds to soften the varnish then wipe off the varnish with vertical strokes. Now trim your nails to an oval shape. Don't cut down too far at the sides or you will weaken the all-important hinge. Finish off by lightly bevelling the nail on both sides with fine emery board, held at right-angles to the nail.

Cuticle removers should seldom be used because they make the cuticle too dry. If the cuticle has got ragged, though, use a very little and rinse it off after a few seconds. Then with the blunt end of a thick orange stick, or one tipped with a rubber band, gently lift the cuticle and wipe away any dead skin. Never cut the cuticle, unless there's a fragment of loose skin hanging down which you can cut off.

There are nail strengtheners for fragile nails. They reinforce the cement and give the nails a chance to grow.

Nails contain protein and benefit from a well balanced diet that includes plenty of protein: a little milk, cheese, meat, fish, pulse vegetables and plenty of fresh fruit and vegetables. Vitamin D is good for nails but too much is toxic so take only the recommended amount. Sunshine encourages the body to make its own vitamin D and helps nails to grow. Don't forget, though, that it's bad for the skin.

Cold weather and bad circulation inhibit nail growth so wear gloves in winter and encourage the circulation by massage and buffing. Better still, go for a long walk or spend an afternoon sawing logs.

Finally if your nails are constantly broken and split take them to an expert. Persistent nail problems are often the sign of something wrong with your insides. Experts have come to the conclusion that taking gelatine to strengthen the nails does not a bit of good.

FEET

Your feet are difficult to keep an eye on – they're so far away and many of us are too plump or out of condition for the contortions necessary to examine our feet properly. It's worth the effort though. Keep an eye open for run-of-the-mill things like corns and calluses and maybe a verruca.

A callus is a painful area of the skin that has become hard and thick.

A corn is a form of callus on or between the toes. It is always the result of pressure or friction from badly fitting shoes.

Verruca is the medical term for a wart: a small growth caused by a virus. A verruca on the sole of the foot is painful because of the pressure from standing and walking, and often builds up a thick callus round it. This type is infectious and should be taken to a doctor. If there is any sign of trouble in the feet you should go to a doctor and get treatment.

Athlete's foot is a chronic disorder of the skin on the feet caused by a fungus infection that likes wet, warm places such as swimming-pools and sweaty toes. You may have splits in the skin, blisters, and sometimes scaling between the toes and sometimes on the soles of the feet and round the heel. The more you perspire the worse it will get. Normally, athlete's foot is only a minor nuisance but sometimes a fungus of the ringworm type infests the foot and it may spread to other parts of the body (under the breasts and in the armpits and groin) where it can produce an annoying rash. This can be treated by frequent washing of the affected parts and with fungicidal creams, powders and sprays. But if the condition persists you should see a doctor.

Gently rub away the scaly or damp peelings and dry the foot. Wash gently then dry the foot again and apply a proprietary fungicidal dusting powder. Try to leave the foot uncovered for as long as possible and let the air get at it. At bedtime and in the morning, rub in a mild fungicidal ointment. Put on clean socks or tights every day and try to avoid nylon; cotton or wool are more absorbent and more satisfactory. Try to wear the sort of shoes which will let in some air; in winter don't wear boots all day long; and try not to let your feet get very hot.

Good daily foot care should prevent most troubles and an occasional visit to a chiropodist will keep your poor feet in good condition for their demanding job.

One chiropodist I spoke to says a trouble he frequently comes across is dirty feet but ironically, another is clean feet: 'People suffer from the modern disease of being overclean.' Some skin specialists tend to think that many modern skin conditions are caused by too much care – by putting substances on the skin which it doesn't like.

People are very unkind to their feet. They soak them in all sorts of detergents or in washing soda, 'Which can produce gorgeous rashes and sores', said my chiropodist. And, people tend to rush off and buy very expensive things to put in the bath. Some are quite good but others are much too detergenty.

If your feet seem dry and scaly, they are not necessarily suffering from athlete's foot. They may just be dry. What the poor darlings could do with is cream smoothed into them. Creams that work on the hands will work quite well on the feet as well.

Drastic self-treatment of feet can be disastrous. Do not use what my chiropodist called those 'cheese-grater affairs' to scrape off old dry skin. The secret of success is even scraping and an expert is the person to do it.

Most people who have problems with their feet should see their chiropodist every four to six weeks. People with no special problems obviously need to go less often. A good chiropodist should be state registered. Check that yours is before you make an appointment. In some areas it is very difficult to set up as a chiropodist without being registered but in others almost anyone can offer his services, whether qualified or not.

When washing your feet, use ordinary plain, mild soap, and not very much of it. If the feet have become very sore and soft or there are sore places between the toes which are beginning to fester, a really huge handful of salt in the water will help to draw out any infection. Soak the feet in this for about ten minutes every evening – not quite up to the ankle.

Air for the feet

Try to give your feet as much air as possible, especially if you work or live in centrally heated buildings.

Don't wear boots all day long, but change into sandals or shoes which will give your toes room to stretch and let the air in. Don't wear the same shoes day after day. It is better for your feet, and for the shoes as well, to alternate. Exercise your feet by rolling them round and round; spread out the toes then relax them; curl them up, then relax them. If nylon irritates your feet try to wear cotton socks instead and make sure they are big enough. Socks and stockings that are too tight can do almost as much damage as shoes that are too small.

Toe-nails

Toe-nails should be cut straight across, just like our mothers taught us. If you can't because it leaves a point at the edges which may stick into tights or feet, cut a roundish nail but never actively cut down the sides. You may otherwise end up with ingrowing toe-nails and then you will certainly need professional help.

The statement that shoes can wreck feet is true. Badly fitting shoes cause corns, bunions and ingrowing toe-nails. They cause poor posture which leads to general tiredness and strain. Do buy shoes that fit – i.e. that give your toes plenty of room to move about in. Some people buy expensive leather shoes only to find they have synthetic linings. Others seem more comfortable in artificial leather anyway. High heels throw the weight right forward on the foot and unless worn for decoration only and for very short periods will eventually damage the foot. Wide-toed shoes are fine.

HAIR

Hair, like nails, is made up of a structure of dead cells filled with tough protein called keratin. Between 100,000 and 200,000 hairs can grow on a human head. Each hair grows from its own individual follicle. A hair grows about 10 mm (half an inch) every month and drops out when it is two to four years old. Then it is replaced by a new one. The base of the follicle is supplied with blood vessels and nerves, though the hair itself is made of dead cells.

The condition of your hair reflects your general state of health.

Hair should be washed at least once every ten days, and more often if it is oily. Cheap shampoos are often made with borax, which may irritate the skin but will help to dry out greasy hair. Expensive shampoos are usually made with soap or detergent.

Shampooing

Use warm not very hot water. Wet the hair thoroughly, then pour some shampoo into the palm of your hand – enough to make a good lather. Never pour shampoo directly on to the hair. Keep a towel next to the basin so you can wipe your eyes if any shampoo gets into them. The hands should massage the scalp gently but firmly, rotating smoothly round the head. Hold your fingers as though you were holding a football and rub the scalp with the pads of your fingers; don't scratch the skin with your finger-nails. Massage the whole head; if you leave out a small area it may feel itchy later on.

Rinse the hair and scalp thoroughly until the hair squeaks when you run it through your fingers. If you wash your hair very often, one shampooing should be enough, though most instructions advise you to repeat the process.

Rub the hair in a towel to get off the excess moisture them comb it gently without pulling or tugging it.

Most shampoos are soapless, made of synthetic detergents. They can be used in hard or soft water. Modern soapless shampoos are gentler than their predecessors but you need use only a little and it is important to rinse the hair well or they will make hair and skin very dry. Some people are allergic to some shampoos and may have to find an alternative.

Oil shampoos (using pine, olive, palm or other oils) are supposed to get the hair clean and leave a little oil in the hair. But it's better to put on a little oil after washing your hair than to expect an oil shampoo to replace lost oils.

You can give yourself an oil treatment by putting warm olive oil on to your hair while it is still dry. Leave it for five to fifteen minutes. Then shampoo your hair as usual. Hot towels will make the hair swell so the oil can penetrate.

Egg shampoo can be made from real egg or lecithin. They emulsify grease and can be rinsed easily. You can use whites or yolks on their own or mixed with a little water or soapless shampoo. Egg shampoos are good for coarse hair.

Lemon shampoo contains citric acid and can be used on any hair, greasy or dry. It is good for really fine hair because it leaves it in a manageable condition. This is why lemon juice or vinegar are often used for rinsing.

Beer and champagne shampoos usually contain acid which gives a manageable finish to the hair. They can be used on dry or greasy hair. Real beer and champagne can be used as a rinse after washing and act as good setting lotions. They are good for fine hair which needs body.

Medicated shampoos are intended to be used to deal with scaly or very dry skin and slight irritations. Most are intended to prevent rather than cure scalp conditions.

Medicated and treatment shampoos, which contain antiseptics, should be used with caution. Some people may be allergic to them; many are toxic and some will darken bleached hair. Any infections or persistent scalp irritation should be treated by a doctor.

If for some reason you can't wash your hair when it needs a wash you can try using a 'dry' shampoo.

The use (mainly by men) of liquid spirit shampoos is like dry-cleaning clothes. The liquid spirit is sprinkled on the hair and then massaged with the hands for a few minutes. The spirit dissolves grease and dirt which is removed by rubbing with a towel.

Dry shampoo powder, which is more common, works like cleaning a fur coat with fuller's earth. The powder is sprinkled on the hair where it absorbs the dirt and grease, and then you brush the whole lot out.

Obviously dry shampooing is second best to washing.

Looking after your hair

You should groom your hair carefully and gently every day and wash it two or three times a week; certainly never less than every ten days.

Your comb should not have any sharp edges. A badly made comb could break the hair and damage the scalp. Some plastic combs produce static electricity which makes your hair rise. When combing wet hair you should use a comb with widely spread teeth. The comb should be used upright – not flattened against the hair. Start at the hair ends and gradually work upwards towards the scalp, very gently teasing out knots and tangles.

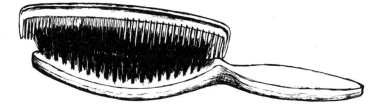

The best type of hairbrush has natural, soft, short bristles, though thin long bristles may be easier to use on long hair. Brushing stimulates the natural oils. To brush correctly you should use a smooth stroking action. Never scrub hard over the hair or hit the scalp with the bristles. The brush should be turned with a rolling wrist action and you should support your head while you are brushing. For blow-drying a round brush with bristles all round is best and easiest. Use a brush that is comfortable to hold.

Clean your combs and brushes at least once a week. Combs can be cleaned with an old toothbrush dipped in warm water and detergent. Brushes can be washed in warm detergenty water. Dry away from direct heat, bristle side up.

Thick, oily hairdressing may clog the pores and irritate the scalp. The best way you can care for your hair is to keep it clean. Dry it in sunlight or with a hair drier, brushing it gently while it's drying. If you want to bleach your hair, use hydrogen peroxide to which a drop of ammonia has been added. Sodium perborate is not good for the hair and may harm the scalp. All bleaching will eventually alter the texture of the hair.

You can tint or dye your hair but there's no completely safe dye which will give hair a permanent natural-looking colour. Always test a small piece of hair first and check that the dye won't irritate your skin by putting a small bit on your arm.

Don't dye eyelashes or eyebrows because the skin round the eyes is sensitive. Mascara does not usually cause any trouble but if it irritates then you should stop using it.

In general, treat your hair gently. Scratching may break hairs off and will certainly damage the scalp. Don't pull your hair very tightly over rollers. Eventually such pulling will bring it out by the roots. Don't use your hair drier too hot and too close to the hair. Comb or brush only as much as is needed to keep the hair in place. Any extra hard brushing and curling will put a strain on the hairs. Use a wide-toothed comb and avoid brushes with nylon bristles. Hot combing, hot curlers and curling irons will all weaken hair.

Shampoos and conditioners containing protein coat each hair with a film of protein. This makes the hair seem thicker and protects it from bleaches and other hair treatments.

BABY

In this age of experts you can't expect to do something as basic as having a baby without being barraged with advice from all quarters. The best advice I know is relax and enjoy your baby in spite of good advice.

One of the worst moments of being a mother for the first time is getting home from hospital and finding you have to bath the baby on your own. Even if you had pre-natal baby-bathing lessons the real thing with your own baby is not the same.

Everything to do with a new baby takes twice as long as you expect, so allow plenty of time for bathing before a feed so there's time for both of you to enjoy the bath.

It doesn't really matter what you bath the baby in. The basin will do if it's big enough and clean. A plastic bath or washtub will do perfectly well. A bath on a stand is best because it's at a convenient height and there's room for baby to splash about, but at one stage I used to put the baby bath in the big bath which meant some bending for me but the baby didn't mind.

Before bathtime get everything together that you will need and lay it all out within reach. A small trolley or table will make this easier. You will need:

The bath
A chair for yourself – a fairly upright one in which you can reach the baby comfortably when it's in the bath

Apron
Large soft towel
Mild soap (baby soap is probably best)
Cotton wool
Soothing cream
Powder
Nappies
Nappy pins
Set of clean clothes
Bucket for dirty nappies
Bucket for used cotton wool, etc.

Make sure the room is warm and if necessary try to screen the bathing area from draughts. If you have a screen you can sew pockets on it to hold some of the accessories such as nappy pins, cotton buds, etc.

Fill the bath, running cold water first and then adding hot. The water should be warm but not hot. My mother's method of testing was to dip her elbow in the water. Babies hate water that's too hot or too cold.

Lay the baby on your lap and gently wipe his face and hands with cotton wool squeezed out in water (no soap). Wipe gently across each eye from the inside towards the outside. Use a clean piece of cotton wool for each eye. Don't clean the baby's ears but if its nose is dirty clean it very gently with a small piece of twisted cotton wool – not with anything stuck on a wooden stick. Babies are tougher than they look but their delicate little skins must be treated gently.

Wash the hair with a little baby shampoo (you don't have to do this every day). Hold the baby's head over the bath with one hand supporting the neck and use a mug to pour water over. Don't get any water on the baby's face or it will think hair washing is something horrible.

Wash and soap the baby's bottom – easier with hands than a flannel. Now you can put baby in the bath, putting one arm under its head and holding the upper arm with that hand. The other hand can hold its ankles. Keep the head supported all the time with one arm and splash gently with the other. Never leave your baby alone in the bath. Even toddlers have been known to drown in only an inch or two of water.

If the baby gets tired or crotchety or when the water's cooling down, take it out and place it on half the towel spread over your lap. Then cover it with the other half and pat it gently dry. Dry in all the folds and cracks of the skin. Sprinkle on baby powder and put on the nappy and clothes.

Some people find it easier to have a table or a platform and to change and dry the baby on this. It's certainly easier in some ways for the mother if you have the space.

A baby's nappy should be changed five or six times a day. Often if a baby cries for no apparent reason it's nothing to do with hunger but because it is in wet or dirty nappies – presumably as uncomfortable for a baby as it would be for you or me. Every time you change a nappy make sure the baby's bottom is thoroughly cleaned and dried. If there are little sore red places treat them with suitable powder or cream.

Wet nappies should be put immediately into a bucket of water. Dirty ones should be rinsed first. Wash nappies once a day in a very hot wash. They may need boiling from time to time.

WASHING SOMEBODY IN BED

Sometimes you may prefer to look after a child or relative at home rather than that they should languish in hospital. Or you may even be looking after an elderly person who isn't very mobile. It's then essential to know how to wash and make them comfortable in bed without in fact making them more uncomfortable or breaking your back.

People who have to lie in bed for any length of time need to be washed frequently because the skin perspires and can cause sore places quickly which are aggravated by being rubbed against the sheets.

Obviously the patient must be kept warm while being washed, so cover all his body except the part you're washing with a thick bath towel or thin blanket and put a towel underneath to catch the splashes. Many patients don't enjoy the washing process but they always feel refreshed and grateful afterwards.

Take off the pyjamas or nightie. Wash, rinse and dry eyes in clean water, and the face, neck and ears. Work quickly and gently. Next wash, rinse and dry the arms, working from the armpit towards the fingers. Let the patient put his hands in the water. Wash and dry the chest and abdomen. Wash rinse and dry each leg washing from thigh to ankle.

Change the water if it gets dirty or cool.

Now wash the groin and between the legs unless the patient is capable or prefers to do this for himself. Wash the feet in the bowl. Now turn the patient on his side and wash and dry his back.

Straighten out the sheets and underblanket before leaving the patient in peace again.

This all sounds very easy. Usually it's not. The patient may be in pain or frightened and cantankerous, and of course, heavy. If you possibly can, try to get someone to help you, at least for the turning of the patient, or to help him to the lavatory. Try also to get someone to 'patient-sit' occasionally so you have the chance to get out for a little. There is no virtue in being a martyr unnecessarily.

Preventing bedsores

Anyone stuck in bed and not allowed to move is susceptible to bedsores. These are nearly always caused by pressure from the weight of the body on the areas where it touches the bed. If the pressure is too prolonged, those areas start to lose their blood supply and the skin covering them becomes inflamed. Sores can also be caused by bedclothes pressing on knees and toes.

Moisure (especially from sweat) and rubbing will produce sores more quickly and once they have formed they are very difficult indeed to get rid of. The main points of pressure are the toes, heels, knees, buttocks, elbows, shoulders and the back of the head. Rub pressure points or any tender places with surgical spirit. Prevention is better than cure. If the patient is likely to be stuck in bed for some time, you should try to get a sheepskin for him to lie on or a synthetic sheepskin which has the advantage of being washable.

You can get inflatable rubber rings to protect pressure points. These should be enclosed in pillowslips. A pillow between the legs of a patient lying on his side prevents them pressing together. New gadgets are being invented all the time. Your local council or the Red Cross may be able to help with equipment.

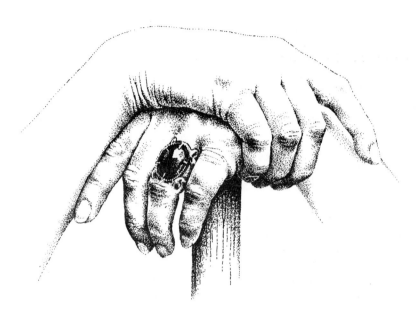

CHAPTER 7

THE LAZY PERSON'S
GUIDE TO HOUSEWORK

Keeping a house clean should be a matter of prevention rather than cure. The more you can keep wiping, mopping and dusting as you go through your home the less heavy cleaning will have to be done later.

I have *The Book of Good Housekeeping* (Waverley Book Co., London) which I bought in 1955, the year I got married. It has some, inevitably, strangely out-of-date budgeting, but none more so than the time-budget in which it suggested the whole day, every day of the week, should be spent preparing, serving and washing-up after meals, making beds, 'daily work' in bedroom, bathroom and landing; tidying and laundrywork. Afternoons, I am happy to see were free for extra shopping, ironing, needlework, gardening, and so on. People nowadays, whether with full-time jobs or children or not, are unlikely to want to spend so much time on the house. I should say two hours in an average day is the most one should expect to have to put in. A far cry from *Keeping House with Elizabeth Craig* (Collins, 1936) who says, 'Each servant should be given a supply of necessary cleaning materials.'

Times have changed and there is perhaps even more sense now in organizing one's time in the house, so as not to waste it doing things in a less efficient way. In fact the less time one has the more organized one should be and everyone has certain priorities to bear in mind: one of mine, for instance, is emptying the cat litter *every* morning no matter what.

People with jobs or outside interests will find their houseworking priorities are simple and few. People with more time may be more fastidious and include daily vacuuming, dusting and shaking the doormat as essential as well.

Even if you find housework a dreadful chore, you will find it pleasant to come home to a house which is relatively ordered, fairly clean, where fires are ready to be lit and the sink is not full of dirty dishes.

Mothers with young children have the most difficult time keeping a house clean. In fact it's a mistake to worry too much about the state of the house unless you have someone to come in and help with the housework. Babies and young children do need attention and are exhausting. For your own sake you should keep the home pleasant but don't break your back trying to create a *House and Garden* atmosphere in the years before they go to school.

Tidy up as you go along is the best advice I can give.

Pick up clothes and put them away before you leave the bedroom; keep children's toys in their own boxes; wipe the stove every time you cook a meal and the worktop every time you scrape a carrot. I used to keep a basket downstairs and carry books, toys, socks etc. back whenever I went upstairs, and a plastic bucket in the bathroom for bath toys. A friend keeps her bath toys strung in a string bag from the ceiling.

Wash up odd mugs or plates when they've been used and don't let a higgledy-piggledy pile of crockery and cutlery put you off washing-up at all. It's much easier to clean up a pleasant home than one where you don't know where to *begin*.

CLEANING EQUIPMENT

The *Book of Good Housekeeping* was certainly right in suggesting you should have the right sort of tools for the job.

In a house with carpets you will need a vacuum cleaner: expensive but essential. Upright ones collect a lot of dirt before they need emptying and suck strongly. They're good for large carpeted areas. Oblong cylinder ones are good for large uncarpeted areas and stairs. Choose one with good suction. Some will blow as well as suck and some will suck up water too. These are adapted from industrial ones and may be cheap, simple and foolproof but noisy. For small flats or bedsitters a carpet sweeper should be enough.

The basic housework tool kit would consist of the vacuum cleaner plus a 'wet' mop of some sort for the kitchen floor, a broom, a dustpan and brush, a bucket and scrubbing brush, a cobweb brush, a window-cleaning squeegee (marvellous tool), a lavatory brush, cloths of various sorts and a collection of detergents, bleaches and so on. (See page 214 for lists of products and tools.) If you have a home on two or more floors, you will find it convenient to have a dustpan and brush, and a duster and broom, upstairs and another downstairs.

'The most labour-saving move you can make', (says *Good Housekeeping*), 'is to have easily cleaned surfaces – for furniture, flooring, tables, etc.' This is true but don't follow it as gospel. Some people prefer polished wood to sealed wood, wood floors to vinyl tiles, wallpaper (even in the kitchen) to gloss paint. If you wipe these surfaces from time to time, they should not get so dirty that they're really hard to clean. In any case things you actually like are not a pain to care for. If you clean because it's your *duty* you may well find it a chore. If you like the finishes and designs in your home, caring for them may even become a pleasure. But that's no reason not to take any short cuts you can!

HOW OFTEN?

Do clean often. Many of the very helpful products on the market are marvellous for keeping a home clean but not quite drastic enough for cleaning up a dirty one. Getting dirt off is hard work whereas it's easy to wipe over walls or doors in an odd half hour just to prevent the dirt settling.

My own method is to have certain priorities and bumble through the rest as best I can. Every day I clear out rubbish, burn paper, shake doormats (we live in the country where there seems to be a lot of mud), wash up and get someone to vacuum. Every week I dust and polish. Every year I look under the beds and the piano and look away again. Every Christmas and before dinner parties I clean the silver. This is a very minimal programme. It leaves a lot to be desired, but at least I know the extreme basics are being done.

A weekly cleaning plan

This plan of campaign for once-a-week cleaning is worth setting down as a checklist. You don't have to follow it religiously but if you do you'll certainly have a clean house that will be welcoming and will not get so dirty that cleaning becomes a Herculean task.

1. Open the windows.
2. Remove flowers, empty ashtrays, waste-paper baskets, etc.
3. Clean out grate and re-lay fire. (An activity that is coming back into fashion now that electricity and oil are so much more expensive, and especially since the discovery of the wood-burning stove.)
4. Vacuum curtains, upholstery and carpets.
5. Mop and polish the surrounds.
6. Clean the windows and the paintwork.
7. Dust window ledges, wainscotting and all polished furniture. Polish where necessary.
8. Shake the rugs before replacing them.

For the bedroom you should:

1. Strip and air the bed. Dust, brush or vacuum the bedstead and mattress. Make the bed.
2. Remove all ornaments from dressing-table and lay them on a newspaper on the bed; cover with dust-sheet.
3. Shake the curtains.
4. Vacuum the carpet or shake the rugs out of doors.
5. Clean windows and wash paintwork if necessary.
6. Mop and polish floor surrounds.
7. Dust and polish furniture.
8. Replace everything.

The kitchen, more than any other room in the house should have energy spent on keeping it clean. Partly of course for the sake of hygiene and partly because there's more grease and dirt floating about in general which, once dried, will be much more difficult to get off. You should always have a couple of cloths at hand, one to wipe cooking-preparation and wall surfaces whenever you've finished a job, and one to wipe things you've spilled on the floor.

The bathroom too should be cleaned often. Try to get other members of the household to clean the bath and the basin and *the loo* every time they use it. Insist that children put toothpaste tops back on the tubes and soap in the soap dishes and hang their dressing-gowns up. The more unpleasant you are about this the more likely they are to remember.

FLOORS

Start with the floor. ('All floors should of course be swept daily or dusted with a dusting mop,' says *Good Housekeeping*.) If you are going to do a thorough job, move the furniture out, roll up rugs and give yourself some elbow-room.

Here are three methods of washing floors. Use the first one on floors which won't be damaged by getting very wet. The others are suitable for more delicate floors. These are methods recommended by professional cleaners. They are useful for kitchens, children's play rooms, work rooms, village halls.

All these methods suggest you have more than one floor mop in the house and this is actually a good idea. If you haven't you can always mop up on your knees with a large cloth or sponge instead.

Heavy-duty wash (for terrazzo, ceramic or quarry tiles, stone, marble, concrete, vinyl).

1. Sweep the floor thoroughly.
2. Make up the detergent as directed on the bottle or packet and apply it with a mop.
3. Allow the detergent to soak for ten to fifteen minutes – do not allow the floor to dry out but *do* check that water isn't running under skirting boards where it may saturate electric wires and sockets.
4. Scrub any very dirty bits and in corners. Use a nylon pad or fine wire wool, if necessary.
5. Wipe over with a nearly dry mop, rinsing the mop frequently. Then apply clean water with a clean mop and then dry with another mop or a dry cloth. (You must rinse the floor properly or you'll leave a film on the floor which will prevent any polish you put on later being absorbed and make the floor dangerously slippery.)

Heavy mopping This will clean the floor fairly thoroughly without removing any existing polish. Use lukewarm water – hot water may damage the polish on the floor. Use a mild detergent, not too concentrated. Otherwise the process is the same as above.

Damp-mopping Most homes don't need more than this. Use a low concentration of detergent solution, lay it on the floor with a clean mop and pick it up with a clean mop a few minutes later.

Polishing

There are three sorts of polish:

> Solid paste (e.g. wax)
> Liquid solvent waxes (liquid wax)
> Water-based emulsion waxes

You can use water-emulsion waxes on all floors (except unsealed wood or cork). But the other two should only be used on certain floors (see specific types of floors).

Wax polishing   Apply the polish evenly and lightly and allow to dry. Then buff up with an electric polisher, a broom head with an old towel tied round it, a weighted hand polisher or elbow-grease. You should not have to apply more polish for a couple of months or so. Just buff up from time to time.

Water-based polishing   Use a very clean cotton or sponge mop. Wet the mop head and leave it damp. Pour the polish on to the mop head and lay thinly on the floor, spreading it so that no bubbles are left. Aim to build up the surface with thin coats. Don't splash the skirting-board. The first coat should cover the whole floor. Further coats need to be applied only to areas walked on. Allow each layer to dry before you put another one on. Don't put too much polish on little-used areas and don't put polish under rugs.

It's best to use two or three thin coats, buffing them up between applications. If you put polish on too thickly it will lead to a build-up of dirty polish and anyway will be very difficult to buff up. You shouldn't need to put more polish on for several months. Just shine it up a bit occasionally.

How to treat different types of floor

Asphalt   A mineral pitch used on floors, specially in basements as it is moisture-proof. Mop with a dry mop or with a wet mop wrung out in cool water. Wash occasionally with warm water and mild detergent, rinse and dry. Don't use abrasives or strong cleaning powders. Don't use oil- or wax-based polishes. Asphalt is damaged by solvents as they tend to soften the surface. Polish with a water-emulsion polish but don't let this build up or the floor will become dangerously slippery.

Concrete   If you have a concrete floor in a room you are actually going to use, say a workshop or a wash room, you can seal the surface. The concrete will be much easier to sweep and wash if you do this and won't get so dusty. Or, if you want to you can wax polish. Don't use soap on unsealed concrete floors.

Cork   Plain cork can be sealed or polished. If polished, use a wax polish from time to time and buff up in between. If sealed you shouldn't need to polish but you can use an emulsion polish, though not too often or you'll have a build-up of polish which will have to be removed eventually or it will get very slippery.

Some cork tiles are covered in a vinyl coat which just needs to be mopped when dirty. Polish should be unnecessary on these but if you do want to polish use an emulsion. Cork can be sanded and then sealed if in bad condition. Don't let cork get too wet, and dry it thoroughly after washing.

Linoleum   Based on linseed oil, finely ground cork and wood flour, mineral fillers, bonded on to a hessian backing. Is supplied in sheet or tile form but for domestic purposes has been largely superseded by vinyl. However, if you do have some left from a previous age, wash it with warm soapy water but don't scrub. Remove marks by rubbing with medium-grade steel wool dipped in turpentine. You can then either polish it or seal it, as for wood. Make sure to dry the floor thoroughly. You can use a sealer on the floor which will make maintenance easier. An oil sealer will bond better than a plastic one.

Marble   A natural stone. Normally laid in slabs rather than tiles. Needs very little maintenance, but you should get expert advice for stained or blistered marble. Avoid abrasives. Oils and fats are harmful. Use diluted washing-up liquid, with a soft mop or cloth.

Painted floors   There are paints available which can be used on vinyl, lino, etc. These can be washed with mild detergent solution. Use as little water as possible. One of the sponge mops which squeezes out well would probably be best. Painted floors can be waxed which makes them easier to clean.

Glossy enamel paint can be washed with hot water. Rub gently. Rub stubborn spots with a very mild scouring powder or a fine wire wool.

Quarry tiles   These are laid on a cement bed and grouted. They resist most substances well. They should be treated with linseed oil when they are new. They are easy to damp-mop with warm soapy water and can be scrubbed if necessary. White patches on newly laid tiles, caused by lime in the cement, can be washed with a weak solution of vinegar and water. Use a silicone polish if you want to. Tiles shouldn't be washed until two weeks after they have been laid. In some cases they are coloured and maintained with red-coloured wax.

Rubber   Rubber should only need washing with a household detergent. You can then polish with emulsion or special rubber polish. Don't use wax polishes, turpentine or paraffin or solvent-based cleaners or polishes. Can be protected with a water-based sealer.

Shellacked floors   These will be ruined by water so never wash them. Use a damp mop. They must always be protected by wax or they will crack and the shellac will wear away.

Slate   Slate can be treated much the same as stone and you can apply a little lemon oil after the slate has been washed and dried. This will give it a lustrous finish. Remove all excess with a clean cloth. Do not use wax near fireplaces. Some people wash their slate floors with milk, which gives it a shiny finish.

Stone   Stone floors may be made of bluestone, slate, flagstone, granite, sandstone, marble, quartzite, etc. Stone floors are porous. Do not use soapy cleaners which will form a scum which you can't get rid of. Wash or scrub with washing-soda or household detergent. You can protect stone floors with a cement sealer and wax-polish them.

Terrazzo   A mixture of marble chips set in cement. Avoid alkaline cleaners which dry into crystals. Washing-up liquid can be used perfectly well. Do not use steel wool.

Varnished floors   Wipe with a damp detergenty mop or cloth. Don't use very much water as the varnish may not be waterproof. Waterproof varnish can be washed like seal. You can wax-polish varnished floors if you want to but it is likely to make them dangerously slippery and there doesn't seem much point.

Vinyl, asbestos and thermoplastic   Mop with floor detergent. Polish with water-emulsion polish. Never use solvent-based cleaners or polishes. These will soften and damage the tiles, and then the dirt will become ingrained.

Wood floors   Wood floors should never be soaked, nor should you use very hot water which has a softening effect. Sanded and sealed floors should only need vacuuming or sweeping and mopping with detergent and water. Eventually the seal will begin to wear off on the heavily trodden parts and you should then give it another coat of seal at once or you will have to sand the floor again and reseal. If you use a D.I.Y. seal you will be able to patch it if it gets worn. But heavy-duty seals, of the kind that have a hardener and seal which you have to mix together, cannot be patched. If one bit gets worn you will have to sand and seal the whole floor.

Polished wood floors should not need washing at all. Use wax polish. You can thin some polishes with turpentine or use a liquid wax. Liquid wax helps to clean the floor too whereas a paste wax, because of its high wax content, will only polish and won't clean as well.

Stains caused by oils and greases can sometimes be removed by mixing a paste of fuller's earth and soap and water. Put this on the stain and leave it for two or three days. The paste is absorbent and will draw out the stain. You may have to do this several times and rub gently to get rid of the stain completely.

CARPETS

Maintenance

It is extraordinary how roughly we treat carpets and still expect them to last for ever. We expose them to all sorts of light, walk on them in heavy and high-heeled shoes, tread mud into them, spill things on them and even burn them with cigarette ends.

A carpet can be made to last several years longer if looked after correctly. Carpets should be vacuumed thoroughly once a week. Anything spilled, and mud, should be cleaned up or swept up at once. Occasionally, say once every six months, you should give all carpets and rugs a shampoo.

Shampooing

Luckily, cleaning carpets has become easier since dry-foam shampoos were invented and it's no longer necessary to let the carpet get so wet that dyes will run. Detergent foam is very important in carpet cleaning and you should be sure to use a carpet shampoo, not just any old detergent, or domestic or industrial washing powder, which contain bleach and alkalis which are very damaging to carpets.

Liquid detergents are not recommended because they make the carpet too wet. It might shrink or the colours might run or you could get a slightly sticky residue which will encourage it to get dirty again quickly.

Dry-foam carpet shampoos which crystallize as they dry have the advantage of absorbing the dirt at the same time.

A hundred kilograms of wool carpeting will absorb about 16 kg of water before the backing becomes saturated and liable to damage. But 100 kg of Acrilan carpet, for instance, will absorb only about $2\frac{1}{2}$ kg before the backing is affected so you have to be specially careful not to get man-made fibre carpets too wet.

There are various shampoos to choose from. Some just come in a bottle. Some have an applicator which looks rather like an upright vacuum cleaner which you brush backwards and forwards. This is quite hard work but effective and there's a satisfying feeling of brushes digging into the carpet fibres. Most sophisticated electric ones can be hired from hire shops and for large carpeted areas one of these will make the job much easier.

Here is the basic shampooing procedure:

1. Take all the furniture off the carpet.
2. Vacuum. You must do this thoroughly. Run the vacuum cleaner over the carpet at least twelve times, overlapping each stroke. If the carpet is loose, vacuum underneath as well as on top, starting on the underside.
3. Test the shampoo on a small piece of carpet usually hidden from view (under a table, for instance) to make sure the colour doesn't run.
4. If all is well, dilute the shampoo with water following the

manufacturer's instructions or if using an aerosol, follow the instructions on the can. *Do not wet the backing of the carpet.*

5. Let the carpet dry. If you want to put the furniture back, put a piece of greaseproof paper or cooking foil under the legs so you won't get rust stains on the carpet.

6. If any areas are particularly dirty, treat them twice or the end result may be patchy.

7. Allow the carpet to dry completely. This may take a few hours or all night, depending on how damp you got it and what sort of heating you have.

8. Vacuum the carpet to remove dry foam and dirt and to raise the pile. Vacuum again the next day.

9. Brush the carpet all over in the direction of the lay of the pile.

Don't let furniture stand on a damp carpet and don't walk on it while it is damp. If you have to walk across it put some brown paper or shelf paper down.

If there are any stains which the shampoo hasn't been able to remove, I'm afraid that's your fault for not dealing with them when they happened. Wine and other wet things can be soaked up with salt. Pour the salt over the stain and let it sit there for a bit and absorb it. If you haven't enough salt, kitchen or other tissues will absorb liquids too. Don't rub, just press the tissue down on the stain.

Small rugs can be cleaned by hand with carpet shampoos. Small cotton rugs can be washed in a washing-machine.

Wool carpets are probably the easiest to clean. They weaken a little when wet but are more resistant to fungus than cellulose fibres so you may find that dry rot in a house has destroyed the back of a carpet but the pile is still unaltered. Cotton pile carpets are not easy to clean at home because they take a long time to dry out. This means there's more chance of the colour running. Acetic acid or white vinegar added to the shampoo might help. Synthetic carpets should be treated with special care: if you brush too hard without enough shampoo, the fibres may crack and too much mechanical action will make the pile crack or frizzle. Man-made fibres also attract static.

Testing for colour-fastness

There's no standard for colour-fastness for carpets, and dyes *are* likely to run, so you should always test before shampooing.

Dyes can fade in sunlight and even the atmosphere may produce a change in colour. Oriental carpets are sometimes touched up by hand with colours which are suspect, so the cost of a rug or carpet doesn't necessarily mean it will keep its colours.

Before testing for colour-fastness, vacuum or beat the carpet very thoroughly. Then dampen a piece of carpet with the shampoo you intend to use. Leave for a little while and then rub a small bit with a white cloth or put several layers of tissue over the damp bit with a weight on them. The longer you leave them, the more thorough your test. If there's no bleeding of colour you can go ahead and shampoo.

If there is slight colour bleeding add salt or white vinegar (50 ml to 2 litres; 2 fluid ounces to half a gallon) to the shampoo.

Professional cleaning

If you have any doubts about cleaning your own carpet, if it is very big, very dirty or very valuable, don't do it. Get a professional to do it for you. (See page 243 for addresses.)

If you wish to have a carpet professionally cleaned, find out whether the price includes moving the furniture or whether you'll be expected to do that. If you decide to move the furniture yourself don't put it back for twelve hours after it's been cleaned. Many cleaning companies offer a discount of ten per cent or so if they don't have to move furniture.

Be ready to show the cleaner where he can get warm and cold water and where the drains and fuse boxes are.

Most firms will offer a silicone treatment to prevent the carpet from getting dirty again very quickly and to make future cleaning easier.

Oriental carpets are often given special 'chemical' washing by professionals to give a sheen to the pile and to alter the light reflections. Wool has a rough surface and because it is dull absorbs light. A smooth fibre reflects light and that's what makes it shine. Rough-surfaced wool fibre can be made smoother if a portion of its outer skin is dissolved away. Chlorine bleaches (hypochlorites) are mostly used for this and you should never attempt to do it yourself. Always get the job professionally done by specialists. Sometimes the dyes are affected and have to be replaced by hand painting.

Chemical cleaning, as you can see, is pretty drastic and if the carpet can be satisfactorily cleaned in the conventional way so much the better. Even so, valuable oriental rugs are best treated by professionals and not cleaned at home. Some firms feel chemical cleaning is too drastic for old carpets and will do the job with detergent using hand brushes.

Making carpets easier to clean

A special treatment is now available for carpets which coats each fibre so that dirt can be removed more easily. Some new carpets are treated with this. It is possible to get an existing carpet treated but it has to be done professionally. The treatment is completely invisible, should last three years and is quite expensive.

Static electricity

Walking or shuffling (or any form of friction) on carpets generates an electrical charge. More often than not this is earthed at once through the carpet. Many synthetics are not good conductors of electricity, though, and then the charge builds up in a person or carpet and only discharges when they touch something which is earthed. That's when you get a mild shock.

Lack of moisture in the atmosphere is the main cause of static. So it is usually worse in centrally heated houses where there is double glazing, and in dry, frosty weather. Dirt acts as a conductor, so having a dirty carpet helps! You can get antistatic sprays which last for about twelve months. However, these usually make the carpet get dirty again more quickly so you can't really win.

Stain removal

The secret of stain removal is speed. The sooner you can catch the stain the better. If there are stains on the carpet when you decide to clean it, try to remove them before shampooing.

Always work from the outside edge to the centre of the stain. Solids should be scraped off and the area vacuumed before attacking the residual stain. Liquids should be spooned up and blotted with some absorbent material such as salt or white tissues.

When applying removers, work with small amounts. Don't get the spot too wet and always blot – do not rub or brush.

Test a piece of carpet for colour-fastness before applying the remover to an obvious bit. Do not use detergents if you don't know what was spilled. When you do use detergents, they should be neutral (pH 7) but most ordinary domestic detergents are anyway.

If you start with one formula and follow it with another, allow the first to dry thoroughly before trying the second. Use Turkish towelling to dry the patch.

In general, remember that a spot remover which is safe to use on wool may destroy certain acetates.

Organic or protein fibres (wool, camel, mohair) prefer acids to alkalis; cellulose or vegetable fibres (cotton, jute, viscose rayon) prefer alkalis to acids and so does silk and nylon.

Polyesters prefer acids.

Dealing with common stains

Alcohol and soft drinks Absorb excess liquid. Mix 25 ml of liquid detergent in 250 ml of lukewarm water (one tablespoonful in half a pint). Apply a small amount and blot the liquid. Apply a half-and-half solution of white vinegar and water, then blot and rinse with clean water. Blot with a clean towel.

Beer Absorb excess liquid. Mix a teaspoon of liquid detergent in half a pint of lukewarm water. Apply a small amount of detergent, blot well. Dry with a clean towel.

Blood Mix 10 ml of liquid detergent in 300 ml of lukewarm water (one teaspoonful in half a pint). Apply a small amount. Blot. Follow with cold water. Blot; rinse; blot. Dry with a clean towel.

Black coffee Flush with a soda siphon and blot quickly. Follow with detergent; blot. Dry with a clean towel.

Cream, ice cream, milk   10 ml detergent to 300 ml of lukewarm water (one teaspoonful to half a pint). Apply small amount of detergent; blot. Rinse with cold water. Blot; rinse; blot. Treat remaining grease or colour stains with proprietary spotting kit.

Grease, oil, tar Apply dry-cleaning solvent in circular motion, working from edge of stain to centre to avoid making a ring. Follow with detergent solution (10 ml of detergent to 300 ml of lukewarm water; one teaspoonful to half a pint). Blot; rinse; blot. Dry with a clean towel.

Ink, ball-point pen Apply small amount of dry-cleaning solvent and blot. Follow with detergent solution (10 ml in 300 ml of water; one teaspoonful in half a pint). Blot; rinse; blot. Dry with a clean towel. Bad marks should be cleaned professionally.

Ink, fountain-pen   10 ml of detergent to 300 ml of lukewarm water (one teaspoonful to half a pint). Apply small amount and blot. Rinse; blot. Dry with a clean towel. The manufacturers of permanent inks should advise about their removal. Stains may need to be removed professionally.

Soot Cover with dry salt. Vacuum up. Apply small amount of detergent solution (10 ml of detergent to 300 ml of lukewarm water; one teaspoonful to half a pint). Blot. Dry with a clean towel.

Tea without milk As for soot.

Urine Sponge with 100 g of salt in a litre of lukewarm water ($2\frac{1}{2}$ oz to 3 pints). Sponge with made-up carpet shampoo adding one eggcupful of white vinegar to each pint, or use a spotting kit.

Vomit Remove deposit, then sponge with detergent solution (10 ml of detergent in 300 ml of lukewarm water; one teaspoonful in half a pint) with a few drops of white vinegar added. Rinse and blot.

Wine As for alcohol and soft drinks.

Dealing with damage

Flood damage hits carpets first. Carpets and rugs will hold a good deal of water and become very heavy and unwieldy. The only way to deal with a saturated carpet is to get a professional cleaner as quickly as possible who will be able to take it away, clean it and dry it out on his special machines. With luck, you will be able to use the carpet again. If you don't do this the carpet will shrink, the colours will run and almost certainly fungus growth will start while the carpet is still wet.

Small rugs may be treated at home. Dry in a warm atmosphere but away from direct heat. If the colour is likely to run, don't hang it up but spread it flat over bricks or duck-boards to allow air to circulate.

For minor *cigarette burns*, snip away charred fibres. Use small

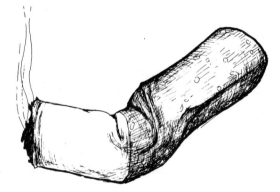

sharp scissors, working carefully to avoid cutting too deeply. Make sure you can see what you're doing, and that there is good lighting. Bad burns may need professional repairing.

Carpet fibres which have been squashed and crushed by heavy furniture can sometimes be revived. Try rubbing the fibres with the edge of a coin. Or iron very lightly with a steam iron or a dry iron over a damp cloth. The carpeting should be protected with a dry cloth, if you're using steam, as a protection against burning or shrinking of wool fibres. After steaming, gently brush the fibres to restore the nap.

If one tuft creeps up above the rest, don't pull it out. Snip it away with a sharp pair of scissors.

Coconut, sisal or rush matting

If you can take them up, shake them out of doors occasionally and vacuum up the enormous quantity of dust that collects under them. If the matting is fitted, vacuum as often as you can. Scrub occasionally with warm soapy water (don't use soda) and dry flat. It is much easier if you can do this outside.

Fur rugs

If on a felt, wool or flannel backing, fur rugs can be cleaned with fuller's earth or French chalk. Spread the stuff over the rug, leave for several hours then brush or shake it out. You can do this with clean powder several times, until you think the fur is clean.

Fur rugs which haven't got a backing should be wiped over with a cloth wrung out in lukewarm mild detergent solution. Don't get the skin wet, just the hair.

Other rugs

Hooked rugs should be vacuumed and swept as for any others but should not be beaten or shaken in case the loops become loose. Any further cleaning should be done by a professional.

Indian numdah rugs are made of matted goats' hair. They are usually on a whitish background with colourful embroidery of birds, animals, trees and flowers. They should not be shaken and should be dry-cleaned. When you vacuum, do so quickly but gently or you will eventually damage the embroidery.

WALLS AND CEILINGS

There are several excellent spray and other products on the market for cleaning walls and other surfaces. But they are all meant for keeping clean houses clean, not for cleaning up very dirty ones. My advice is to spend the odd ten minutes or so, whenever you have a moment, wiping over the surfaces in your home. Thus it will never get really dirty and never need a hard clean. Kitchen walls which get greasy splashes on them should be wiped most often. Cobweb brushes will get dirt off the tops of high walls and out of ceiling corners. You can even get radiator brushes to deal with radiators themselves. This is a counsel of perfection, but here are some suggestions for necessary cleaning.

Always wash walls from the bottom up (except ceramic tiles). Use a clean sponge mop so you can reach the ceiling without having to stand on steps. Always rinse the wall, after washing, with clean warm water.

Different wall finishes need different cleaning methods. These are the ones you are most likely to need:

Distemper or whitewash   Thank goodness these are hardly ever used now. They have been largely replaced by emulsion paints. They're impossible to clean because they just come off as a fine powder. It you want to repaint or paper you have to scrape off all the old distemper first.

Emulsion paints   Can be washed using household detergent or aerosol products for the purpose. If the ceilings are high and you can't reach the top of the wall, you can use a sponge floor mop quite satisfactorily. On very dirty walls, particularly in the kitchen where greasy splatters get dried on, I have used plastic scourers on emulsion paints. But the fact is, it is quite hard work getting very dirty walls clean, even with the help of new miracle products.

Ceramic wall tiles and gloss paints   Remove the surface dust often with a clean duster tied over a broom head or with a cobweb brush. Wash with warm water and soapless detergent or an aerosol product, starting at the top and working down. A sponge mop is good for tiled walls. Rubber-based paints should be washed with soap and water with a little borax added (45 g borax to 1 litre of water; or 1 tablespoon to 1 quart). Rinse with clean water and a clean sponge. Work on a small area at a time. Remove stains with a paste cleaner. An old-fashioned way of cleaning splattered tiles is to rub them with a cut lemon. Leave for a quarter of an hour or more and then polish with a soft dry cloth.

If you're preparing a wall for repainting there are special tacky cloths you can buy which will remove specks of dust, grit and fluff. This leaves a perfectly clean surface ready for the first coat of paint. You can use it before each coat to get a really professional-looking finish.

Wallcoverings There are comparatively few paper wallpapers about now. A lot of what you see is vinyl.

Ordinary wallpaper is not washable. You should brush it down with a cobweb brush or soft broom head covered with a duster. Any definite marks can be rubbed lightly with a damp cloth. Grease marks should be sponged with a cloth moistened with a dry-cleaning solvent. Start well outside the stain, as you would on fabric, and rub gently over and round it.

You can use a ball of bread to remove surface dirt. Or use a proprietary cleaning dough or make your own using about 50 g (3 level tablespoons) flour with 50 ml ($1\frac{1}{2}$ tablespoons) white spirit and 50 ml water. Add the liquids bit by bit and knead well. Rub the dough on the wall with a wide, sweeping movement and overlap each area as you work. As the dough gets grubby, turn it so that a clean bit is on the outside. An india rubber may do the trick too, but use a soft one.

To prevent non-washable wallpaper getting too dirty you can brush it over while still new and/or clean with an invisible fabric or wallpaper protector. Use a large distemper brush and let it dry. Test for colour-fastness first.

Washable wallpapers can be cleaned with a sponge squeezed out tightly in mild detergent solution.

Vinyls may be treated comparatively roughly. Wash with household detergent and rinse with a clean sponge.

Fabric-coated walls should be cleaned according to manufacturers' instructions. If you don't know where the covering came from, a local wallcovering shop may be able to suggest a suitable cleaner.

Most families, sooner or later, will have to deal with crayons all over the wall. Try sponging with a soft cloth dipped in dry-cleaning solvent (but test the wallcovering first for colour-fastness). If the cleaning fluid leaves a ring, try making a paste with fuller's earth or French chalk and cleaning fluid. Test this too and if the colours don't bleed, smooth the mixture over the crayon marks. Allow it to dry out thoroughly, then brush out.

WINDOWS

The obvious moment to clean windows is on the first sunny day in spring when suddenly you see how perfectly filthy they are. But you are advised to choose a dull day for best results, or a time when the sun is off the window. In sunshine the glass dries too fast and produces streaks. You should not clean windows on a frosty day when the glass is brittle and more likely to break. All you need in the way of cloths is a good window leather (i.e. chamois) and soft cleaning polishing duster for inside windows. After use wash it in warm soapy water (not detergent) and leave some soap in the leather so that it won't become hard; squeeze it out and hang it to dry.

There are several different window-cleaning preparations in the shops which don't need a leather. Probably the most expensive way, but perhaps the easiest, is to use an aerosol which you spray on to the glass and then wipe off with paper tissues or a non-linty cloth. Proprietary window-cleaners are for use on *dry* windows. If you have condensation you'll waste money using a window-cleaning aerosol and get poor results. Other shop-bought window-cleaners should be used sparingly and when almost dry polished up with a soft duster. (You can use a liquid silver-cleaning polish that way.) Don't use a dry cloth on dirty glass; you will scratch the panes.

If you resent the cost of these products, try mixing your own cleaner using equal proportions of methylated spirit, paraffin and water. Put it into a bottle and shake it hard and often. Some people say cold water on its own is as good as anything. Water containing borax or vinegar is very effective and cheap, though. A leather is the best cloth to use with water.

The best tool I know for cleaning windows is one with a flat head. It has a rubber squeegee on one end and a sponge on the other. The head pivots so that you can scrape down the window with the flat-edged rubber bit and soak up any extra cleaning fluid with the sponge. It works like magic. But a chamois leather and water are still the cheapest way.

Outsides of first-floor windows can be cleaned by you if you're prepared to do it yourself and are not afraid of heights. Get someone below to hold the ladder. Anything higher than that should be tackled by a professional.

You could try cleaning your first-floor windows from the inside using a squeegee on a telescopic lightweight handle.

A traditional method of removing *paint stains* from window panes was to rub them well with the edge of a penny or with a pencil eraser. If that doesn't work move on to fine steel wool or scrape them off with an old razor blade or a craft knife.

If you suffer from *condensation* on windows you are supposed to be able to prevent droplets forming by rubbing the pane over with a cloth dipped in equal parts of glycerine and methylated spirit or with

a proprietary anti-mist cloth. Bad condensation is caused by dampness in the atmosphere condensing on cold surfaces and the only way
to cure this properly is to get some ventilation into the room and more
efficient heating.

Blinds

Some Venetian blinds can be lifted down and washed but it's
probably easier to get a gadget a bit like a pair of scissors with foam
pads with which to grasp the top and bottom of each slat and wipe it
clean. Dip the foam heads into a detergent solution and then wipe.
Plastic blinds can be rinsed with detergent solution.

Roller blinds should be sponged with detergent solution before
they become too grubby. They are very difficult to get clean if they
are really ingrained with dirt. Some are washable, in which case you
can lift them down and scrub with a stiff lather, using a cloth or brush.
Wash a small bit at a time, as you would a wall, and overlap the
strokes. Don't get the fabric too wet. Rinse with a damp cloth or
sponge and hang up to dry. Don't roll the blind up until it is
absolutely dry.

Non-washable blinds can be cleaned with oatmeal, a rubber,
cleaning dough (see recipe on page 151 under Wallcoverings). But a
very dirty blind probably won't respond to any of those. You should
then wash it and stiffen it again with a D.I.Y. spray stiffener, following
the instructions on the can.

Window screens   The kind that keep flies out, for instance, should
be cleaned from time to time. They can be brushed with one of the
vacuum-cleaner brushes.

STAIRS

Labour Saving Hints and Ideas for the Home (George Routledge &
Son, London, 1924) says: 'Try sweeping the stairs with a paintbrush
instead of an ordinary dustpan brush. A soft, medium-sized paintbrush gets into corners and between rails better than anything else.'
(Unless you have a vacuum cleaner.)

FIREPLACES

Fireplaces, thank goodness, are coming back. Gone are the days of blocking them up and using electricity instead. People are opening up blocked-in fireplaces, installing new ones and even learning to heat their rooms, their water and cook their food on solid-fuel or wood-burning stoves. Suddenly there's a need for blacking for grates and nobody knows where to get it.

Hearths   The hearth should be brushed while the damper is closed so the dust won't blow about. Use blacking or a proprietary cleaner for black hearths and for modern metal free-standing fireplaces. Clean brick with water only, or a proprietary cleaner, not soap or detergent which would leave a scum. You can also wash with neat vinegar and rinse thoroughly.

   Stone fireplaces should be wiped with clean water only, as for brick. If stained, use a cleaning powder or bleach, wipe with clean water and dry. Bad stains may be scraped off with pumice stone or with powdered carborundum and water.

   Alternatively, 'Soot stains can be removed from stone fireplaces by mixing about a quart [1 litre] of hot water to 4 ounces [120 g] of yellow laundry soap and heating in a cauldron until the soap has dissolved,' says Alma Chestnut Moore in her book *How to Clean Everything* (London: Stacey, 1972; first published in the U.S.A. in 1953). 'When the mixture has cooled add half a pound [225 g] of powdered pumice and half a cup [120 ml] of household ammonia. Mix well.' Proprietary cleaners do exist for getting soot and smoke marks off stone.

   Ceramic tile surrounds should be washed with hot water and detergent. Stains may be removed with steel wool or a scouring powder, used gently.

Chimneys   Wood is more likely to cause chimney fires than coal because the resin gets stuck on the walls of the chimney and eventually catches fire and burns like fury. Modern flues, which are built with two 'skins' help to prevent this to a large extent but you should still have your chimney swept twice a year, *especially* if you are burning wood.

Stoves   'To keep polished stoves in good condition without using blacklead,' says *Labour Saving Hints*, 'Oil the parts of the stove with good salad oil, dust over it some unslaked lime from a muslin bag; let it remain a few days. Then rub off with a fine rag. Polish with a leather. The stove will then be quite smooth and look like enamel, only needing a daily dusting.'

   In fact proprietary blacking in tubes is available in hardware stores which will blacken up the black metal parts of a stove, fireplace or grate.

Fire-guard Dust with a brush. If very dirty, rub with a cloth dipped in paraffin or wash with hot water and detergent. Don't do this in front of the fire. Fire-guards with brass fenders should be cleaned as for brass.

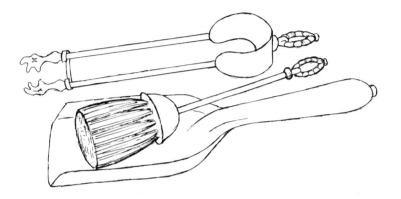

Fire-irons Rub the iron with a cloth moistened with paraffin. This will help to prevent rust. Clean the handles with metal polish.

Most polishes are flammable so don't do the cleaning in the obvious place – in front of the fire. For cleaning brass irons, see Brass on page 182.

Steel and cast-iron fenders, grates, hearths and irons can often be burnished by professional metal renovators. A local ironmongery might know someone who would do such a job. Or look in the telephone book.

BATHROOMS AND LOOS

Lavatory

You may not be carrying dangerous bacteria, but you are certainly carrying bacteria of some form or another – we all are, not only in faeces and urine but on clothes, hands and feet. Hands touch lavatory handles, doorknobs, taps, towels, switches and soap, and the organisms may live for several weeks. Many of the bacteria we harbour are quite beneficial but in case there is an infection in the house it is important to keep everything as clean as possible.

The flushing of a lavatory produces a fine spray of infected water droplets whether the lid is closed or not. These spread through the atmosphere and land on floors and walls. Careless or hurried men and boys spray the surrounds even more and it is a good thing to clean the loo at least once a day. If you feel queasy about this wear rubber gloves, but don't be put off. One soon gets used to it – like washing babies' nappies and cleaning their little bums.

The lavatory should be cleaned regularly at least once a week using a powder cleanser. This is an all-round cleaner which cleans and disinfects above and below the water-line. To maintain the cleanliness it's a good idea to suspend a small block, containing detergent, sanitizer and a light perfume, under the rim of the bowl. Every time you flush the loo some of the cleaner is released.

Most W.C. bowls are made of earthenware or chinaware glazed with a hard brittle surface which is resistant to many chemicals but may be scratched if abrasive scouring powders are used. The surface is not easily soiled but deposits can form and these vary according to hardness and chemical content of the water. A cleaner needs to remove anything not flushed away and provide a disinfectant against bacteria and viruses.

Wash all surfaces with water and detergent. Rinse well. Disinfect.

There are several cleaners which make it unnecessary to brush the lavatory bowl. Since brushing is unhygienic and unpleasant this is a happy thought. The best cleaners incorporate both acid and bleach and are usually in powder form. *Never mix two sorts of loo cleaners.* I know of a man who was blown clean off his W.C. because he threw a match down while sitting on one in which two incompatible cleaners had been left to soak.

Baths

Try to get the members of your household to clean the bath every time they use it while it's still warm, using a paste bath cleaner. It's easier if you use a long-handled bath brush. The bath should be rinsed after cleaning. If you live in a hard-water area use a water softener such as Calgon. Bath salts also make the water soft but since they are often made of coloured and scented washing soda they may damage enamel baths if used too much.

Never use steel wool, lavatory cleansers or bleaches on your bath, and don't allow dripping taps – replace the washers.

Lime scale can be removed with one of several treatments available in hardware shops. You are supposed to leave these on the stain for a bit and then wash off. (Don't do what I did – forget I'd done it until someone had had a bath. Presumably the stuff was very diluted by the bath water because there were no ill effects.) You are advised not to, but will probably have to, repeat this process several times before you win. They are acid and should be used with caution, following the manufacturer's instructions.

If you are really in despair you can have your bath chemically cleaned, or repaired, or resprayed. There are several firms who do this work. It will not be as satisfactory as the original, new bath but the finish should last several years if treated with care.

Don't wash sharp-edged objects (Venetian blinds for instance) in the bath and don't let anyone use it for developing photographs, because developing solution will damage enamel baths. Don't leave non-slip mats sitting in the bath. They may stain it permanently.

Acrylic baths I.C.I.'s advice for cleaning their own acrylic 'Perspex' runs along these lines: wash the bath in warm water and detergent using a soft cloth or cotton wool. If there's a lot of grease to be removed, soda or other alkalis may be added but they should not be necessary.

You can use scouring powders (or even if desperately necessary wire wool or emery paper) on opaque acrylic for stubborn stains but you'll lose a little of the polish. You can get the polish back if you use a good liquid metal polish on a soft cloth or cotton wool.

If you use scouring powders on clear acrylic the surface will look more scratched and you will lose the clearness. You can use metal polish to help restore the surface but it's difficult to get it as transparent as it was before.

You can safely use diluted sterilizing and bleaching agents based on sodium hypochlorite (chlorine bleach) or hydrogen peroxide on coloured perspex, as long as you don't leave it there.

Perspex will not be stained by dripping taps; it will not rust or corrode. It is not affected by bath salts and is non-porous so won't retain bacteria.

Baths made of acrylic are affected by extremes of heat; lighted cigarettes and burning matches will damage the surface. Some dry-cleaning solvents and paint stripper will damage it too.

KITCHENS

Stove enamel is smooth, hard and durable. But it can be damaged so be careful not to chip or scratch it. Once damaged it will never be the same again even if you have it resurfaced. When acids of any kind – vinegar, salad dressing or fruit juices – are spilled they should be wiped off at once, even if the enamel is 'acid-resistant'.

A chlorine bleach (used according to the instructions on the pack) can be used to clean most modern enamel sinks but old enamel on cast-iron sinks can be damaged or discoloured by bleach.

Laminated plastic used on tables and worktops and other surfaces provides a stain- and heat-resistant surface but it won't resist all stains nor the heat from a pan taken directly off the cooker. Don't use harsh abrasives, nor chlorine or hydrogen peroxide bleaches, sink or bathroom cleaners. Don't let berry juices fall on laminated plastics; if this happens, wipe if off at once.

Keep worktops regularly wiped with a damp cloth and occasionally put on a coat of cream wax cleaner. For cleaning of specific stains use a one-step car cleaner/polisher.

Stove

Your cooker should be wiped frequently. Follow the instructions in the manufacturer's booklet. If the stove is second-hand or you've lost the booklet these general rules should produce a clean stove without damaging the materials it's made of.

It is important to clean up as you go along. Keep a damp sponge or cloth next to the stove so that you can wipe up anything you've spilled at the time. Once food has dried on to the stove it may be very difficult to remove.

Electric and gas cookers   After every cooking session take off removeable parts. This specially applies to gas burners but some electric rings are removeable. Wash them in hot water and detergent in the sink. Wipe over the whole surface. Most things spilled, if got at soon enough, will only need a wash in hot water and detergent – use a nylon scourer for stubborn spots of grease and burned-on food. But it should not be necessary to use scourers or scouring powder on the enamel. Never scrape the surfaces with a knife or anything sharp. Once the surface of the stove has been scratched it is damaged for good. If the hob is very dirty with burned-on food, clean it with a caustic jelly applied with an old toothbrush. Leave for one or two hours then rinse off with warm water. Wear gloves.

Oven   There are various oven-cleaning preparations on the market for ovens which don't clean themselves. Follow the manufacturer's instructions and wear rubber gloves. If the oven is very dirty you may have to rub with wire wool as well. The oven will be easier to clean if it is warm. If you have a self-cleaning oven or one with detachable non-stick walls, follow the manufacturer's instructions and don't use an oven cleaner. Glass doors can be cleaned with a cloth dipped in bicarbonate of soda and if necessary a boosting rub with wire wool.

No electrical part should ever be soaked in water, of course. Before cleaning, switch off at the mains plug.

Grills These should burn themselves clean.

Solid-fuel cookers These have very flat hot-plates and you should use heavy, flat-bottomed pans on them. The two surfaces must sit close on each other – a small crumb will prevent the pan heating up efficiently. Keep the hotplates clean by brushing them often with a stiff wire brush. The oven of these cookers are virtually self-cleaning since they are so hot they burn away any deposits. This applies too to the underside of the lid of the hotplate. The simmering-plate lid should be brushed occasionally with a stiff wire brush to keep its shine. Clean vitreous enamel parts with liquid detergent and hot water. An occasional rub with wire wool should do no harm but will damage the enamel if used too often or too vigorously.

Refrigerator

It is very important to follow the instruction book. If you haven't got one, find out from the manufacturers what to do. If you have an automatically defrosting model find out where the pan is into which the defrost water evaporates, because you must wash it from time to time. Non-automatic fridges should be defrosted once a week or a fortnight. A fridge covered in ice is inefficient. But the condenser (freezing section) should only need cleaning twice a year.

Wipe up anything you spill at once. When you do the defrosting, lift out all removeable trays, drawers and shelves and wash them in warm water and detergent, rinse and dry. Don't use scourers or abrasives. Wash the inside with 50 g of baking soda to 450 ml of water (a tablespoon to a pint) or with liquid detergent and water. Rinse and dry. Don't use abrasives.

The outside should be wiped over with detergent solution and polished, if you like, with a clear silicone furniture cream or water-emulsion polish. The back of the fridge can be cleaned with the brush attachment of the vacuum cleaner, but switch off the electricity first.

If you are the sort of person who forgets to cover food in the fridge so that smells transfer from the fish, say, to the butter, you need one of those little bags with carbon inside which absorb smells. They're available from hardware departments and stores and will need replacing every six months or so.

If you are going away and leaving the house empty, remove *all* food from the refrigerator, unplug it and *leave the door open* or what you find when you return will be a fridge full of evil-smelling green mould which is almost impossible to get rid of.

Freezers

A freezer, if kept tightly closed, should only need defrosting once a year. Choose a time when stock is low – January and February are usually good months when you've used up a lot of food at Christmas and garden produce is mostly eaten up. In any case, the freezer should be unfrosted when frost has built up to a thickness of 5 mm ($\frac{1}{4}$ inch).

To clean the freezer, disconnect the electricity, remove any frozen food and wrap it in several layers of old newspaper and round them put a blanket.

If you want to hasten the unfreezing, put one or two large pans of hot water into the compartment. Tempting though it is, *do not* use a sharp metal tool for chipping off the ice to get the job done more quickly.

Mop up the water and frost (a big old towel will save a lot of cloth wringing). Wipe the interior clean and dry, switch on and put the food back. Wipe down the outside of the cabinet with warm water and detergent.

PESTS

You may be worried to see moths in your wardrobe. Or you may be plagued by mice, rats, fleas, flies, spiders, silver-fish, cockroaches and/or ants.

One way to discourage pests is not to provide anything for them to eat. So wipe up crumbs after each meal, keep all food covered, do the washing-up regularly and don't leave uneaten cat or dog food on the floor. Fill cracks or holes in floors and walls, brush walls and ceilings fairly often to prevent cobwebs. Don't keep stagnant water in or near the house (mosquitoes love it); disinfect your garbage bin and keep it covered. Clean drains weekly with soda crystals washed down with boiling water, or with chlorine bleach. If in spite of your care you are plagued, the following paragraphs provide methods for dealing with specific pests. If you're in real trouble you can call in the local health authority or a professional exterminator.

Ants

Follow the route march until you find their nest and destroy it with an insecticide, following the instructions. If you can't find the nest but you can find the hole where they come in, block it up with a piece of cotton wool soaked in paraffin. This will deter ants but not kill them. So spray generously behind and beneath skirtings, round sinks and windowsills. (Take care that children or pets can't get at it.) Ants love jams, sugars and fats and wouldn't turn up in the first place if there wasn't something left over worth coming for. Another type of ant killer is poured on to a piece of wood or a stone. This attracts the ants and then kills them but is not poisonous to animals or humans.

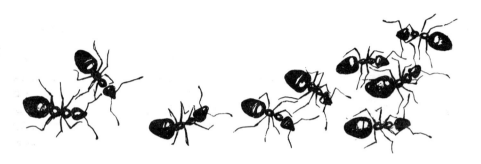

Bats

Bats are usually harmless, but they do carry fleas, are subject to rabies and don't smell very good so you're better off without them in the house. You can try introducing them to your cat.

But if you sprinkle paradichlorobenzene crystals (the same can be used for moths) the bats should leave. Stop up any gaps through which they might return. If you can't get rid of them this way, get in touch with your local health authority or a professional vermin exterminator.

Bedbugs

These are a bit like lice. They're small, brown and ugly, and smell bad. They hide during the day in cracks in walls and ceilings and come out at night to suck your blood.

They may be found in the seams of mattresses, in crevices in bedsteads and eventually behind window and door frames, skirtings, picture mouldings, furniture, loose wallpaper and cracks in plaster.

Bedbugs have made a comeback recently in new houses where the shrinking building materials have left cracks.

Insecticides containing malathion, lindane or pyrethrum should be used and should be sprayed into all possible hiding places: the springs, frames, webbing and slats of beds, so they are thoroughly wet. Don't actually soak the mattress but spray it, with particular attention to the seams and the tufts. Spray skirtings and cracks in walls and floor boards. Don't spray near food; make sure the spray you use is suitable – a too high concentration of some insecticides is dangerous to humans.

At any sign of another bedbug, spray the whole lot again with equal thoroughness.

Cockroaches

Sprinkle the place where the cockroaches are found with pyrethrum powder or use a special aerosol insecticide. Follow the instructions and protect children and pets. Sprinkle or spray every day until they have all gone, and don't leave bits of food lying around to attract others.

Cockroaches are big, black beetles. They come out at night and eat food, starch, fabrics and paper.

If the house is badly infested, spray first and then sprinkle insecticide powder, blowing it into cracks and openings.

Fleas

Fleas like warm homes. Otherwise they are fairly indiscriminate and will multiply readily in clean or squalid conditions if the house is warm enough.

All pets that walk through grass will get fleas at some time. There's nothing embarrassing or shameful about it.

If your animal scratches a lot, especially sudden scratching in response to bites, it's time you had a look for fleas on it. Part the hair and if the animal is infested you will see possibly the small dark flea itself scurrying to get away or its dandruff-like droppings. Infection with fleas may lead to dermatitis or tapeworm and fleas may produce a violent allergic reaction in some dogs or cats.

There are several flea powders in the shops but *always* follow the instructions and never use those intended for one sort of animal on another sort. Some anti-flea powders for dogs, for instance, must *never* be used on cats. Cats can absorb a number of toxic substances through their skin and both cats and dogs may be made ill by preparations which are wrongly applied. You should be specially careful not to let the powder come into contact with the animal's eyes or mouth.

You can get impregnated anti-flea brushes, collars and discs; or you can get the stuff in powder or aerosol form and occasionally as tablets. You *must* follow the instructions and don't use more than you're told to. If you are in any doubt about your ability to treat your animal correctly, take it to the vet. And *tell* him if you've been treating it yourself and what you've been using because some insecticides react badly with others.

Eggs of the flea can produce larvae in two to twelve days in warm conditions but in cool temperatures may remain dormant for two months or much longer. So while treating your pet, make sure you clean the house thoroughly at the same time.

Use the vacuum cleaner thoroughly, not just for carpets and floors but in other places where fleas and their eggs may lurk; in crevices in furniture, around skirting boards, cushions, upholstery and anything soft and warm. Vacuum regularly and then burn the contents of the bag. If you can't, seal it up in a plastic bag before putting it with the refuse. You can, if you like, apply a suitable insecticide to furniture and furnishings.

Wash, burn or throw away the animal's own bedding and substitute cotton sheeting or paper. Or use disposable bed and bedding (a cardboard box from your grocer will do) until the fleas have gone. The box should be burned and replaced every few days.

If all this fails, your local health authority should be notified and will come and sort out the problem.

Flies

Flies are filthy. They can spread at least thirty different diseases to animals and people. They breed in garbage and rotting meat, and especially in hot weather. So always keep all food and all garbage tightly covered and take particular care in summer. Treat the garbage bin with disinfectant regularly. Don't let manure sit near the house. If you use fly screens, make sure they are in good condition.

It's not really possible to get rid of all flies. And if it were, it should be remembered that flies are among the insects responsible for pollination of many food crops.

There are various fly-killers on the market. They are mainly divided into two types: stomach and internal system poisons and contact poisons. Aerosol sprays are the easiest to use. These usually catch the insect in flight and act as contact poisons.

Slow-release vaporized insect-killers should last six months or so without health hazard to animals or people, though it is advised not to put them in rooms where young babies or old people will spend much time. All insecticides *must* be used strictly according to instructions. If you get any on the skin, wash it off at once and on no account let any get near your mouth.

Mice

The odd cheeky mouse may seem harmless. But before long the whole extended family will be pattering about in your sugar and cheese, climbing and chewing flexes and leaving little droppings in unwelcome places.

No matter how sweet, at this stage mice are unhygienic and smelly. Block any holes you think they come in by. These are often inside cupboards where the pipes run. Keep all food stored in sealed jars and tins. Keep all garbage tightly covered. Keep a cat. Often just the catty smell will keep mice at bay.

If you can't or won't keep a cat, and you think there are only one or two mice to deal with, you can set traps. Bait them carefully; a clever mouse will soon learn how to snatch the cheese from a carelessly baited trap. Peanut butter is a good bait. Bacon and cake are popular too. Put the traps at right-angles to the walls in places you know are visited by mice.

If you fail with the traps or are too squeamish to use them you can use poisoned bait. Buy an anticoagulant specifically formulated for mice and follow the directions to the letter. You may have to persevere for several weeks. Don't let the poison get near food and don't let children or pets get near the poison. Lock cupboard doors behind which you've laid down the stuff or put the bait in places where you can safely seal it off. Other mouse poisons are very dangerous and should only be used by professionals.

Mites

These are teeny spiders which get into the soft warm folds of the body and bite, causing itching, swelling and even fever. They may be present where there are birds (in or nesting on the house), mice or rats. House martins nesting in the eaves can sometimes be the cause, in which case you'll have to destroy the nests. Otherwise clean up bird cages and spray with a suitable insecticide.

Mosquitoes

Mosquitoes breed in water so try to cover water butts, puddles, rain gutters, etc. Pyrethrum is a suitable insecticide for mosquitoes. Fish ponds and pools with larvae can be sprayed with a pyrethrum solution, which will kill the larvae but won't affect the fish or plants.

A quick squirt of a suitable insecticide at night should get rid of mosquitoes in the bedroom, providing you don't let more in by keeping the windows open.

You can get an itch-reducing cream to rub on the skin if you *have* been bitten.

Moths

Moths like furs and woollen fabrics. All man-made fibres are mothproof, but when blended with natural fibre, the fabric is still liable to damage by moths. The moths that cause the trouble are small silvery inconspicuous ones that fly softly about in the house. It's not actually the moth, but the larvae which do the damage. Before it dies in early autumn the moth lays its tiny flat eggs in the material. And the material is what the larvae feed on when they emerge in the spring. There's not much risk of moths attacking clothes which are in use all the time. The things that need watching are woollen clothes, curtains, blankets, eiderdowns and furs which are being stored away during the summer. Though it shouldn't be necessary to do a big spring-clean nowadays it is useful to turn out drawers and wardrobes periodically and look at every item for moth marks.

Clothes stored in polythene are usually safe because the moths can't get in. If you have forgotten to moth-proof and the larvae are lying around in the creases and folds (they are off-white and fluffy and nestle in little groups), shake the garment and brush off the fluff and with it the eggs before packing it up again. Dust and dirt are breeding grounds for moths, so clear out the storage chest, tip out old fluff and bits and vacuum every six months.

There are several types of sachets of moth deterrent, available from chemists, to put into drawers, chests or wardrobes. These do not smell. They only last for six months but are not expensive.

Moth-proofing aerosols are also available. These do smell for a little while but the smell soon wears off. Leave the clothes in an airy place after spraying before you put them away. Aerosols are not recommended for furs.

Camphor, turpentine and naphthalene are all smells which have been used in the past to keep moths at bay.

Another traditional method was to 'Mix two ounces of ground cloves, cinammon, black pepper and orris root, and place them in small muslin bags among the articles to be stored. It is said moths detest this mixture.'

Another way was to put dried orange peel among the clothing. 'Also a few drops of lavender oil is a powerful enemy to the moths and a delightful perfume to the clothes.'

Rats

Rats will appear wherever there's food or somewhere to make a nest. Old rags left to rot in a shed will encourage them; so will open garbage cans or compost heaps with too much food waste on them. I once discovered a whole family of rats nesting in an old cushion in the woodshed.

The occasional rat can be dealt with by using poisoned baits. Some rats are developing an immunity to poisons and it may be sensible to use two different kinds: anticoagulants and multiple-dose poisons. You can get rat poison in chemists and agricultural merchants. Some are ready to use, some have to be mixed with bait. Follow the directions to the letter. Don't let children and pets get at the poison, and get rid of the dead rats at once.

If you have a real infestation of rats don't hesitate to get a professional to deal with them either through your local health authority or privately.

Silver-fish

These are silvery insects about 10 mm (half an inch) long which you often find in bathrooms and basements as they like damp, cool places.

They feed on sugar and starch, and can do quite a lot of damage to starched cotton and other fabrics (especially rayon which is made of wood pulp) and to books, because they eat the starchy glue used for binding.

They can be dealt with by using household insecticides in either spray or powder form, though you may have to repeat the treatment. Success may take two or three weeks. Spray doors and windows, skirtings, cupboards and pipes.

Spiders

Spiders are your friends, which perhaps accounts for the superstition that if you kill a spider it will rain for a week. They eat flies and other unfriendly insects and are harmless. If you must kill them spray with a suitable insecticide.

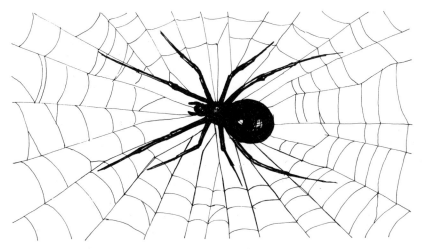

Wasps and hornets

You may not want to believe it, but wasps and hornets are our friends most of the time and destroy many garden pests. However, if you should find a nest, as I did, under the eaves by your bedroom window, you must get rid of it. The menacing buzzing is disturbing anyway. But towards the end of the season when the weather gets cold and the insects sleepy, they will find ways into the house (through the flue in my case) and sleepily fall on and into the bed. Several times I woke up being stung in the dark. The nests are circular combs of off-white papery cells or may be made of mud.

We got rid of one nest by using a flame thrower but a much safer way is to use an insecticide. Get a suitable one and follow the instructions. Store it out of reach of mischievous fingers; don't smoke while spraying, wear rubber gloves and remember that it is poisonous.

Woodworm

Woodworm is recognizable by small round holes each of about the size of a pin head with dust coming out of them. They may be in wooden furniture or in the beams of a house – anything wooden in fact. When redecorating or relaying floors always check for these holes so you can stop the worm before it gets too bad. Treatment is best done by professionals though you can treat small infestations with a D.I.Y. kit. Don't breathe the stuff, don't allow it to touch mouth, eyes or skin. Wear gloves while applying it. If you can, work outside, if not keep windows open.

CLEANING AND STORING YOUR EQUIPMENT

Bottles and jars of cleaners and chemicals should be kept on a high shelf out of reach of children. All substances should be correctly labelled and if you don't know what something is you should throw it out. Don't store domestic bleaches, detergents or other poisonous substances in old soft-drink bottles or they could be mistaken for the real thing.

Dusters and cloths should be washed from time to time. Even paper cloths will last quite a long time (and cost less in replacements) if kept clean.

Brooms should not be left to stand on their bristles. If there is no hanger at the end of the handle you can get one to fit on to it or just screw a hook into the end. Carpet sweepers will hang up and so will upright vacuum cleaners. The more of these items you can get off the ground the better.

New bristle brooms should last longer if dipped in cold salted water before use. (Don't do it to nylon or plastic.) Nylon brooms should be washed from time to time in warm water and detergent and dried in the open air. Small brushes and dustpans should also be washed out from time to time.

The *vacuum cleaner* should be emptied before it gets too full, and so should the carpet sweeper. Wipe the machine on the outside with hot water and detergent.

Mop heads should be thoroughly rinsed and allowed to dry before being put away.

Clean the *broom cupboard* occasionally with a solution of disinfect-ant or chlorine bleach. Leave the door open until the cupboard is quite dry again before putting the equipment back.

Food cupboards, like the refrigerator, should be cleaned fairly often. It's amazing how quickly loose flour, crumbs and sticky bottles can accumulate and how quickly small wildlife will get to know about it. Take everything off the shelves and clean thoroughly inside the cupboard with a solution of chlorine bleach, especially in the corners. Leave the doors open while the surfaces dry.

Wipe over sticky bottles, before you put them back, with warm water and detergent. Check that all dried food is in good condition and throw out anything you feel doubtful about.

Do the same thing, though you don't need to do it nearly so often for *china cupboards*. You can get rid of tannin stains in china teapots or cups by filling them with a solution of Chempro 'T' cleaning tablets or Calgon, following the instructions on the packet. Wash in hot soapy water and rinse well.

Bathroom cupboards should be cleaned out and checked frequently. Wipe thoroughly with a disinfectant solution. Throw out any medicines no longer in use or without labels. Wash old bottles and take them back to your chemist. Wipe other bottles before you put them back. Check the first-aid kit and top up with plasters, cotton wool, disinfectants, etc., if necessary.

You should remove all the clothes from *wardrobes* twice a year and wipe the inside of the cupboard with a solution of household bleach. Leave the doors open while the inside dries.

Check all clothes and shoes. Throw away those nobody will wear again and put useable ones into carrier bags for the local charity shop. Take this opportunity to clean, mend, sew on buttons and assess a garment's usefulness.

For everyone's sake, the *toy cupboard* should be cleared out periodically. If possible keep toys in drawers or boxes in special categories so that larger, heavy ones don't crush small flimsy ones. Allow your children to help you. It's good training and only fair to both parties. After all, only they can tell which toys they care most about and why should you do all the work?

UPHOLSTERY

As with all fabrics, the more regularly you clean upholstery the less rigorously you will have to attack the fabric when you do. In any case, accumulations of surface dirt, dust, perspiration, hair oil, etc., will discolour and damage the fabric.

Vacuum the cushions every week. Clean arm rests, backs and crevices.

Mop up anything spilled at once before it stains the fabric. Many things are quite easy to get rid of at the time but impossible later on. Blot up liquids and scrape off other things immediately.

Turn the cushions from time to time so that they wear evenly. I wouldn't dream of suggesting you keep your upholstery out of the sun, but the fabric may fade if it gets a lot of sun. Shampoo chairs and seats two or three times a year. Do it *before* the furniture looks dirty.

The furniture industry has adopted a standard cleaning code to indicate the proper cleaning method for different types of upholstery fabric. Look for the code when choosing furniture.

W means clean only with the foam of an upholstery shampoo or other water-base cleaner specifically designed for upholstery. Don't use laundry products, household cleaners or solvents.

S means clean with a water-free solvent (dry-cleaning product) or get the upholstery professionally cleaned. Do not use detergent or water-based cleaners.

S-W means clean only with upholstery shampoo or a water-free solvent.

X means vacuum often. Do not use other cleaners (except possibly an absorbent like fuller's earth or salt).

If you have cats or dogs you may find vacuuming doesn't easily get the hairs off the upholstery. An effective way of picking them up (though expensive if there's a lot to do) is to plaster sticky tape all over the furniture. As you tear it off the hairs come off too.

Some people imagine that cleaned upholstery gets dirty faster. This can happen if the cleaning product is a bit sticky and isn't rinsed off thoroughly. Then bits of dust will indeed be attracted to this stickiness. Silicone sprays are often recommended to prevent upholstery getting dirty again so quickly. But because of people's clothes constantly rubbing against the fabric, the treatment doesn't last long and you should treat the fabric every few weeks. It's certainly better than nothing.

For cleaning upholstery you can use a special product which includes a special soil retardant coating. Some of these have an applicator which I've found does make the cleaning process very much easier, more convenient and efficient.

First, remove as much surface dirt as you can by giving the furniture a thorough vacuuming, getting into all corners and crannies. Spot-clean stains at this stage if you didn't do that at the time they occurred.

Test the fabric for colour-fastness in an inconspicuous area. To do this, treat the area with a little of your upholstery shampoo, leave for a short time and than dab with tissues. If no colour comes off on the tissue you can go ahead with your cleaning.

Whatever product you are using, follow the instructions that came with it. Treat a small area at a time, using as little moisture as possible so you won't wet the padding. 'Dry' foams are certainly the easiest and safest to use in this respect.

Rub the foam well in. Rub up and down, overlapping your strokes, and then across in the same way. Any obstinate stains can be rubbed with the applicator brush or with an old soft (clean) toothbrush.

Wipe the entire surface vigorously with a damp (not wet) towel to take off the foam residue and loosened dirt. A Turkish towel, which is both rough and absorbent, is excellent.

Allow to dry and then vacuum again thoroughly.

For delicate fabrics you should not use a brush, just a sponge. If, after shampooing there are still stains, use dry-cleaning solvent for oily and greasy stains. Water-based stains should have been loosened by the shampoo. But if that hasn't worked you could try a solution of 10 ml (1 teaspoon) of detergent or soap powder, 10 ml (1 teaspoon) white vinegar in 1 litre (1 quart) of water.

For details of dry-cleaning spot-removal techniques see Chapter 4. General tips:

1. Use a small amount of cleaning fluid at a time.
2. Blot between applications with clean white tissues. Do not rub.
3. Blot with tepid water to rinse. Do not get the fabric too wet.

Leather upholstery should be dusted or vacuumed, then cleaned with saddle soap when necessary. Use as little water as possible. When quite dry, polish up briskly with a soft cloth. Rub the leather once or twice a year with castor oil or neat's-foot oil or on pale leather use Vaseline. Rub the oil in with the fingertips and wipe off every trace with a soft cloth. Don't wax leather furniture.

SPRING-CLEANING

My Edinburgh landlady had a passion for cleaning. She cleaned all the time, moaning as she did it. I'd hear her halfway downstairs: 'Oh me, my back's breaking. This'll kill me. I'm not well.' Every spring, she changed the curtains. Replacing a perfectly miserable set of mud-coloured woven ones for an even more depressing couple of chicken-shit see-throughs.

This heralded the great spring-clean and she'd spend the next three weeks working herself to death polishing and scrubbing an already spotless house.

Thank goodness it's no longer necessary to change the curtains with the season and if you've followed my previous advice about cleaning and tidying as you go along it shouldn't be necessary to spring-clean at all in the way the Victorians meant it.

But when the first rays of spring sun shine down it is apparent that grubby windows need attention, dust and dirty marks seem to appear from nowhere and there does seem some sense in having a sort out and a clean-up. Take it seriously but not too earnestly. There's no *need* to break one's back.

'The right way to begin spring-cleaning is to have any repairs done on the roof, such as retiling,' wrote Elizabeth Craig in *Keeping House* (Collins, 1936). Quite true. In fact one's spring-cleaning list should possibly read something like this:

1. Check the roof for loose or missing slates or tiles.
2. Clear out gutters with a trowel and put the compost that has formed up there on to your rose beds.
3. Check the pointing on outside walls. Damaged pointing allows the walls to absorb water which will eventually damage the material and bring damp into the house.
4. Check windows for joints and crevices where water might lodge. Clean down window frames and use a rust primer for rusty patches on metal windows or an aluminium primer on wood before the normal undercoat.
5. Clear drain gullies at ground level (see page 173).
6. Clean the carpets or get them cleaned (see page 142).
7. Wash walls and paintwork if you haven't kept them wiped and clean.
8. Clean upholstery and curtains.
9. Clean windows.
10. Give each room a thorough going-over as described earlier in this chapter.
11. Turn out cupboards and ruthlessly throw away what you haven't used for the past year.
12. Sort out clothes and get rid of those you never use.
13. Clear out larder and kitchen cupboards and drawers.

After this you really can feel you have done your duty.

CHAPTER 8

OUTDOOR CLEANING

Outdoor inspections and cleaning of the exterior of the house, the drains, outhouses, paths, vehicles and so on are an important part of caring for one's personal environment.

Not only will you make the place look a lot better but you will also have a chance to discover when the tiles need mending on the roof; when you need a new grille for the drain, whether the greenhouse needs repairing or repainting and whether your tyres are going bald.

You should inspect and thoroughly clean up roof, gutters, outside drains, window frames, paintwork etc., twice a year. Cars and bikes will obviously need cleaning and inspecting much oftener than that.

This is a guide to the basic cleaning every householder has to do outside.

DRAINS

If you have drains at ground level, clear the drain gullies regularly, especially in the autumn as earth and debris may collect at the bottom underneath the grid. Remove the grid and scoop out any silt with a trowel. Put the grid back afterwards. Pour undiluted chlorine bleach down the sides of the drain gullies. This will dissolve grease, destroy germs and prevent unpleasant smells. You should do this quite often in summer.

Make sure that any manhole covers can be raised easily, then check regularly inside and out so you can keep them clean and free of grease, by scrubbing with hot water and washing-soda or a solution of two capfuls of chlorine bleach to one gallon of water. Use a long-handled brush. A broken or badly fitting cover will allow debris and silt into the chamber. Damaged rendering on the concrete will also allow debris to get in and should be repaired.

Leaves, rags, metal objects, bricks and dolls' arms and marbles are often put in gullies by young children. Clear out any foreign bodies of this kind.

Don't allow birds to nest in gullies or the tops of soil vent pipes. You can buy a wire covering which will stop them.

Don't plant trees near drains. The roots often break them up and cause blockages.

GUTTERS AND DOWNPIPES

You should clear rainwater gutters about twice a year. Leaves and odd bits that fall into them will soon turn to soil, and then grass and other seeds will grow. Then the water will not be able to run along the gutter and will overflow and run down the wall, creating damp patches both inside and outside the house.

Place a ladder so that you can reach the gutter but never rest a ladder against a gutter – it's not strong enough. Use a garden trowel to scoop out the muck in the gutter. Late autumn is the best time, when leaves have stopped falling and before the weather gets too cold, and again in the spring. The debris will make excellent compost, being rich in birdlime, so tip it on to a flower bed.

Scrape off as much rust as you can from old galvanized iron gutters using a wire brush. Touch in the scraped parts with a rust inhibitor and give them a coat of zinc chromate primer. Then put on a coat of bituminous paint.

EXTERIOR WALLS

An annual cleaning of outside decoration will remove industrial deposits which bite in, dust which abrades, chalking which dulls the gloss and efflorescence which stains. If you live near the sea, wash the walls to take off salt, which has a bleaching effect on paint.

New cement building slabs are often greasy because of the non-stick agent used in moulding them. If you decide to clean the surface, allow six months or a year before decorating with emulsion, stone or cement paint, to allow the agent to leach out and disperse. If any remains, scrub with white spirit.

Glazed and terrazzo tiles   Mop down with a mild detergent solution. Avoid all abrasive cleaners.

Wall Stains

These are some of the stains most often seen on outside walls.

Cement splashes on bricks   Try acetic acid (white vinegar) or use the acid treatment described for rust stains on concrete.

Copper stains   These are caused by water from copper fittings leaking on to a painted surface. The stains are green. Treat with a weak solution of hydrogen peroxide and rinse afterwards with clear water.

Iron stains   You may see these on doors with metal studs – stable doors for instance. Use citric acid or lemon juice to remove them.

Moss   Moss may grow on various materials outside. Brush off all such growths with a wire brush and if they are obstinate, treat green patches with a fungicide which you can get from many paint shops. Ordinary household bleach will do the job too. Wash off with clear water before painting.

Paint splashes on bricks   Paint stripper will remove the surface paint. You may have to use a wire brush or rub with a brick of the same texture to get bits out of the pores.

Rust stains on concrete   First try citric acid or lemon juice as for iron stains from stable doors.

If that doesn't work try diluted bleach mixed with whiting to form a poultice which you can leave on the stain for some hours.

Tar stains   If you are intending to paint over a previously bituminous or creosoted surface use an emulsion paint. The solvents in an oil paint may make the creosote or tar bleed through. If you must use oil paint, seal the previous surface with aluminium primer/sealer.

GARDEN PATHS

Use a weed-killer on paths. Coarse weeds can break up the surface and fresh seeds will take root in the compost left when they die back.

GREENHOUSE

It is very important to keep your greenhouse clean and hygienic. You won't grow healthy plants unless your greenhouse is well cared for. This means immediately removing diseased material, dead leaves and rubbish of all kinds, killing and removing weeds and insect pests and the annual scrubbing down of both the glass and the frame.

The time to have a really thorough annual clean-up is late autumn when nothing is growing in the greenhouse.

Glass and woodwork should be scrubbed with soft soap and water or a weak solution of carbolic or a similar strong disinfectant. If the greenhouse can be completely emptied for a few days you can do what commercial growers do, which is to spray with a one per cent solution of cresylic acid in water. This is quicker than scrubbing. If the greenhouse staging is made of wood, scrub it thoroughly with soap and water or disinfectant as above. With solid benches, the material used on the stage should be removed, or if shingle, washed.

You may choose to do any painting and minor repairs now, though it may be more convenient to do this in spring or summer. The clean-up should include washing all the plant pots, seed trays and pans, sterilization of seed boxes, stakes and canes.

Control of the weeds both inside and outside the greenhouse is more important than you may think. Weeds often harbour pests and diseases and if these multiply and breed on the doorstep it won't be long before they get into the house. Greenfly and blackfly, for instance, flourish on a number of weeds and so do white fly and red spider during hot, sunny weather. So keep the weeds at bay. Put them on the compost heap with thinnings, soft prunings and other greenhouse vegetable rubbish.

The best way of cleaning the glass is with a car cleaning brush. This way you can scrub down, remove the stippling in autumn or clean off soot and dirt in winter. The brush is fixed to the end of the hose, water pours up the handle, through the brush head on to the glass.

As for getting rid of pests remember that some insecticides are highly poisonous and all should be used with care. Always follow the manufacturer's instructions to the letter.

The quickest and most effective way of dealing with pests in the greenhouse is to fumigate. First make a note of the cubic capacity of the house. Measure the height to the ridge and to the gutter. Add these measurements and divide by two to get the average height. Multiply this by the length of the house and then by the width. Once you know the cubic capacity your local garden shop should be able to sell you the right amount of 'smoke'.

If there are any gaps in the house, block them up with sticky tape. Fumigate on a warm, windless evening (the temperature should be about 15 to 21°C, 60 to 70°F). Leave the house locked and tightly shut until the next morning, when you should open up all doors and vents and let a great draught blow the smoke out.

The 'smokes' themselves are in the form of pellets for small greenhouses and canisters for larger ones. Take off the paper and cap and light the wick. Certain chemicals which are suitable for common pests such as aphis, thrips, leaf-hoppers and leaf-miners should not be used on certain plants. Ask the advice of your local garden shop or centre when buying fumigating chemicals.

Liquid insecticides are lethal to many pests. Always follow the manufacturer's instructions. Deal with the pest as soon as you notice it and cover every part of the plant. The sucking insects should be sprayed with a contact wash such as malathion and eating insects dealt with by stomach poison sprayed on to the plant.

White oil emulsions are useful on tough leathery-leaved plants but can damage those with waxy surfaces such as carnations.

CARS

Engine

It will help you to maintain your car properly if you don't have to look at the engine through layers of grease and dirt.

There are several engine-cleaning products, including one called Gunk. These have a solvent which will dissolve the grease so you can wipe the dirt off easily.

Body

Cleaning the bodywork is not difficult and it is important not just for the look of the car or to keep up the resale value but also because you can then spot any bits of damage that need to be repaired. A weekly wash with water and a little liquid detergent should be enough. Hose off all mud and grit before you use a cloth, or bits of grit may scratch the paintwork. Never use a dry cloth. Wash from the roof downwards. Remove tar spots with white spirit and rinse with clean water.

Polish is usually not necessary as a protective measure but can't do any harm. The easiest way of polishing a car is to put a sachet of special liquid into a bucket of clean water and swill it over the bodywork. Some kinds will dry shiny; others will have to be rubbed over afterwards with a soft cloth.

Abrasive polishes are available but you should use them with care and not very often. Eventually they will remove the paint and on metallic paints will affect the finish. The car's instruction book should give details about the kind of polish to use.

Chrome is usually fairly high quality these days and shouldn't need more than washing once a week, though you can get chrome polishes if you want utter perfection. Stainless steel is even easier to deal with than chrome.

Rust spots should be removed immediately, treated with a rust inhibitor and touched up with the appropriate car paint.

Windows

Wipe the windows with a clean chamois leather and make sure no wax polish or domestic window cleaners get on to the windscreen or rear window.

Inside

Car insides should be cleaned out once a week and thoroughly cleaned out twice a year. Vacuum if you can. Take out the floor coverings and shake them. The seats and trim are nearly always made of some sort of plastic and you can clean them with a special cleaner available from car accessory shops. Check that the one you buy is suitable for the fabric. An upholstery cleaner is usually a detergent which you rub into the material, leave for a minute or two and then remove with a damp sponge. Dilute for normal cleaning but use neat for bad stains. Never use a cleaner containing bleach. Don't use too much water or you will get condensation. Otherwise simply use warm water and liquid detergent in the same way.

Empty the ashtrays. The carpet and underfelt help to muffle road noise. If they become badly worn they won't be so insulating. Make sure when replacing the carpets that the one near the driver's feet is properly fixed and won't fall back over the pedals.

Remove the seat back and frame, and brush with a small stiff brush.

Wipe leather with a damp cloth or sponge with tepid soapy water. If the leather is badly stained clean with saddle soap following the instructions on the tin.

Don't use much water on the front panels which may warp if they get too wet.

Cloth roof linings should be vacuumed gently. Modern plastic ones can be wiped as for upholstery.

Boot

Don't forget the boot. It needs cleaning just as much as the interior. While cleaning, check that all the spare parts you intend to carry are actually there: spare tyre (inflated); jack; jack spanner; jump leads; spare windscreen; spare fanbelt; torch. A footpump and a tyre-pressure gauge can be useful.

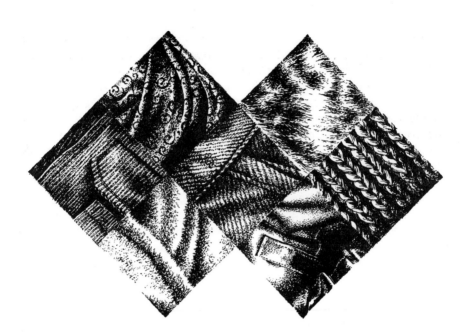

CHAPTER 9

A to Z OF HOUSEHOLD MATERIALS AND HOW TO CLEAN THEM

This chapter includes all the objects lying around the house, and deals with the treatment of various metals and other materials. I will give general cleaning techniques for each type of object and emergency advice for dealing with accidents. I hope I have included most of the objects and materials likely to be found in most homes but I have not dealt with antiques or valuable objects which nearly always need specialist attention.

Acrylic Wash in water and washing-up liquid. Shallow scratches can be rubbed with metal polish on a soft cloth. (For acrylic baths, see page 157).

Alabaster Egyptian alabaster is hard and rather like marble. The alabaster normally used these days is softer and slightly soluble in water. It is often used for small ornaments, ashtrays, lamp bases etc.

Wash gently using a soft cloth or sponge squeezed out in warm water and soap-flakes. Afterwards wipe all soap off with a clean damp cloth and polish. Don't get the object too wet.

Aluminium (See also Pots and Pans.) Many kitchen pans are made of aluminium. Aluminium pans should be washed in mild detergent and water. Rinse in hot water and drain or dry with a soft tea-towel. If the pan has food burned on to it, leave it to soak overnight, scrape out the softened food with a wooden spoon and use a soap-filled steel-wool pad. Aluminium can be washed in dish-washers.

An aluminium pan can be brightened by boiling in it certain acid foods, such as apples, rhubarb and lemons. Another method is to add a tablespoon of vinegar in the egg-boiling water. Or add one teaspoon of cream of tartar to a pint of water, bring to the boil and simmer for two minutes.

Don't keep cooked food in an aluminium pan after cooking. Chemicals in the food may cause the metal to corrode. You won't get food poisoning but the pan will be spoiled.

Aluminium roasting-tins should be treated in the same way though they need a lot of scouring to get rid of burned-on grease.

Amethyst See Jewellery.

Asbestos Asbestos is a fibrous, fireproof mineral substance. It is used in flue pipes and for heat-resistant stove mats. Asbestos fibres cause cancer and if you do have asbestos in the house, you must have it painted to keep small asbestos dust particles from getting into the atmosphere. Once it has been painted you can wipe it clean with a cloth wrung out in detergent and warm water.

Bamboo See Cane Furniture.

Baskets See Cane Furniture.

Blanket, Electric See page 188.

Books Vacuum with the dusting brush or a slightly damp paint-brush to pick up the dust. A feather duster will be better than nothing. Take each book out and dust outwards from the bindings both top and bottom. Wipe the covers with a soft cloth. You can ruffle the pages to dislodge dust, but don't bang them together, fun though this is, because you will trap folded over pages and permanently crease them.

A centrally heated atmosphere is not good for books. It damages the backings, pages and bindings. Dampness on the other hand will cause mildew. If you have central heating perhaps a humidifier in the room where the books are kept would help. Even a bowl of water will evaporate providing a little moisture in the atmosphere.

Leather bindings should be polished with a little colourless wax on a soft cloth about once a year. Use saddle soap or petroleum jelly and rub on with the fingers or a piece of cheesecloth. Rub only a little into the leather. Wait for several hours, then repeat. Two sparing layers are better than one thick one. Allow the books to dry out for a day or two before putting them back in the bookcase.

You can remove grease spots from a page by putting a piece of blotting paper on either side of the page and pressing gently with a warm iron. Books that have been left in the damp or damaged by flood should be treated bit by bit. Put sheets of tissue paper or blotting paper between the pages. Put a weight on top and leave in warm, dry air (the airing cupboard would be ideal) or in a room with a fan heater on but *not* directed towards them.

Books look their best lined up at the front edge of the shelf. Keep them upright, not tilted over at all angles which is bad for their bindings. Don't squash them up too tightly together. You should be able to take them out and put them back easily. Don't pull them out by their spines.

Fresh mildew on pages can often be wiped off with a soft dry cloth or one with a tiny bit of white spirit on it. Or dust the pages with cornflour or French chalk. Leave this for several days before brushing it out. If mildew is bad and has been there for some time you probably won't be able to get rid of it.

Brass An alloy of copper and zinc. It is used in horse brasses, fire irons, fenders, candlesticks, trays, warming pans and handles on furniture. If a brass object is very dirty, wash it first in a household ammonia solution. Then clean with vinegar and salt or a piece of lemon. (You can use oxalic acid and salt but the acid is poisonous and you are more likely to have vinegar at home.) Wash carefully and polish with an essential oil (from chemists or herb shops) on a soft cloth. If you prefer to use a proprietary metal polish, you can, of course, but it will be more expensive.

Lacquered brass will not need cleaning in this way. It should be washed occasionally in warm water and detergent. Unfortunately lacquer often becomes damaged and the metal will corrode under the remaining lacquer. It will then have to be removed with acetone or amyl acetate. Re-lacquering is difficult and best done by a professional but I would say it's better not to lacquer at all but remember to polish and care for the brass regularly.

Very dirty brass objects, such as fire tongs, may have to be rubbed with steel wool or very fine emery cloth. Rub the metal up and down, not round and round and expect the job to take some time. Afterwards, wash thoroughly in hot water and detergent.

Brass preserving pans should be cleaned inside with vinegar and kitchen salt. Wash and rinse thoroughly after cooking and dry. Use a soft steel wool pad if necessary. Metal polish should never be used on the inside of a brass pan which is intended for cooking, but you can use it for the outside. Rub it on, rinse off at once then wipe the pan. An old pan which has not been used recently should be cleaned professionally if you intend to use it for cooking. Catering or kitchen shops, or shops that specialize in brass should be able to tell you where this can be done.

Bronze An alloy of copper and tin. The colour of new bronze varies from dark brown to light gold. Nowadays solid bronze is often lacquered in the factory. Bronze with this sort of finish will only need dusting and, occasionally, a wipe with a damp cloth. If the lacquer cracks or peels you will have to have all the lacquer removed and the object relacquered. Unlacquered bronze can be washed with mild detergent and water, or hot vinegar. Rinse and wipe dry.

Bronze corrodes easily, forming a light green patina or sometimes even red, black or blue. This patination in antique bronzes is considered to be desirable. Antique bronzes require professional treatment.

Brushes Paintbrushes should be kept clean. Always clean them immediately after use. The brush should be rinsed in the correct solvent, which is whatever you've been using as a thinner, or the solvent recommended by the paint manufacturer, and then cleaned with warm water and soap. Large brushes should be hung up or the hairs will be spread and distorted. If you stand them upside down the liquid flows back, weakening the mounting and making the hairs fall out. Drill a hole in the handle to hang it up; alternatively, two nails sticking out of the wall about 25 mm (1 inch) apart will hold a large brush. If you wrap a damp paintbrush in a paper kitchen towel it will stop the bristles from spraying out. Brushes should be stored flat if not hung up.

Brushes used for oil paint, which you have allowed to dry, can be cleaned with acetone but they won't be good for much afterwards. A proprietary paint stripper may be used to clean hardened paint off brushes.

Clean brushes used for *shellac* with white spirit, then soap and water. *Water-type paints* need only water or detergent and water. *Lacquer* needs a lacquer thinner or acetone. *Oil paints, varnishes and enamels* need turpentine or white spirit.

Rubberized and *synthetic resin* paints should be cleaned with detergent and water. Pour a little of the solution on to the brush, work it with gloved fingers and then paint as much as possible off on to old newspaper. Some brushes may have to be left in thinner overnight.

Do not use spirit to clean nylon brushes and do not use nylon brushes for shellac.

Hairbrushes made of animal bristles should be washed once a week in warm water and mild detergent, or warm water with a teaspoon of household ammonia added. Rinse well and dry on a towel, bristles down. When nearly dry turn the bristles to the sun.

Brushes with nylon bristles should be washed in warm water and detergent and rinsed well.

Brooms should be washed in warm water and mild detergent, with a little washing-soda if you like. Splodge them up and down in the water (change the water if necessary). Then rinse a couple of times. Then soak for five minutes in a bucket of water with 30 g (two tablespoonfuls) of kitchen salt, shake and hang to dry head down. Don't bother with the salt and water if the broom is nylon or plastic. Similar treatment is correct for dustpan brushes.

Shoe brushes can be soaked in warm water and detergent with a little household ammonia. Wash. Rinse well and dry head down. If the brush is caked with hardened shoe polish then soak it in a saucer of white spirit, rub on newspaper or old rags and then wash.

Cane furniture (also bamboo, wicker and rattan)   Dust with a duster or a feather duster or vacuum. Rub occasionally with a cloth squeezed out in water.

Untreated cane should be wet thoroughly about once a year so it doesn't dry out. Put it outside on a sunny day and play the hose over it or put it under the bathroom shower. If it looks a bit grubby, wash it with mild detergent and water with a little household ammonia added. Dry it thoroughly. Polish it with furniture cream if you like.

China, porcelain and pottery   For earthenware made from china clay, use clean hot water and washing-up liquid. Wash fine china by hand in a plastic bowl to prevent chipping. Rinse and dry. You should not need to soak or to rub hard or use cleaning powders or scourers. If you do you will damage the glaze and the pattern.

Cracks in fine porcelain can often be made much less obvious by removing the dirt. Cover the crack with a cotton wool pad soaked in a solution of household ammonia or chlorine bleach. Leave for several days, wetting the pad from time to time with more solution. Scrub gently if necessary with a fine-bristle brush dipped in the solution.

Don't pour cold water on to hot china dishes or vice versa in case they break.

Very fine china kept on display but not used should only be wiped over occasionally with first a damp and then a dry cloth. China with a raised pattern can be cleaned with a soft brush.

Egg should be rinsed in *cold* water. Hot water cooks the egg on to the plate.

Get rid of tea and coffee stains by rubbing them with a soft wet cloth dipped in bicarbonate of soda. There are some proprietary products for removing these stains but bicarbonate is cheaper. (If you don't let the drink stand in the cup you won't get the stain in the first place.)

Earthenware, stoneware, salt-glaze ware, etc. is tougher than fine china and is often ovenproof and won't be harmed by boiling water or soaking and can be washed satisfactorily and often in a dishwasher.

Unglazed pottery should not be washed. Partially glazed bowls and dishes should be washed by hand and not soaked.

Chromium A soft silvery metal, which does not tarnish in air and can be highly polished. It is used as a plating on handles, electrical appliances, tubular and other metal furniture, car finishes, light fittings, etc.

Wipe with a soft damp cloth and polish with a dry one. If necessary, wash with warm water and detergent. A little paraffin on a damp cloth will help to clean kitchen chromework (light fittings or chair legs) that has become greasy and fly-blown.

More expensively you can buy chrome cleaners from car and bike accessory shops or hardware shops.

Clocks and watches I'm afraid the quick answer to this is don't attempt to clean the workings of clocks and watches yourself. If you want to practise, try on a worthless old jumble-sale clock.

The movement can be immersed in paraffin then cleaned with a soft brush dipped in petrol. When the movement has drained and the petrol evaporated lubricate the parts with clock oil applied on a feather. *Don't over-oil.* Paraffin is highly flammable. Never work with it indoors.

Electric clocks are sealed and should not need cleaning.

A good clockwork clock or watch should be cleaned and oiled about once a year unless the works are sealed. You may have difficulty finding someone reliable to do this. Modern watches and clocks are usually sent to the manufacturers to be overhauled. Otherwise you will have to rely on the yellow pages or word of mouth to find a good cleaner/repairer.

Old clocks often have fret-cut panels in the sides. These should be backed with a panel of fine-mesh fabric which catches the dust. If this fabric is missing or damaged it should be replaced. Cracks and openings in the case should be sealed up. Thirty-hour clocks are often driven by weights suspended from ropes, and fluff from the ropes eventually gets into the movement. Replace them with chains if possible.

Clothes-pegs   If you leave wooden pegs on the line they will need to be washed in hot water and detergent occasionally. You can put them all in a mesh bag or a pillowcase in the washing machine. Or wash them by hand in the same way, shaking the bag about in the water.

Plastic ones will not need washing so often if at all. If you do wash them, do it in warm, not hot water.

Coffee-maker   It's wise to wash the inside every time you've made coffee or the traces of oil will begin to give future brews a bitter taste.

Wash any removeable pieces in washing-up liquid and rinse well. Wring out a cloth or sponge in soapy water and wipe the outside. Don't get the electric element wet, if there is one.

Don't tip your coffee grounds down the drain. They *will* clog it up and so will tea-leaves.

Copper   A lustrous red-brown metal used for kitchen pans, warming pans, jugs, bowls, ornaments, jelly moulds, paraffin lamps.

In air, copper forms a greenish surface film which can cause nausea and vomiting if eaten. Copper pans must be kept scrupulously clean, should never have food left standing in them. In fact most modern copper pans are lined with chromium or tin.

New pans may have a protective lacquer coating which should be removed before you use the pan. Cover the pan with boiling water and let it stand until the water has cooled. The lacquer should then peel off. Instructions will come with the pan.

Wash copper utensils and ornaments with water and detergent, rinse and dry well. Use a nylon scourer or nylon brush for burned-on food. Never cook food containing vinegar, lemon juice, rhubarb or other acids in a copper pan as they will react with the metal and taint the food, though you may remove any corroded spots with vinegar or lemon juice and salt or a proprietary copper cleaner or buttermilk. Rinse at once and dry well.

Equal parts of salt, vinegar and flour will make a satisfactory copper polish. Always wash thoroughly with detergent and water after using the polish or the copper will quickly tarnish again. Copper can be burnished professionally and you can get damaged tin linings stripped. Kitchen shops that sell to professional caterers should be able to advise.

Copper can be lacquered but this is rarely satisfactory since it inevitably chips, and air and tarnish creep in under the skin. Also, the layer of lacquer does alter the shine. There are various proprietary metal polishes on the market that are suitable for copper.

Coral   The skeletal remains of coral polyp colonies. It is mainly composed of calcium carbonate – like pearls. Clean it as you would pearls (see Jewellery).

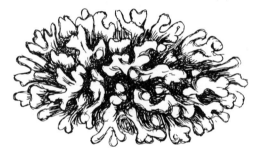

Cork and corks   Sterilize in boiling water. Other cork objects, ice boxes for instance can be rubbed with fine emery paper or emery cloth.

Combs   Soak for a few minutes in one dessertspoonful of household ammonia to one pint of warm water. Wash with a nailbrush. (You can get special comb brushes, but why bother?) Rinse well. Dry away from heat.

Ivory or tortoiseshell combs should be treated as for ivory and tortoiseshell.

Costume jewellery   See Jewellery.

Crockery   See China.

Crystal   See Glass.

Decanters   Decanters and vases with narrow necks do need cleaning and are of course difficult to get into. One method is to shake tea-leaves and vinegar in the vase, another is to fill the base with ball-bearings and rattle these around in it.

One recommended method is to fill the vessel with water into which you put 10 ml (two teaspoonsful) of household ammonia. Stand overnight. Wash and rinse.

Another method is to use a little clean sand (sandpit sand, sea sand or fine aquarium gravel) with a squeeze of washing-up liquid and a little warm water. Shake well, leave it to soak for a few minutes, shake again. Rinse and repeat if necessary. This is supposed to get rid of flower and plant verdigris, and wine sediment.

Or fill the vase with a proprietary cleaner, leave it to soak and then rinse it out.

For more details on cleaning glass see under glass.

Diamonds   See Jewellery.

Dishes   See Washing-up and China.

Drains   See page 173.

Dustbins   Dirty dustbins attract rats, flies and other disease-carrying and smelly creatures. Keep your dustbin clean and tightly covered. This applies to swing bins and other smaller bins in the kitchen too.

Some local authorities provide dustbin liners. Do see that *everyone* in the household knows about them and will line the bin before starting to fill it with garbage. If the local authority doesn't supply liners, get your own. It will save you that filthy job of cleaning out your own bin and the bin itself will smell sweeter.

Wash the bin anyway from time to time with hot water and detergent, and use a little disinfectant, especially in the summer.

Plastic bins are light to carry but rats can and do gnaw through them so if you think you may have rats locally it would be better to get a metal one.

Electrical equipment
BLANKETS   Never fold an electric blanket or crush it into a cupboard or you may break the wires. You should have the blanket serviced once a year by the manufacturer. Some electric blankets are washable, though often they must be returned to the manufacturer for laundering. Follow the manufacturer's instructions.

FANS   An electric fan will need a drop or two of oil about once a year.

Always disconnect the electricity supply first. Then wipe the blades and the motor casing with a cloth squeezed out in warm soapy water. Don't let any water get inside the casing.

HEATERS Dust will make your heater less efficient and more expensive to run. Disconnect the heater first. When it is cold, dust with a feather duster or the dusting tool of the vacuum cleaner. The fan of a fan heater should be oiled at least once a year with a very little fine oil.

Reflectors of sun-bowl lamps should be brightly polished to reflect as much heat as possible. Use a proprietary impregnated wadding which you cannot spill.

IRONS The bases of modern irons are either aluminium or chrome-plated and so do not tarnish but may acquire residues of various things which make them less smooth. It is essential to clean them immediately or ironing will be difficult and delicate fabrics may suffer. Always disconnect the iron when you have finished ironing and especially before cleaning the iron.

If the base has dried starch on it, wipe it with a damp cloth. You can also clean the sole plate with metal polish. Melted nylon or other synthetic fibres can be removed by heating the nylon until it becomes soft. Then you can scrape it off with a wooden spatula. Don't use a metal knife.

If necessary you can use a very fine steel wool but do so cautiously because it is very easy to damage the sole plate. Don't use steel wool on chromium-plated irons. From time to time you can rub the sole plate over with beeswax and wipe off the surplus with a piece of kitchen tissue.

Take care not to run the iron carelessly over zips, buttons, hooks and eyes, etc., or you may scratch the sole plate. If this does happen you should take it back to where you bought it and get a new plate fitted.

Steam irons which have been filled with tap-water may acquire a scale, as do kettles. The water will have difficulty in heating up properly and deposits of scale will come out through the vents, and leave a hard residue on the sole plate.

There are products available (from hardware stores) which will clear scale out but you can prevent it by only using distilled water in the iron.

Read the manufacturer's instructions. Don't overfill the reservoir. If the opening of the spinkler nozzle becomes blocked, clear it with a fine sewing needle. When you've finished you should empty the reservoir. Let the iron cool in an upright position on its heel rest. Always keep it like this when it's resting during the ironing sessions too, so you don't waste the steam.

KITCHEN EQUIPMENT   Always follow the manufacturer's instructions for each individual item. If you have lost them stick to a few basic rules.

ALWAYS disconnect the equipment from the electricity supply before you clean it.

Wipe the exterior and the motor housing with a cloth squeezed out in warm water and detergent. Then dry it with a clean damp cloth. Wash any removeable parts. Dry and put them back again. Only oil if the manufacturer says you should. Never let the electrical parts come into contact with water.

LIGHT BULBS   Dust regularly when you clean the room. Wipe them about once a month if you want to get the full value from them, with a damp cloth rung out in warm suds. *Switch off the light and take the bulb out of its socket first,* or you will electrocute yourself. Don't get the metal part wet and dry the bulb well.

The reflecting interior of a shade should be wiped too. Dusty shades and reflectors will absorb a lot of the light.

SUN-LAMPS   Follow the manufacturer's instructions. Here are a few general hints. Dust the reflector and keep it clean and polished, using a suitable metal polish. Wipe the bulb once a month or so with a cloth damped with spirit. Make sure the lamp is disconnected and the bulb is cold. Don't use soap and water and don't handle it or you'll leave grease on the glass.

WASTE-DISPOSAL UNITS   A waste-disposal unit won't need cleaning because the unit scours itself every time you use it. But you should flush it out about once a week. Close the opening, run 50–75 mm (2–3 inches) of cold water into the sink and while the water is still running turn the unit to the 'on' position. Keep it on until the sink is empty of water. Do *not* use drain-cleaning chemicals.

Enamel   Enamel is a tough finish produced by fusing a special kind of glass on to a metal base. For pans, baths, etc., the base is cast iron or steel. For jewellery it may be silver or gold.

Enamel can be chipped quite easily so should not be treated carelessly or knocked about. Sudden changes of temperature may crack the enamel so pans should be heated slowly and hot pans should not be put down on to a cold surface.

Enamel plates, bowls and mugs, etc., should be washed in warm water and detergent. Do not use metal scrapers or scourers, scouring powders or steel wool. If food is stuck to the enamel, soak it in water for a few hours. Pans should be soaked for a few hours then washed with hot water and detergent. You can safely use a nylon scourer. If food is burned on hard, fill the pan with water, add a couple of teaspoons of bicarbonate of soda and boil. Wash thoroughly afterwards.

Enamel doesn't like acids so don't let tomatoes, rhubarb or citrus fruits sit in an enamel pan. (See also Pots and Pans.)

Light stains can often be removed by rubbing the enamel with a damp cloth dipped in bicarbonate of soda. Wash thoroughly afterwards.

For enamel baths see page 156.

For enamel jewellery see Jewellery.

Floor polisher   Wash the polishing brushes before they get very dirty. Stand the bristles in a shallow bowl of white spirit until the polish has softened then rub them clean on a piece of old sheet or newspaper. Let them dry completely before you use them again.

Foam rubber   Used for mattresses, cushions, pillows, backings for rugs and children's toys. It is mildew-proof, non-allergenic, light, soft and porous. If you use the vacuum cleaner to dust pillows, cushions, etc., they shouldn't need washing.

However, if someone has been sick or spilled something really vile you can wash the foam in lukewarm water and a mild detergent. Keep it in its cover. Handle the object carefully because it will be weaker when wet. If you wash it in the machine choose the coolest and shortest programme. It will take a long time to dry, because you must on no account use heat. Keep it out of sunlight. To speed up the drying, you can use an electric fan, or a fan heater set to circulate cold air only, or a tumble drier set to cold. Take great care that the foam cannot catch fire. Black clouds of poisonous smoke can quickly asphyxiate.

Some firms make pillows with extra-dense covers to prevent hair oil and other stains getting through to the foam.

Frames   See Picture Frames.

Garden tools   Try to remember to put your tools away after each session in the garden and to clean all the mud and bits of garden off first.

Before putting them away for winter, rub with steel wool to get rid of any bits of rust and coat the metal with lubricating oil.

Don't leave fertilizers or insecticides in watering cans or other spreaders. Rinse these vessels out carefully after each use.

Empty hoses of water, coil them up and hang them in the garage or tool-shed.

Drain any fuel from the motor mower, cultivator or garden tractor, and drain off the oil while the engine is warm. Refill the crank case with fresh oil. Take out the spark plug, squirt a little oil into the firing chamber, turn the flywheel a few times to spread the oil and put the spark plug back. Cover the exhaust pipe so the damp won't get in. Yours may be the only mower to start first time next spring.

Glass

TABLE GLASS   When washing up, wash glasses first (see page 210). when the water will be at its hottest and cleanest. Use washing-up liquid and rinse in clear, hot water. Drain dry on a soft cloth. Glasses with stems should be held by the stem. Wash each piece separately.
CUT-GLASS   Bowls should be washed in warm water and liquid detergent. Use a soft brush to get into the crevices. After drying, polish with a silver cloth or stainless-steel cleaner.

Badly stained cut glass may be left to soak for several hours in warm water and detergent to which you have added a few drops of household ammonia.

For glass vessels with narrow necks, see Decanters and Vases.
GLASS OVENWARE can be cleaned as for any other pans. Soak off any burned-on food. Scour if necessary with a nylon pad or steel wool. Don't put a cold pan straight on to a hot stove and don't put a hot pan straight on to a cold surface.

Glass may become clouded or stained. Fill the object with water and add a teaspoon of ammonia. Let it stand overnight. Wash and rinse.

Scratched glass surfaces should be rubbed with chamois leather impregnated with jeweller's rouge, pressing lightly. Scratches on the feet of old wineglasses should be left alone as evidence of the great age.

Glass surfaces of shelves, clocks, barometers, and picture frames can be cleaned with a proprietary polish, or aerosol, or vinegar and water.

Gold   See Jewellery.

Hinges   Door and cupboard hinges should be checked from time to time. Remove dirt with a small clean paintbrush; smear with petroleum jelly working it into the joints (use a swab of cotton wool on a matchstick). This should stop squeaks or possible rusting. Remove surplus with paper tissues.

Horn   Usually made into snuff boxes, knife handles or shoehorns. Wash in warm water and detergent. Don't let the horn soak. Rinse and dry as quickly as possible. Don't put cutlery with horn handles into the dishwasher.

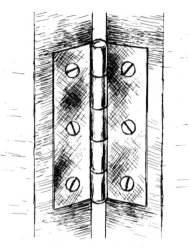

Hot-water bottles   Rubber-ridged bottles and covered ones may get grubby. You can dunk them for two or three minutes in hot water and mild liquid detergent. Scrub with a soft nail-brush or a sponge (for covered ones). They will dry more quickly if you fill them with hot water. In summer, store them away from light and heat, preferably hanging up.

Ivory   Ivory should not be immersed in water as it is made up of layers and the layers may separate when wet. Wipe it over with a cloth squeezed out in warm water and mild detergent. Never allow knives with ivory handles to soak in hot water as this may damage the glue and loosen the handles.

Ivory yellows as it grows older and will grow yellower more quickly if kept out of the sun. Yellowed or roughened ivory can be smoothed with glass paper then rubbed with pumice but this should be done by an expert.

Ivory carvings may be polished with whiting on a soft brush. If it's just yellowed, you can bleach it by rubbing in a little hydrogen peroxide and leaving it in the sun to dry. But do not try to do too much with ancient ivory. Get a professional to do the work.

Old glue stains can be treated with a stiff paste of whiting and hydrogen peroxide. Cover the stain. Don't make the paste too runny. Stand the object outside until the paste is dry. Wipe off the paste and dry thoroughly with a clean cloth. Almond oil put on with a soft rag will give the ivory a protective coating for the future.

Jade   A gem mineral, varying in colour from white to dark green, which is very popular in the Far East. It is either jadeite, a sodium aluminium silicate, or nephrite, a calcium magnesium iron silicate. Green jadeite is the most prized variety.

Jade shouldn't need washing. If it does, wash in warm water and mild detergent. Rinse and dry with a clean cloth. Otherwise dust with a feather duster.

Jewellery   I once had a friend with an enormous hoard of exquisite jewellery – family heirlooms passed down to her through the years. She kept her treasure in the top drawer of her dressing-table, all jumbled up together and would poke around with her forefinger to find the one she wanted. 'Shall I wear the rubies?' she would say, frowning.

Whether you've got a lot of jewellery or only a little and whether it's valuable or only valuable to you, it deserves better treatment than that.

Keep rings in separate little boxes or compartments in your jewellery case. If there's any chance of things getting scratched or knotted together, wrap them individually in tissue paper or cotton wool. You can hang necklaces from hooks. Gold and platinum scratch quite easily – gold is particularly soft and diamonds may scratch other stones or their settings. Stone settings often get worn, broken or pushed out of position and usually you can't see what's happening. Get good jewellery inspected and mended from time to time.

Don't wear your best jewellery every day if you are an energetic and careless wearer. My jewellery box is full of rings which are oblong instead of round because I've caught them on door handles or otherwise mistreated them. Hands are much tougher than jewellery it seems.

As a general rule it is cheap and quite satisfactory to wash jewellery in hot water and mild detergent using a soft tooth-brush to get into the intricate bits. A little household ammonia in the water helps to loosen the dirt. *Do not* use ammonia on pearls. Rinse in hot water and dry on a cloth. Don't use very hot water which may expand the settings so that the stones fall out. This is specially true of claw settings.

There are jewellery cleaning products on the market which make jewellery cleaning even easier and more foolproof but they are of course more expensive. Follow the manufacturer's instructions.

The following hints concern specific kinds of jewellery.

Gold and platinum should be rubbed gently with a clean piece of chamois. Ordinary cloths may harbour bits of grit which could damage the metal. Gold plate should be treated with the tenderest care. I had a silver flower ring with gold plate; the gold has now completely worn off merely because I have worn it a lot.

After washing, polish with a suitable polish, wash and rinse again.

Long bead and stone necklaces should be restrung about once a year, especially if they are heavy ones which you wear a lot. You can clean stones and old beads with dry baking-soda (sodium bicarbonate) on a brush.

Costume jewellery should be washed in warm water. (Hot water may crack the stones.) Don't leave any jewellery in the water for longer than necessary or the cement may come loose. If it does use an epoxy resin glue to fix it again.

Acrylic jewellery should be sponged with lukewarm water and mild detergent. Wipe dry with a clean damp cloth.

Plaster jewellery should *not* be washed in very hot water or cleaned with alcohol or ammonia.

Wooden jewellery shouldn't be washed, just wiped with a damp cloth and polished with a little wax polish or rubbed with olive oil.

Dirty diamonds are not a girl's best friend. Take special care to get them clean or the light won't be reflected from every facet and won't shine with that special brilliance diamonds should have. Use an eyebrow brush or very soft toothbrush to loosen any dirt at the back of the setting.

Diamonds may even be boiled in a weak solution of soapsuds plus a few drops of ammonia. Dip the object into the boiling liquid in a tea strainer or a piece of muslin (like a bouquet garni). Leave it there for just a moment and then let it cool. Then dip it into an eggcupful of white spirit and lay it on paper tissues to dry.

Don't boil diamonds if there are other stones in the object too!

Pearls Most pearls are found in oysters though some are also found in clams. The oyster is sometimes attacked by a minute parasitic worm and builds the pearl round it to relieve the irritation. The pearl is built up in thin layers of mostly calcium carbonate. Pearls dissolve in weak acid.

Natural pearls may be white, yellow, rose, blue or grey. They may be pear-shaped, dome-shaped or irregular.

Cultured pearls are made in Japan, where a tiny bit of mother-of-pearl is put inside the oyster who covers it with pearl.

Artificial pearls are made from hollow glass. The inside is covered with a special finish made from fish scales.

If you want to test your pearls, real or cultured ones will feel rough if you draw them across your teeth. Artificial ones will feel smooth. If you have dentures I don't know how you test them!

Pearl necklaces should be restrung at least once a year or whenever they begin to get loose. Pearls are nearly always strung with a knot between each, as are any valuable stones, so that if the string breaks the whole lot won't tumble to the ground.

To keep pearls clean, rub them gently with a clean soft chamois leather, taking care to rub between the beads. This will remove the film of dirt picked up from you and the atmosphere every time you wear them.

Although pearls may be washed in warm water and mild detergent (*not* ammonia), pearl necklaces should not be washed because the water may rot the thread.

Jet (black amber) is a sort of glossy black lignite (brown coal) which became popular for jewellery when Prince Albert died! Soft breadcrumbs can be used to clean pieces of jet. If it is not decorated with materials that water damages, then it can be washed.

Kettles   Kettles often scale up in hard-water areas. You can loosen scale with boiling water and vinegar (half and half). Let this stand in the kettle for several hours or overnight, then scrape out the deposit with steel wool.

There are dozens of old wives' recommendations for preventing your kettle from scaling up. You can put in a marble or a piece of loofah. Or you can buy a little wire ball from hardware shops. If yours is a hard-water area I doubt if anything will actually prevent scale. But a scaled-up kettle is inefficient and slow, and bits of scale get into soups and coffee. You can get rid of it by using a proprietary descaler. Follow the manufacturer's instructions. If you prefer an old household remedy fill the kettle with cold water, add a level dessertspoonful of borax and boil. Pour the water away, rub off the softened scale and rinse the kettle out.

A gentler method, which may be better for electric kettles, is to add a few tablespoons of water softener to the water instead of borax.

Lacquer   The art of lacquering comes from China and Japan. Lacquer is made from the resin of a tree. It's used mostly as coloured decoration on little boxes and ashtrays, but can be found on furniture and screens.

You can make a paste, which will clean and polish lacquer, from flour and olive oil. Apply with a soft cloth and wipe off, then polish with a soft rag. Silk is best because it leaves no linty bits.

Another method is to apply a little liquid wax with a soft cloth then polish gently with a clean soft cloth.

Lamps, electric   See under Electrical Equipment, and Lampshades, and the name of the material from which the base has been made.

Lampshades   Most can be vacuumed or dusted. Some washable fabrics may be stuck together with unwashable glues, so don't plunge a lampshade into water unless you know it is safe.

Plastics and glass can be washed or wiped with cloth squeezed out in warm water and detergent.

Kitchen shades get dirtier and greasier than others. Use a strong detergent – carpet detergent in a strong solution is good.

Paper, Chinese and Japanese shades should be brushed *often* with a feather duster.

Parchment should be wiped with a cloth wrung out in vinegar and water. Leave to dry before you touch it.

Raffia and straw: vacuum *often*.

Silk lampshades should be cleaned professionally – *before* they get very grubby. Don't attempt to clean them yourself. The Association of British Launderers and Cleaners (address on p. 69) should be able to give you the name and address of a specialist cleaner.

Leather   Leather-covered furniture should be dusted with a clean cloth or feather duster and cleaned with saddle soap. When quite dry, polish up with a soft, dry cloth.

Leather may dry out, especially in a centrally heated atmosphere. To prevent this, rub it once a year with castor oil, or petroleum jelly. If you want a duller shine use neat's-foot oil. Do not use paraffin and don't wax leather furniture.

Leather luggage, bags, etc., should be dusted or wiped over with a cloth wrung out in soapsuds. Oily spots should be removed with a dry-cleaning solvent. Apply neat's-foot oil while the leather is still a bit damp. Rub it in with the fingers. On glossy leather use castor oil. Use white Vaseline on pale leather. (These directions do not apply to patent leather (q.v.), suede or artificial leather.)

Leather, artificial: do not treat stains with a grease solvent. Use instead a thick paste of French chalk and water. Leave until dry and then brush off. Professional dry-cleaning is best.

Leathercloth should be wiped with a damp cloth wrung out in soapy water. Then wipe down with the cloth after rinsing it in clear warm water, and rub dry. If you want to polish it use an emulsion floor polish.

Patent leather should be cleaned with a soft damp cloth and mild detergent. Do not wax or polish it as this will crack the leather.

Suede should be brushed with a special bristle, rubber or wire suede brush, working in a circular motion. Rub gently or you will damage the surface. There are aerosol sprays to raise the nap.

Loofahs   See Sponges and Loofahs.

Marble   Wipe regularly with a cloth wrung out in water and mild detergent. Wipe dry and polish with a soft duster.

Marble is not stain resistant so don't encourage people to put cups of coffee and tea or wineglasses on marble table tops or mantlepieces. Badly treated marble is difficult to deal with. If you can find a professional, do.

Otherwise you can rub the marble with wire wool and then polish it with an electric polishing pad to bring back the dull shine.

Marble which has been painted – and for some reason quite a number of old marble fireplaces have been painted – may have to be treated with a paint stripper to take off the paint. Follow the instructions on the bottle or tin. You may need to do this several times. Protect neighbouring plasters or polished surfaces and your own skin and eyes. Put out all naked lights including cigarettes. Carefully scrape the paint off. Then rub over with wire wool and polish with an electric polisher.

This method is frowned upon by perfectionists but I really don't know how else you'd get the job done and I have seen it work perfectly well.

Melamine   Melamine plastic is used for plates, cups, tumblers, jugs, cutlery handles, etc. It is tasteless, non-poisonous and doesn't smell. Boiling water won't damage it and it can be put in the dishwasher. Melamine should be washed as other tableware. It does stain rather easily and you can remove stubborn stains with a little toothpaste rubbed on with your finger or an old toothbrush. Melamine is easily scratched so don't use scouring powders or pads. From time to time you can treat it with a special product for plastic available from department stores or ironmongers. But baking-soda (sodium bicarbonate) will often remove light stains. Sodium perborate is usually effective for heavy stains. See also washing-up.

Mirrors   Mirrors can be cleaned with a special window-cleaning product, but it's cheaper to use a mixture of equal quantities of water, methylated spirit, and paraffin. Or use water with a little vinegar or ammonia added. Polish with a chamois leather if you have one. If you haven't it may be worth investing in one for window panes as well.

Chromed parts on bathroom and car mirrors may be rubbed with Vaseline from time to time to stop them getting rusty. You can get hair lacquer off a mirror with surgical spirit.

When cleaning mirrors, never let the backing get wet or let water seep between the frame and the glass or the glass and the backing. Once the silvering at the back is damaged the only solution is to get a new glass.

It is possible to have mirrors resilvered but this reduces the value of antique mirrors to some extent. For modern mirrors it's probably best to get new glass.

Mother-of-pearl This is the substance that lines the shells of the oyster and the nautilus. It's made up mainly of calcium carbonate – like pearls.

It's used for inlaying, for small decorative articles, for tiny knife handles, etc. Wash in warm water and detergent. Don't use ammonia. Don't soak mother-of-pearl handles in water or you will loosen the cement, and don't put them in the dishwater.

Nylon plastic This is a very tough plastic. It is opaque or nearly white or tinted. It is not affected by freezing, is lightweight and rigid but slightly resilient. It is used for unbreakable tumblers, brushes and bristles. Nylon cutlery and crockery can be put in the dishwasher. Nylon brushes can be boiled. (If you are not sure if they *are* nylon don't boil or put in a dishwasher. Acrylic and ordinary plastic won't stand up to such rough treatment.)

Nylon utensils used to hold coffee or brightly coloured food should be washed quickly before they become permanently stained. Don't use abrasives. Don't use them for cooking.

Oilcloth Used to be made by coating a fabric with linseed oil and whiting. Nowadays P.V.C.-coated fabrics have taken over and do a better job. If you have some old oilcloth you feel affectionate towards you will find it has a tendency to crack along the folds and at corners. To avoid any more cracks, don't fold while damp. Sunlight and strong heat will damage it too. Don't put hot dishes on it. Wipe with a damp cloth wrung out in warm water and washing-up liquid. Alcohol is damaging to the finish and so are acetone and amyl acetate.

Paintings
Oil paintings You can certainly clean up the odd ancestor without

doing too much harm but *do not* tamper with any painting you think may be valuable. Get it dealt with by a professional. Local art shops or art dealers may be able to advise.

If you do attempt to clean up an oil painting, start on one you don't value too much and get some practice in because it's a complicated and exacting job.

You can still buy old and fairly worthless paintings in charity shops, jumble sales or junk shops and that's the way to start.

There are no absolute rules. The techniques and materials used will depend on the paints used and the canvas they were painted on.

The canvas is nearly always nailed on to a wooden frame which is called a stretcher. Old canvases were nearly always made of linen; modern ones may be of cotton but they are not such good quality.

The surface of canvas is always primed with a solution of glue and water and then painted with white-lead paint. Otherwise the paint used damages the canvas.

Oil paints are colour pigments ground in linseed or poppy-seed oil. When the picture is finished and dry it is varnished.

First dust the painting by lightly brushing with a cotton rag, a soft brush or a feather duster. Don't use soap, water, breadcrumbs, or any of the other 'rubbers' sometimes recommended. A very thin film of cream furniture polish may brighten the surface and won't do the painting any harm. Make sure the canvas is supported from the back while you are cleaning the front.

Most experts disapprove of any further cleaning being done by amateurs, and understandably. So from here on it's your responsibility.

Many paintings look dirty because the varnish has changed colour and become opaque. It may only be necessary to take off the old varnish and put on a new coat.

The method described here is extremely simplified. If you are at all doubtful about your ability go to further-education classes. There's nothing like watching someone do a skilled job, to help you understand the problem.

To remove the varnish you will first have to soften it with the correct solvent. You will have to experiment to see which solvent you want to use. Do this on a piece of painting normally hidden by the frame.

Apply the solvent gently by dabbing – don't rub – on a piece of cotton wool. If the varnish comes away at once the solvent is too strong.

You should be able to get a suitable alcohol solvent in art shops. Have ready a 'stop' for the solvent, turpentine acts as a stop for an alcohol solvent, and if the varnish comes away too quickly, stop it at once. Proprietary solvents don't give you the flexibility of those you mix up yourself and if you go on to more sophisticated cleaning you will want to learn to make up your own. It is best for an expert to tell you about this.

Start at the top left-hand corner (or top right-hand corner if you are left-handed) and rub gently with solvent in a circular motion on a pad of cotton wool. As soon as the cotton wool is covered with varnish throw it away and start with a clean piece. If *any* paint colour shows on the pad, stop the solvent action with turpentine and start on the next patch.

Work from left to right (or vice versa) and try to leave a thin film of varnish so you can't possibly damage the paint. Now wash the painting over with turpentine and allow it to dry. When completely dry, brush with a coat of varnish.

Working on small sections at a time does make it difficult to get an even finish, however, and it is difficult to tell whether you've reached the paint or not.

You must work in strong light and with a good magnifying glass. Daylight is best. If good daylight is not available then good fluorescent lighting is effective and cheap.

Of course, there's much more to cleaning pictures than this very basic method. If you've tried on unworthy pictures and want to take it further, get some proper teaching from experts.

While cleaning you may come across holes and tears. You can stick these together with a glue made of five parts beeswax, five parts resin, one part Venice turpentine. Melt them all in a durable saucepan and don't smoke or light a match. The mixture is highly flammable. Coat a small patch of cotton with this mixture and place it over the tear on the back of the canvas. Press with a warm iron. The iron should be warm enough to melt the adhesive but not so hot as to damage the paint. Then allow the adhesive to harden and scrape off any surplus wax.

Water-colours   I have several water-colours painted by an extremely talented great-aunt. Unfortunately water-colours are often left lying around unframed and some very beautiful ones painted by our Victorian ancestors are in quite poor state.

Sad to say, water-colours are very difficult to clean. New bread can be rubbed gently over the surface and will absorb some dust and grime. This won't damage the paper or the paint. Rubbers are too rough and crude.

If the painting has been framed but the glue has deteriorated and discoloured the paper, then you will have to take the painting from its mount to remove the glue and stain. Such paintings are usually mounted on stiff paper or cardboard and stuck with paste. Soak a bit of blotting-paper in water and leave it over the back of the mount. Be patient, it will take some time to loosen the paste. If the adhesive was the runny kind you may loosen it by holding the painting over the steam from a kettle spout. Dab the paper with cotton wool soaked in water to loosen the paste.

If the colour still persists you may want to try bleaching the painting. You can get most stains out with a sodium hypochlorite solution. For rust and ink stains you should use oxalic acid (poisonous) and for grease stains you will need benzene.

Water-colours should never be only partially wetted. If you *have* to wet them you should flood them completely. After using any of the bleaches, or solvents mentioned above, you will have to rinse afterwards. As you will understand, this is no job for an amateur on a picture of any monetary or sentimental value. Immersion in water will make some water-colours run and others bleach. So clean as much as possible without using water, but be prepared to put up with the grubbiness of time and put the painting behind glass to prevent it getting any worse.

Patent leather   Clean with a soft, damp cloth and a mild soap. Do not use waxes or polishes which will crack the leather.

Pearls   See Jewellery.

Perspex   I.C.I. trade name for an acrylic (q.v.).

Pewter   Pewter is an alloy of tin and various other metals, including lead, antimony, copper, bismuth and zinc. It was used in ancient times in the Far East, and pieces have survived from Roman times. Production virtually ceased at the end of the nineteenth century but there has recently been a revival of interest in it.

Many people nowadays prefer their pewter to be dullish though originally it was made to look as much like silver as possible.

If it's kept in a humid atmosphere pewter will quickly develop what's called a 'hume' with a grey film and tarnishing. Heavy oxide scale is usually found on valuable antique pieces and it's better to leave these uncleaned on account of their historic interest. Tarnishing can be removed by immersion in solvent chemicals but this should be done by someone with a specialist knowledge of pewter.

Sometimes tarnishing can be faked with chemicals, so don't buy a piece simply because it looks old.

Ordinary pewter can be polished with a suitable proprietary metal polish or with whiting and a little household ammonia or a similar mild abrasive. You shouldn't need to do this more than two or three times a year.

Piano Many homes have a piano and most pianos are sadly neglected. Even a common-or-garden second-hand upright bought for the children to practice on deserves to be kept clean and tuned. Anybody who plays the piano (or has to listen) deserves to have it tuned too.

A piano should be tuned not less than three times a year. Once each season is better. Pianos go out of tune whether they're used or not.

Hang a bag of anti-moth crystals inside the piano where it won't touch any of the strings or hammers to prevent moths getting at the felt. If the piano is new it may already be mothproofed.

Vacuum the inside from time to time but be careful not to touch the strings or hammers.

Keep the piano in a normal temperature and not in a damp atmosphere, nor against hot pipes, or stoves and not where the temperature often changes. (And don't expect anyone to play with pleasure if you keep the piano in a little-used, cold room.) Mine is kept in the kitchen, largely because that's where we have space for it. It gets played a lot.

Dust *keys* with a feather duster as often as you can. Occasionally wipe with a cloth wrung out in warm water and washing-up liquid. If the keys are stained or sticky, wipe them with a cloth moistened with methylated spirit. The more sunlight that falls on the keys the less yellow they will become.

You are advised not to stand vases and other things on a piano which might leave pressure marks. If you *do* stand a vase on it, make sure there's a mat underneath to prevent any water from damaging the wood.

Always close the lid when the piano's not being used.

Dust the casing as often as possible. Old, varnished wooden pianos can be cleaned with a cream polish. Pianos with a sealed finish should not be polished, just wiped over to remove greasy marks with a damp cloth. Then rub with a dry cloth or chamois leather. Modern piano cases are often made of plastic or similar materials. Clean them as above for sealed wood.

Picture frames Wash the glass as you would window or mirrors with an aerosol spray or a chamois or soft cloth wrung out in ammonia and water or vinegar and water or just warm water. Don't get the glass very wet or water may get inside the frame and damage the picture. Polish with a dry chamois or with paper tissues.

Wooden frames should be wiped with a cloth squeezed out in warm water and washing-up liquid and polished with a little cream furniture polish occasionally. Occasionally a wooden frame is varnished with clear varnish or sealed. This is a pity as it gives the wood an artificial shine not nearly as delicate as the shine of polished wood. But of course you will not need to polish it.

Gilt frames, if not valuable, can be cleaned with a dry-cleaning solvent. If the gilt is worn you can get a small pot of gold from art shops to rub on to the frame with your fingers. This stuff is poisonous so wash your hands thoroughly afterwards.

Platinum A metal with a greyish white lustre, slightly heavier than gold, often used nowadays in jewellery. It is corroded by chlorine, sulphur and phosphorous. For cleaning, see Jewellery.

Pots and pans For aluminium pans, see Aluminium. Most pots and pans, whether non-stick or not will be easy to clean if you leave them to soak for a few hours. Frying-pans with a lot of fat left in are difficult to deal with. If you don't want to keep the fat for further cooking, *don't* put it down the sink, because it will congeal and block the outlet. Scrape or pour the bulk into the rubbish bin, squirt a good squirt of detergent or a handful of soda crystals into the remaining fat, fill up with hot water. Then you can pour it down the sink. In winter don't waste it, give it to the birds. Never put a hot frying pan straight into cold water.

Roasting- and baking-tins should not be scrubbed with wire wool or abrasive powders except very occasionally. If a tin has a lot of baked-on-grease, soak it for about half an hour in one pint of very hot water poured over one dessertspoon of washing-soda crystals. Then scrub with a nylon scourer, rinse well and dry.

Enamel roasting-pans with burnt-on grease should be soaked in hot water and detergent (not washing soda). Then use a washing-up brush or nylon scourer if necessary.

Pottery See China.

Prints All cleaning of pictures requires practice and skill. Always experiment and practice on worthless prints before trying your hand at something you really care about and *if in doubt* get professional advice.

Printing ink can usually be immersed in water quite safely and won't suffer from very gentle bleaching. Which makes prints easier to deal with than water-colours. Japanese prints need special care as the colours are not always fast and will bleach. New bread or dough can be used to get marks off a print and you can try washing it in distilled water with a large camel-hair paintbrush. Lay the print on a sheet of glass while you're working on it, then cover it with blotting-paper with a slight weight on top. Never cut off any part of the margin of a print. This destroys its value.

Quartz (silica)   Rock crystal, amethyst, rose quartz, agate, onyx, sardonyx and cat's eyes are all forms of quartz. They are often used in jewellery. For general hints on jewellery care, see Jewellery.

Records   If you care at all about the sound you listen to you must keep your records clean. Also your cassettes. Always put a record back in its cover as soon as you have played it. If you haven't got a cleaner fixed to the arm of the record player keep one next to it and gently clean each record before you play it. Washing records is difficult because it usually leaves a deposit of mud deep in the grooves. Do as much cleaning as possible with a hand-held record-cleaning brush. Clean the stylus of your pickup regularly – a record shop will sell you a kit with a suitable brush and some isopropyl alcohol for this.

Roasting-tins   See Pots and Pans.

Rubber   Store rubber things in a cool dark place. Rubber gloves don't stand up to chemical cleaners very well. It's better to use plastic ones for cleaning metals. The hands sweat a good deal in rubber and plastic gloves so you should wash and powder the insides with talc every time you use them.

Rubber boots should be washed in water or detergent and water. Wipe, and dry in a cool airy place. If boots get wet inside, stuff them with crumpled newspaper and dry them upside down in the airing cupboard.

Saucepans See Pots and Pans.

Shoes Shoes will last longer and go out of shape less quickly if you buy the right size. They must give your feet and toes plenty of room across the instep and should be 5 mm ($\frac{1}{4}$ inch) longer than your longest toe.

You should *not* be able to feel the end of the shoe with your toes when you stand up. Use shoe trees if you have the patience. Keep heels mended. Worn heels look dreadful and make shoes uncomfortable when walking.

Keep your shoes always cleaned and polished with the correct dressing. Badly treated shoes do mar one's whole appearance and won't last as long.

Wet *leather shoes* should be stuffed with crumpled newspaper which will absorb some of the moisture and help the shoes keep their shape. Dry away from direct heat. Rub a little leather conditioner or castor oil on to the soles and uppers of leather shoes which have got wet. This will soften the leather.

Suede shoes should be brushed with a rubber, bristle or wire brush. Work in a circular motion and don't rub too hard. When you've brushed the whole shoe, smooth the nap in one direction. There are aerosols to raise the nap but these shouldn't be necessary if you clean your shoes regularly. It may be difficult to remove oil or grease stains from suede. Try a spot of cleaning fluid. If this does not work alone, mix the fluid with fuller's earth or salt and leave the paste on the stain for several hours.

Muddy shoes should be allowed to dry. Then brush the dried mud off on to a piece of newspaper. Wipe any residue with a damp cloth.

Patent leather can be cleaned with a soft damp cloth and detergent. Don't use wax, it will crack the leather.

Apply a small amount of the appropriate polish with a shoe brush. Rub well in and buff up with a soft cloth.

Clean *sports shoes* with soap or detergent and water. White shoes will have to be rubbed with a special white cleaner or whiting mixed to a paste with water.

Silver Silver will tarnish. Tarnish is caused by the action of gases in the air on the surface of the metal. Silver will tarnish more quickly in a damp or salty atmosphere. You can buy various bags, wraps and rolls of cloth impregnated with a tarnish preventer for sterling silver. These are available from jewellers. Or wrap closely in self-stick transparent film.

Silver needs constant care. Always wash it as soon as you can after use in hot water and washing-up liquid. Rinse in hot water and dry at once.

The best way to clean tarnished silver is to rub it with a proprietary silver polish. Dip cleaners are suitable for cutlery in daily use and are useful for etched and embossed pieces. If you can't get the object into the dip jar, dab it with cotton wool saturated in cleaner. Don't leave the silver in any longer than necessary.

In my experience it is best to get out the whole lot together and spend a relaxed hour listening to the radio and rubbing the silver gently and polishing it afterwards. Wear cotton gloves and treat your silver gently. Old silver has often been worn leaf thin because it was cleaned with home-made slightly abrasive products using whiting. It was difficult not to rub off some of the silver at the same time. Modern treatments should take off only the tarnish. A soft toothbrush is useful to get into chased surfaces. Rub each piece with straight strokes, don't use a circular motion. Afterwards rub the silver with a clean, soft flannel cloth or chamois leather. Then wash again. If you leave any polish on the silver it will tarnish again more quickly.

Gold linings in silver bowls should be wiped gently with a soft cloth. Gold is soft and such linings are thin and easily worn away.

Lacquered silver will not tarnish. But the butler at Woburn Abbey, who once took me round the silver vaults, had no good word to say about lacquering at all. If the lacquer becomes damaged, tarnish will occur where the air gets in and will creep along under the lacquer where you can't reach to clean it. Removing the lacquer is very difficult indeed.

Never use rubber bands for securing the wrappings round silver. Rubber can corrode silver through several layers of cloth and the damage is permanent.

Salt, eggs, olives, salad dressings, gas, vinegar, fruit juices, perfumes, etc. all have a tarnishing effect on silver. Sea air is bad for it too, because of the salt. Silver rose bowls should be kept clean and the flowers kept fresh. Acids from decaying flowers will damage silver quickly.

Never use silver cleaner on metals other than silver, gold or platinum. Work near an open window as tarnished silver gives off a sulphurous smell.

Long-term polishes are now available. Depending on where you live, your silver shouldn't need cleaning for several weeks or even months after you've used it.

Silver plate (electroplate) This is not solid silver, of course. A coating of silver has been applied to another metal. Treat silver plate as for silver but treat it more gently and protect it more carefully.

Sheffield plate is a sheet of silver fused to copper and then rolled thin. After about 1850 when electroplate was invented, Sheffield plate was no longer used and pieces are now quite valuable. Clean as for silver plate.

Soap dishes Soak for two minutes in 100 g of washing-soda crystals dissolved in $3\frac{1}{2}$ litres of very hot water (one tablespoonful in half a gallon). Scrub with a stiff washing-up brush. Rinse and dry.

Spectacles Wash your glasses occasionally with warm water and soap to remove the grease that they acquire from your skin. Use a soft brush to clean round the rims. Polish with a soft cloth or tissues or lens paper from your optician.

Sponges and loofahs Sea sponges are the skeletons of little sea animals which grow among the rocks. Wash sea sponges in soapy water or detergent and water. If you've let them get slimy with old soap, soak them in cold salt water (15 g to 500 ml, one tablespoon to one pint). Squeeze out well and rinse. Sponges should be hung up or kept on a bath rack where the air can get at them and they can dry out. Don't bleach.

Loofahs, like sponges, often get a bit smelly and slimy through sitting around in the wet. Loofahs can be boiled in water and detergent. Allow to cool and rinse well.

Plastic sponges can be cleaned with a mild household-ammonia solution (25 ml per litre; one tablespoon per quart). This sometimes improves the colour and disinfects them. Don't use strong bleaches or strong detergents.

Synthetic or rubber sponge mops should be soaked before using because they're brittle when dry. Rinse them well after use. In fact if you can struggle with the clip-in mechanism, put them in the washing-machine with the dirty socks. Hang up the mop when you're not using it and let it dry naturally, away from direct heat or sunlight.

Suede See under Leather.

Sun-lamps See Electrical Equipment.

Teapots *Aluminium* Fill with water and 100 g (two tablespoons-ful) borax, boil and then wash as usual.

China See China. See also Washing-up.

Chrome Clean inside with a cloth moistened with vinegar and dipped in salt. Rinse in very hot water.

Silver Clean the inside with hot water and borax (15 g borax to

500 ml of water; one teaspoonful per pint). Leave for about an hour then clean with a washing-up brush and bottle brush for the spout. Rinse thoroughly. Clean the outside as you would for silver (q.v.).

Taps   A few drops of paraffin on a damp cloth should keep chrome taps, outlets, etc., clean and bright if you treat them regularly. Paraffin dries quickly and leaves no drops, and the smell disappears almost at once. Metal polish isn't necessary and is hard work. If the chrome is stained rub it with a damp cloth dipped in bicarbonate of soda. Then rub with a dry cloth.

Telephone   Use a feather duster on the telephone every day. Eventually, in spite of this it will need a real clean. Wipe it with a damp cloth and mild detergent.

Television   Clean the glass with a cloth wrung out in water and washing-up liquid. Wipe dry. Dust attaches itself very quickly to the screen. Never use chemical cleaning fluids. Polish the cabinet with furniture polish (don't get any on the glass). Never let anything hang over the back or it will cover the ventilation holes and overheat the appliance.

Tortoiseshell   Should be cleaned with a paste made by moistening jeweller's rouge with one or two drops of olive oil. Rub on gently with a soft cloth, leave for a few minutes, then polish with a clean duster. Imitation tortoiseshell may be washed in warm soapy water, rinsed and dried.

Typewriters   Keep your typewriter covered whenever it is not in use. Dust it with a feather duster every day. Once a week clean the platen (roller) and the little rubber rollers that feed the paper in by wiping with a cloth moistened in alcohol. Some platens are removeable which makes them easier to clean. Clean the type with alcohol or proprietary cleaning fluid (from stationers). Slip a piece of blotting-paper or tissue over the platen and scrub the type with a stiff bristle typewriter or toothbrush. You can get dough-type cleaners and spray-on cleaners for the type if you prefer.
   Once a month, oil the carriage rails by moving the carriage right over to the left and putting one drop of oil on the rails. Do not oil the type bars, and don't over-oil the rails. Too much oil will only make your paper dirty. Brush out dust and bits of eraser every day.

Vacuum cleaner   Empty the bag before it gets too full. If the cleaner has a small bag you may need to empty it every time you vacuum. If the cleaner uses disposable bags, keep a good supply. You cannot always rely on manufacturers to estimate correctly how many they should make, or retailers to stock up when they should. Unfortunately, disposable bags are so designed that it's almost impossible to make your own in an emergency.

If your vacuum cleaner has a cloth bag, take it out to the dustbin to empty it because bits of dust inevitably get out and float around. For the same reason, tie your hair up in a scarf before emptying the bag. Wipe the case with a cloth wrung out in detergent and water once a week or so. Keep the attachment brushes clean by washing them in hot water and detergent occasionally.

Vacuum flask   Clean the inside with hot water and detergent, or water and baking-soda (sodium bicarbonate). *Always* leave the bottle uncapped or it will smell musty and grow mouldy. If the flask does have a musty smell, pour in warm water, a squeeze of washing-up liquid and a little silver sand, or water, 60 ml (two tablespoons) of vinegar and a crushed eggshell. Shake well, leave to soak, shake again and rinse. Then pour in a pint of hot water and 10 g (two teaspoons) of bicarbonate of soda, cork the flask, leave for several hours. Rinse thoroughly.

A bottle brush will help to get the neck clean. Do not immerse the whole flask or water may seep between the inner and outer compartments. If the flask has a cork stopper which becomes discoloured or mouldy you can sterilize it by putting it in a pan of boiling water for five minutes or so.

Vases and decanters with narrow necks   See Decanters.

Washing-up   For some reason many people find washing-up a dreadful chore. It need not be.

Stack all dirty dishes and utensils systematically; plates of a size all together; cutlery in a bowl or saucepan; saucers and cups neatly stacked. Make sure the plate rack and draining-board are clear and within reach before you begin. Use hot water and only just enough detergent to deal with grease. Wash the cleaner items first, e.g. glasses. That way one lot of water will last longer.

Rinse everything after washing; a bowl of clean water is less wasteful for this than holding the things under a running tap.

Cutlery should be put directly into a cutlery drainer; cooking knives in or on a knife rack. Put pointed knives in upside down so people will not cut their wrists when reaching for a spoon.

Leave plates to drain dry. The hotter the washing-up water the quicker it will evaporate.

Burned-on food should be soaked overnight and should then come off quite easily.

Put items away as soon as they are dry.

Milk bottles should be rinsed out immediately they are emptied.

Cutlery should be washed as soon as possible after each meal. Use hot water and washing-up liquid and dry at once.

Wood, bone and ivory handles should be kept out of the water. In my experience even wooden handles which are supposed to be dishwasher-proof will keep their shine better if washed by hand.

Plastic handles can be put in hand-hot water but not in a dishwasher.

Stainless-steel cutlery can be corroded by salt in very hot water and by rhubarb, lemon juice or vinegar. Rinse it as soon as possible even if you aren't going to wash it at once. The salt you put in your dishwasher is to activate the water softener and should not damage stainless steel cutlery.

Silver cutlery should be cleaned from time to time with a proprietary silver cleaner. Wash afterwards. Most of these products will damage stainless steel so do your cleaning on old newspapers or a table or worktop and not in a stainless steel sink. If you do get any on stainless steel sink or cutlery, rinse it off at once.

Fine blades should be sharpened occasionally by a professional grinder. Failing him, sharpen them yourself on a butcher's steel or with a rotary knife sharpener. If using a steel hold the blade at an angle of about $15°$. If the rotary sharpener pull the blade right through several times, don't just push it backwards and forwards.

Steel knives which are not stainless, some cooking knives for instance and elderly handed-down cutlery, are difficult to deal with. They should be washed as soon as they have been used and dried immediately and kept in a dry place or they will rust or go black. Steel wool will remove this corrosion as will rubbing the knife with salt and greaseproof paper. Better still is to rub with a cork dipped in scouring powder.

Knives with serrated edges should never be sharpened.

Watches   See Clocks and Watches.

Wicker   See Cane Furniture.

Wood   Wood is a pleasant, natural material, used for all sorts of things: draining-boards; worktops; bread-, cheese- and chopping-boards; bowls; spoons; wall panelling etc.

Wood absorbs water and will crack, warp or go soft if left wet for a long time. Unpolished wood can be washed after use, then dried thoroughly and put away upright. Don't soak it or put it in the dishwasher. Don't stack wooden bowls until they are absolutely dry. Salad bowls may be rubbed with a little olive oil to keep the wood in good condition.

Wooden work surfaces can be varnished or sealed, but if you prefer a less 'hard' look you can rub in linseed oil instead. Remove any finish the wood may have already, then heat the linseed oil (ask for *boiled* linseed oil when you buy it) in a double boiler or in a small bowl in a pan of boiling water. Linseed oil is highly flammable so watch out. Don't heat it over an open flame or near the gas pilot light. Apply the hot oil to the wood then rub it down with steel wool. Wait twenty-four hours, then do it again. Wait another twenty-four hours and give it a third coat. Re-oil occasionally. This surface can now be wiped with a cloth or sponge wrung out in lukewarm water or detergent and water.

French polish or shellac finish should be dusted with a clean soft cloth or feather duster. Don't use oiled or treated dusters. Polish with a wax polish used very sparingly and buff up well with a soft clean cloth. Rub with the grain. The harder you rub the better the polish. French polish shows every mark: heat, water, spirits, scratches. Leave serious stains and marks to professionals – look in the Yellow Pages under furniture repairers and restorers.

Wax polish should be treated like French polish. If a table has white ring marks because something hot or wet has been standing on it, try leaving a paste of salt and olive oil on the mark overnight, then remove it and polish the wood as usual. If some mark is left you may be able to cover it with a paste of colour available in hardware shops. Do not use silicone polishes or sprays on waxed furniture.

All furniture will eventually accumulate dirt and will need to be cleaned. For waxed and French polished furniture use rich suds of soap-flakes and warm water. Squeeze a soft cloth dry in this and wipe a small area at a time and wipe it dry as you work. Use a soft toothbrush on carved wood. Polish when dry.

Oiled wood such as teak should be cleaned with a soft, dry duster. Stains may be rubbed with a fast-drying oil such as teak oil. Oil should be applied sparingly once or twice a year. Put a few drops of oil on a cloth and rub it in. For a thorough cleaning or if the oil has made the wood too shiny, rub the wood with a cloth moistened with white spirit. Then apply a little teak oil. Rub the oil gently along the grain with fine sandpaper or steel wool. Wipe off excess oil and rub with a circular movement to get the oil into the pores of the wood. Throw away oily rags. They are combustible.

Most *kitchen tables* bought now are varnished or sealed. Don't put very hot things on them – they are only heat-resistant for teacups and things like that. These tables need only to be wiped down frequently with a damp cloth. Surfaces covered with laminate should also be wiped frequently. You can scrub them occasionally with hot water and detergent. You can use a paste cleaner if the surface is really filthy but don't use scouring powder or scouring pads. Unvarnished wood should be scrubbed along the grain. Wipe with a cloth wrung out in cold salt water. Wipe dry or the wood will become soft.

Wrought iron Either polish with a liquid wax which should prevent it from getting rusty, or treat it with a rust inhibitor and then paint it with a paint specially made for iron. If rusty spots *do* appear, rub them with steel wool and paraffin. If you're dealing with an old very rusty piece of wrought ironwork, soak the piece in paraffin for an hour or so and then rub with steel wool.

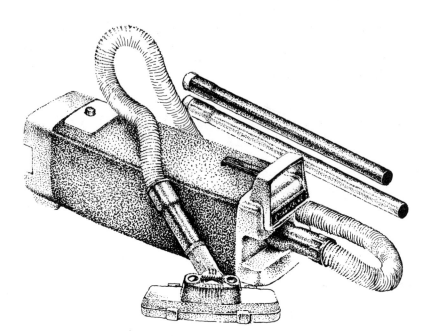

CHAPTER 10

CHOOSING CLEANING EQUIPMENT

What do you need in the way of implements to keep a house clean? The answer is, actually not much. Dirty homes are often untidy ones. It doesn't matter how many carpet sweepers you have, if you can't get at the floor, you won't be able to clean it.

However, there are certain basic things without which cleaning is really difficult. These I have listed plus some of the luxuries which really do make life easier. I've tried to give the pros and cons of the various types, or at least point out what variations are available.

With electrical equipment the choice is more complicated since there are the running costs to consider as well as the initial outlay and they do usually take up rather a lot of space and can be irritatingly noisy too.

The answer is to start off with the basics: broom, dustpan and brush, dusters, sponge mop and progress as you discover what you need.

Don't feel guilty about getting what you do need. A machine which really helps you and does the job better than you could or would, is worth its weight in gold. Equally one that is inefficient and bulky is a complete waste of money.

The choice is yours; here are some of the options.

WHAT TO LOOK FOR WHEN BUYING ELECTRICAL EQUIPMENT

Most large electrical equipment costs so much that you'll have to put up with your choice for some years, so choose carefully and take your time.

Dishwasher

A dishwasher usually runs off cold water and heats the water up. A small table-top model may use about 2.5 litres but a large machine will use about 5.5 litres for a 'normal' wash. The machine should be plumbed in unless it's a small, mobile one, for which you may need a tap adaptor and a longer hose.

The most expensive machines have rinse programmes, an intensive 'bio' programme for baked-on food and cooking-pans, and even a gentle programme for glasses. Others have a selection from these. The final rinse is always hot so that the water evaporates to leave the plates and other things dry. Some models may have an economy programme, said to save thirty per cent on costs and use less water.

Check that the interior is convenient for the particular things you want to wash. People who use a lot of glasses will need different spaces to those who use more cereal bowls.

Worktop models will wash up for two people; really big ones will take up to twelve place settings.

Washing-machines

You can still get simple washers which just agitate the water and have an electric mangle on top. They're cheaper in every way but limited.

The two main types to choose from are twin-tub or fully automatic. A twin-tub is cheaper to buy and also to run because the same water can be used for two loads; there's less to go wrong and they may spin-dry better and wash quicker. The major disadvantage of a twin-tub is that you do have to stay with the wash and move the clothes from one tub to the other.

When buying one, check that castors run smoothly and hoses are long enough to reach the taps. An extra drain hose will allow the spinner and washer to drain at the same time.

Fully automatic machines will wash, rinse, spin and turn themselves off without needing any attention once you've set the programme. All automatics have at least seven washing programmes – some as many as sixteen.

There are programmes to deal with anything from working overalls to very delicate clothes, even washable wool. They rinse better than twin-tubs and are less likely to crease clothes and may take a large load (9 lb compared with 6 lb, say). Spinning may not be quite as fast and therefore efficient as with a twin-tub. Most machines will take one and a half to two hours for a cotton wash and about half that time for synthetics.

You can get automatics that have an economy programme which uses about a third less water. Controls are best located on the front of the machine. To be fully automatic a machine should have dispensers, for washing powder, etc., for each stage of the programme, including fabric conditioners. The filter trap should be easy to get at and easy to clean.

Spin-driers

If your washing-machine has no spin-drier you might get a separate one. They are invaluable. The best ones get articles practically ready for ironing.

There are two types: those that empty by gravity into a bowl and those that pump water into the sink. Each takes about $2\frac{1}{2}$ kg (6 lb) of clothes. The faster the spin the better. A spin of 2000 r.p.m. is excellent. It should not be possible to open the lid when the drum is going faster than 60 r.p.m.

Irons

There are about fifty electric irons on the market in the U.K. There are three main types: dry, steam and spray.

Most irons have thermostats. The former H.L.C.C. code was changed recently to conform to the international 'dot' code (see page 28). Both are fairly easy to understand though the dots give fewer choices of settings.

A few irons have a 'very hot' (above 200°C) setting which you should use only on very damp cottons or linens. A cold or off setting is useful if you have to answer the phone or the front door while in the middle of ironing but I wouldn't want to use it with children or young animals who might start to play with the flex.

Weight varies from about $\frac{1}{2}$ kg to $1\frac{1}{2}$ kg (1.25 to 4 lb). Irons under about 1 kg (2 lb) are usually for use when travelling. Choose one that feels comfortable. It's temperature, moisture and a bit of pressure that take out creases – you don't need a heavy iron.

Narrow or fat is your choice. If you have lots of tucks and pleats to deal with then choose an iron with a slim point. If you're ironing sheets and pillowcases the squat ones will cover the area quicker. Grooves on either side of the point will make ironing round buttons easier.

Left-handed people should choose an iron with the flex attached to the top of the handle or where the flex can be moved from the right to the left side.

Sole plates may be of aluminium, stainless steel or coated with P.T.F.E. A few are still chrome-plated. Some steam irons have water gauges to show how much water is in the iron; their capacity varies from 175 to 225 ml (6 to 8 fl oz).

Steam irons are invaluable to those who do any delicate ironing, though even steam won't smooth out very dry, creased areas. Spray irons can send a stream of steam on to such areas and this does usually work.

Travel irons have drop-down handles to pack easily. Get an earthed model with three-core flex to be safe, and one with a voltage selector or you may not be able to use it abroad.

Ironing machines

For the expert, ironing machines are a quick and efficient way of dealing with a large wash. They are much more expensive to buy and quite a lot more expensive to run than ordinary irons. And you have to learn how to use them. They may be heavy, awkward to move and awkward to use. Flat irons seem to be easier to use than rotary ones.

Ironer press

An ironer press will get wrinkles out of trousers and maintain creases in wool and synthetic trousers. It won't set creases and won't cope well with jeans (but who needs to press jeans anyway?). An unnecessary and rather ugly luxury in my opinion.

Ironing-boards

Height is important. The iron handle should be about level with your elbow according to *Which?* magazine, February 1978. They said none of the ironing-boards they tested were high enough. Some boards are adjustable, usually with three different heights.

A really useful board will have quite a narrow tapered end which you can get skirts and dresses over. The cover should fit well and some covers (Milium and Nitex) have a heat-reflecting surface, usually silvery grey, but they don't seem to make much difference to the ironing.

Avoid asbestos iron-rests. Metal wire rests lift off or pull out from the end of the board but you can't stand the iron up well in them. Some boards have solid-metal iron-rests.

A sheet rail can be useful when ironing sheets, tablecloths, duvet covers, etc. It makes the board wide and stops things trailing on the floor.

A sleeve-board attachment is useful but not essential.

Vacuum cleaners

The original upright which beats-as-it-sweeps-as-it-cleans is still probably the most satisfactory for a fully carpeted house or flat. But cylinder cleaners may be more convenient for houses with a mixture of smooth floors and carpet. If you have a lot of vacuuming to do or live in a particularly dusty environment or where there are a lot of animal hairs, get one with a powerful motor. These usually have a variable suction control and may have an indicator to tell you when the bag's full. Many cleaners now have paper bags which makes emptying easier but, beware, if you can't get the bags you won't be able to use the machine because they can't be home-made. It is best to buy a large stock at a time and get more before you run out. Not all modern vacuum cleaners need bags of this kind.

Large circular cylinder cleaners, which look a bit like robots, may be rather bulky for most homes. They are often used by car windscreen replacement firms for sucking up bits of broken glass. Some will even suck up water. They are bulky, basic, powerful and not likely to go wrong but noisy.

WHAT TO LOOK FOR WHEN BUYING HAND TOOLS

Brooms and brushes

Brooms with stiff bristles are best for out of doors or if you have no vacuum cleaner and have to brush matting or rugs. Soft-bristled brushes are better for smooth floors. Handles may be painted wood or plastic-coated steel. A broom with a hook on the end can be hung up for storage.

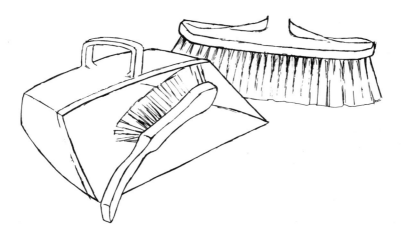

Hand brushes may also be soft or hard bristled. You may find it useful to have one of each. Horsehair is good for hard floors and so is a mixture of natural fibres and nylon; a mixture of natural fibres and polypropylene is good for carpets.

A lavatory brush usually has its own holder. There are various different shapes. Find one that seems to get into the corners of your particular loo.

Dustpans and brushes are often made to slot together for storage which is an advantage.

For people who find it difficult to bend, there are long handled dustpans and brushes. If you have difficulty getting these locally write to Sabco Hardware (U.K.) Ltd, Colville Road, Kelvin Industrial Estate, East Kilbride, Glasgow G75 oRP who make one version.

There are various special brushes for specific uses: Venetian-blind brushes to fit between the slats, drain brushes on long wire, radiator brushes, flue brushes, scrubbing brushes, shoe brushes, carpet brushes, bottle brushes. Cobweb brushes may have telescopic handles which make storage easier.

Carpet sweepers

Most modern carpet sweepers are very efficient. The most sophisticated will get close to a smooth carpet or rise a bit higher for long-pile carpets, and have little brushes at the side to get close to the walls. The pans slot out easily for emptying and so do the brushes for cleaning. The very small ones are not so satisfactory except for a tiny area. You can get replacement brushes, handles and tyres. Get one with a handle that swings flat for sweeping under sofas and sideboards.

Carpet and upholstery shampooers

These vary from little hand-held hand operated rollers to big electrically operated ones that look like upright vacuum cleaners.

Obviously for a small area you won't need a big shampoo applicator. But if you do have a large or very dirty carpet a big one might be a wise investment, but you can hire them from Home Service hire shops (look in the Yellow Pages). Replacement parts include the foam brush, handle, shampoo bag, etc.

Mops

The simplest mop is one with a cotton head for dry mopping and shaking out of the window. One such has a flexible handle which allows you to mop in the most awkward places. But there are dozens of squeeze mops for washing floors. You can get a mop with a shaggy cotton head and its own bucket and a special fitting halfway up the handle into which you draw the mop to squeeze it. I've found this very effective. Another draws up into a sacking bag which squeezes the water out when you twist it.

Sponge mops are less robust than the cotton-headed ones and unless your floor is very smooth will soon wear out. Replacement sponge heads are easy to fit, however. There are various different methods of squeezing them. Find the one that suits you. Some of them need stronger muscles to squeeze than others.

Window-cleaning implements

A chamois leather is good and all you really need. But a squeegee on a handle does make life easier, especially when cleaning windows above the ground floor. You can get squeegees with long, short, telescopic or specially curved handles. A squeegee is a flat angled head with a strip of rubber at one end and a sponge on the other. Wash the window with the sponge and scrape the dirt and water off with the rubber strip. Simple and effective.

Magnetic cleaners clean the outside of the window while you clean the inside. They are much more difficult to use effectively than you might think.

Cloths and dusters

There's a lot to be said for using old sheets, vests and underpants as cloths. They cost nothing, are washable and it's a sort or recycling which must be good! Don't use wool except for buffing up furniture. Don't use synthetic fabrics, which don't absorb water well. Cotton and linen are good. Silk is good for glass because it leaves no linty bits.

Kitchen paper is very convenient for mopping up and polishing but expensive.

Most disposable type cloths are made of viscose. They can be washed and used again quite often before they have to be thrown away. They are absorbent and don't leave bits of lint.

There is also a synthetic chamois which can be used for glass, mirrors, windows, etc., and a larger version for car cleaning.

There are a whole lot of small products which might fit into this category: sponges; thin sponge cloths; wash and wax sponges for car washing.

Feather dusters are excellent for homes with a lot of books and ornaments you don't want to take down every time you dust. They look decorative when not in use, too, which is more than can be said for most cloths.

There are tacky cloths for cleaning walls before repainting. You'll find them in D.I.Y. shops rather than hardware stores. They pick up all dirt and fluff and give a smooth surface for painting.

Scourers

There are so many scouring pads it's difficult to list them all. Very fine steel wool can be used safely on aluminium pans; steel-wool pads impregnated with detergent will not rust so quickly and will dissolve grease while scouring.

Nylon scourers are less abrasive and safer for enamel pans and the tops of cookers. Small fat sponges with a scouring surface one side are also good for pans and cooker tops and even cleaning painted kitchen walls if they're greasy and difficult to get clean with a sponge mop.

Always use the less abrasive scourers first and only use the harsh ones if you have to.

CHAPTER 11

GLOSSARY AND GUIDE

This glossary was not easy to compile. There seems to be no obvious source of information on the chemicals and techniques used in household cleaning. Very few chemicals are mentioned by name on branded products, as though people using them would be too dim to understand. Yet it is important that we should know what we are using in our homes. Some of these products are toxic, others will badly burn the skin and clothes. Many chemicals are dangerous when used in conjunction with others and may explode if used together. The more we know about the products we use, the more freedom of choice do we have and the safer we shall be.

I have therefore included all the substances likely to be used during normal home cleaning work. Even the really dangerous ones like carbon tetrachloride – so that people will know why something that until a few years ago was thought to be perfectly safe, should on no account be used any more.

The glossary includes substances and techniques and also explains such things as 'acid' and 'alkali' in terms of detergents and what a 'neutral' detergent is.

Abrasive Anything rough or gritty used to rub out stains or raise the nap of a fabric (whiting; pumice; scourers; sandpapers, etc.).

Absorbent Any material which will soak up liquids, thus removing most of the stain at the same time. (Salt; fuller's earth; French chalk; talcum powder; silver sand, etc.)

Acetic acid A colourless liquid used to remove blue and to brighten coloured fabrics, by rinsing away alkaline residues caused by hard water calcium soap deposits which make coloured fabrics dull. Vinegar is a form of acetic acid. You can buy acetic acid from chemists. Dilute this by 1 tablespoon to a gallon of water. It will neutralize any alkali effects on silk and improve the lustre.

Acetone A very flammable solvent for animal and vegetable oils and for nail varnish. Useful paint remover. Remember that it will dissolve acetate fabrics.

Acid A substance that dissolves in water, producing a solution which tastes sour (though many acids are far too poisonous to taste) and turns litmus paper red. The acids used in cleaning (acetic acid, citric acid, etc.) are usually mild; they can counteract the colour change made by an alkali on a fabric. Others can be violently poisonous and corrosive. Acidity and alkalinity of water solutions are measured by a number from 0 to 14 called pH. Pure water is pH 7 or neutral. Acidity is represented by a pH below 7 (the lower the pH, the more acid). Alkalinity has a number above 7. The pH of solution for washing depends on the detergent used. Mild alkali soaps give a pH of 8 to 10 (causing them to sting the eye) while a soapless detergent can have a pH of almost 7 (neutral). Strong alkali wash powder may have a pH of 10 or 11 and is mainly used for white cotton and linen. Wool, silk, rayon and coloured fabrics require a pH between 7 and 8.

Air fresheners Won't make the room more hygienic but will counteract cat smells, bathroom smells, kitchen smells, etc. There are aerosols or those which refresh from a 'wick' and those which hang inside the lavatory and are activated whenever it is flushed. See also deodorants.

Alcohols Large class of organic chemicals of which the most important is ethanol, which is produced by yeast during the fermentation of sugar. A seventy per cent solution of ethanol in water is an excellent disinfectant. It is useful in cleaning because it dissolves grease and evaporates rapidly. Useful for cleaning glass. See Methylated Spirit, Surgical Spirit.

Alkalis 'Opposite' to acids. Soluble in water, their water solutions taste bitter, feel slippery and turn litmus paper blue. Alkalis neutralize acids, will rot animal and vegetable substances (wool and silk or rayon for instance), and will change colours in many dyes. See Ammonia, Caustic Soda and other soda compounds.

Ammonia A colourless gas with a pungent, penetrating odour. It dissolves readily in water to form ammonium hydroxide, which is an alkali and grease solvent. Always buy household ammonia which is ammonia solution specially prepared for domestic use; cloudy ammonia is household ammonia with a little soap added. *Do not use* it on silk, wool, aluminium or sisal. Use with care. Try not to get it on the skin or near the eyes. If you do, wash with plenty of cold water. Then you can use a dilute acid (10 g boric acid per 400 ml of water (one level teaspoon per pint) for the eyes; 25 ml of vinegar per 500 ml of water (one tablespoon per pint) for the skin) and more cold water. Wear gloves if you expect to get any on your hands.

Many metal polishes contain ammonium hydroxide which removes any metal oxides, especially of copper. Never smell the liquid and always handle with caution.

Amyl acetate A solvent for celluloid and cellulose paint. Used as a nail-varnish remover and an ingredient in paint removers. It should be safe on acetate fabrics but if the spilled lacquer contains acetone it may already have damaged the material. Smells of pear-drops. Highly flammable, toxic. Don't breathe the fumes and keep the windows open. Get it from chemists.

Anti-static rinse This is useful for treating man-made fibres which are inclined to cling to the body and even spark, especially in cold weather. From chemists and department stores.

Bathroom cleaners and kitchen cleaners There are various different kinds of cleaner: slightly abrasive cleaners, cream cleaners and liquid cleaners. If a cleaner is specified for either bathroom or kitchen use then probably the bathroom one is slightly acid and the kitchen one slightly alkali.

Bath-stain removers These are available in a sort of jelly form or as a liquid. They are caustic and should be left on the stain only as long as necessary to remove it and shouldn't be used too often. Follow the manufacturer's instructions. Available from hardware stores.

Beeswax Comes from honeycombs. White, waxy, solid. Sold in 1 oz blocks in chemists and hardware shops. Used for waxing cotton and silk thread, for making candles and in some furniture polishes. You can make your own furniture polish using 30 g (1 oz) of beeswax and 140 ml ($\frac{1}{4}$ pint) of turpentine. Scrape the beeswax into little bits and leave them to dissolve in the turpentine for several days. Then shake well and use.

Benzene (Used to be known as benzol, though that is also used as the name of a mixture of benzene and other hydrocarbons.) A mineral oil (hydrocarbon) obtained from coal tar. Used as a solvent for gums, resins and fats and as an ingredient in paint removers. It is highly flammable and has been found to be very toxic to the liver, so do not use it. Benzine is a different solvent used in dry-cleaning and usually obtained from petroleum.

Blacklead A black mineral also known as graphite or plumbago used in making pencils, blacking grates, etc. It is a natural crystalline form of carbon and has nothing to do with lead. In the old days one had to mix it with cold water, turpentine or vinegar to reduce it to a thick cream. Modern versions are available in tubes from hardware stores.

Bleaches Bleaching is a process of oxidization which takes the colour out of fabrics or materials. If used in too strong a solution bleaches will damage fabrics. Don't use bleach in a metal container. For specific bleaches see Chlorine Bleach, Hydrogen Peroxide, Sodium Perborate, and Sunlight. See also Chapter 4.

Blue or washing blue The effect of a trace of blue colour is to change a yellowish colour to pale grey – which makes it look whiter. The blue is usually a water-soluble dye. Blueing should not be necessary with properly washed garments. Many washing powders contain small amounts of blue anyway. However, if you do think your wash would benefit there are cheap powder blues and liquid blues available from supermarkets.

Borax An alkali mineral salt. White crystalline, slightly soluble in water. Used as a water softener for laundry, bath and shampoos and as an antiseptic. It loosens dirt and grease and retards the growth of many moulds and bacteria.

Bran The inner husks of corn sifted from flour. Used as an absorbent and a dry shampoo for fur coats and hats, etc. (See page 40.)

Builders Builders are substances added to bar soap, soap powders and laundry soaps to increase cleaning efficiency. They include sodium carbonate, borax, sodium silicate and sodium phosphates. Soaps with these additives are 'built' soaps and should not be used for washing the face or hands or for washing delicate fabrics.

Calgon Trade name for a water softener that is essentially a complex phosphate of sodium. Follow directions on the packet. From chemists. (See also Sodium Sesquicarbonate.)

Carbolic acid (phenol) A weak acid and a powerful disinfectant. Used in general disinfectants for cleaning floors, drains and W.C.s, and in timber preservatives. Cresols are similar. The efficiency of a disinfectant is measured against phenol which is used as a standard comparison.

Carbon tetrachloride A derivative of mineral oil. It is not flammable and used to be used as a grease solvent for dry-cleaning. It is extremely poisonous and should not be used. There are many solvents less dangerous and just as efficient. If you *do* have any lying around at home, don't pour it down the drain but take it back to the chemist and ask him to get rid of it for you. Proprietary spot removers bought some time ago may contain carbon tetrachloride. These same brands now use other ingredients. If you are not sure how long you have had such a cleaner, get rid of it and buy a new one.

Carborundum Silicon carbide. An abrasive that is nearly as hard as diamond. From tool shops. It's uses are similar to emery paper.

Car-cleaning products
Damp-proofing aerosols Spray them on plugs, battery terminals, coil and under the distributor head cap to prevent electrical troubles in wet weather.
Polishes and waxes Different polishes seem to do better on different types of car finish. Most don't last as long as the manufacturers say they will.
Car-washing products You can wash your car with any mild household detergent and polish the car afterwards. Or you can use a wash-wax liquid. In fact to wash first and polish afterwards, though it sounds like harder work, is probably most effective. If a product has enough wax in it to improve the gloss it will leave smears of wax on the glass in the windscreen, mirrors, etc. Products are available in sachets or bottles but are cheaper by the bottle.
Chrome cleaners Research seems to indicate that chrome cleaners do a fairly good job but no better than detergents or polishes, though they may, by filling in nicks in the chrome, prevent rust better than other cleaners.
Colour restorers These consist of small abrasive particles suspended in a liquid designed to remove a thin surface layer of paint. You can also buy even more abrasive products called rubbing compounds. They improve the glossiness of dull paint but, of course, shouldn't be used too often or eventually you'll wear off all the paint.
Tar removers There are various specific tar-removing products for cars but you should find that petrol, engine cleaner and paintbrush cleaner should work just as well, so why buy them? Wash off as soon as possible and polish.
Engine cleaners Spray-on solvents which should make it easier to see what's going on under the bonnet.
Rust removers and inhibitors These products won't work miracles but will help enormously to prevent rust and to get rid of any that exists. Look for rust especially after a spell of cold weather when salt put on the roads may do a lot of damage to the car.
De-icers Sprays usually, which soften the ice on windscreens and near and side windows. Some have a scraper incorporated in the lid. Use these products sparingly or they make a sticky gunge which the windscreen wipers will have difficulty in removing.

Carnauba wax See Wax.

Carpet shampoos Form of foamy detergent which doesn't make the carpet too wet. Leave to dry to a powder then brush or vacuum off. May be put on with a special applicator. Upholstery shampoos are also available, with or without special applicators, which work on the same principle. Always follow the instructions. Available from department stores.

Castor oil Comes from the bean of the castor oil plant. It is a good leather conditioner, especially for polished leather. Clean the leather first. Apply a small amount of oil with a cotton-wool pad or the fingertips. Rub it in well and take off any surplus with a cloth or tissue.

Caustic soda (or lye or sodium hydrate) A strong alkali used for cleaning ovens and bad stains on baths and basins caused by the minerals in hard water. It can be bought as a jelly or as a stick cleaner or a liquid. Used in many lavatory cleaners and for unblocking drains. Do not use it for unblocking the kitchen sink, because it could combine with grease to form a hard soap which will block the drain completely. (Use washing-soda and boiling water.) When using caustic soda, wear rubber gloves, and follow the manufacturer's instructions carefully. Take care not to get it on your skin or near your eyes. If you do, wash it with lots of cold water. It will burn through cloth, enamel surfaces, bristle brushes, rubber gloves, and damage aluminium.

Charcoal A form of carbon which absorbs smells. A block of charcoal in the fridge will absorb the smells of fish and cheese, for example. Or you can buy special products which hold activated carbon, which works rather more efficiently. The carbon should be renewed every six months or so. (If you keep your food well sealed and covered and your refrigerator cleaned regularly you shouldn't need these products!)

Chlorine bleach Chlorine is a yellowish-green gas with a peculiar and suffocating odour. Sodium hypochlorite is a chlorine compound used in bleaching and disinfecting. Useful as a bleach for white cottons, linens and synthetics. Do not use it on silk, wool, mohair, leather, elastane or resin-treated fabrics.

Resin is used in some drip-dry fabrics and the fabric may turn yellow and will be weakened by bleach. You *can* use chlorine bleach in a weak solution on coloured linens and cottons to remove stains. Always test a sample of the fabric first and don't let the fabric stay in the bleach for too long. Even cotton and linen fibres will weaken in that case.

A mild solution of chlorine bleach would be 10 ml of liquid bleach to 300 ml of cool water (one teaspoonful to half a pint). A strong solution would be equal parts of liquid bleach and water.

Soak washable fabrics in mild bleach for five to fifteen minutes. Rinse thoroughly.

Chlorine bleach will remove many stains from baths, sinks, enamelware, tiles and woodwork. Use a solution of about 50 ml of bleach to 500 ml of water (two tablespoons to a pint). If the stain is obstinate, soak a pad of cotton wool in the bleach solution and leave it on the stain for five minutes or so.

If you use bleach as a lavatory cleaner *do not* use other cleaners at the same time. Chlorine and ammonia and other preparations used in lavatory cleaners produce a chemical action and a poisonous gas, which may make you very ill and even kill you.

Cleansing lotions (face) See Cosmetics.

Colour removers These remove colours from fabrics which you want to dye. Always test the remover on a small piece of cloth and don't mix it in a metal container. They are available from shops which sell dyes.

Cosmetics
Soap Use only very simple, pure soap preferably with no colour and no smell. The main additives found in soaps are deodorant chemicals and heavy perfumes. Both of these should be avoided but the deodorants are the worst. The most common deodorant additive, hexachlorophene, was recently found to have toxic effects and is now hardly used in Britain. Many deodorant additives

may produce a rash on the sensitive skin on your face and even hands. All soaps are basically made from the same materials so look for a soap that is white and unscented.

Cleansing lotions Above all, choose one that will rinse off easily. It is *very* important to get *all* the cleanser off, whether soap or lotion. Choosing a cleansing lotion is one of the most confusing things in the world. Don't believe a label which says a cleanser also acts as a moisturizer. You have to rinse off all the cleanser so how can it moisturize too? It is true they are less drying than soaps but that doesn't mean that they moisturize. Free-flowing face lotions are better than stiff, heavy creams. They spread more easily and evenly, and are much easier to rinse off.

Don't buy a cleanser with added medications, antiseptics, etc. As you have to wash the cleanser off, the medications won't stay on the skin long enough to do any good. Anyway, unless you have some special skin conditions, your face does not need antiseptic. You may even find you get a skin problem by being allergic to it. Never clean your skin more than twice a day and do it as quickly as possible. The water used for rinsing should always be lukewarm, never hot and you don't have to splash your face with cold water afterwards.

Moisturizers When you clean your face you inevitably remove some of the substances that keep the skin supple and healthy, the natural moisturizers and protectors which are secreted by the oil glands and rise by way of the pores to the surface of the skin. So you need to replace these natural moisturizers with something that will prevent moisture from escaping from the skin and contaminants from the air from getting at it. In other words a moisturizer is a sort of barrier cream. Moisturizers also lubricate the skin, making it look and feel better and making it much easier to put on make-up. Some women prefer to use a heavy moisturizing cream at night and a lighter one during the day. If you're going to be outside, in sunny, windy or very cold weather, you should use a heavy cream and renew it fairly often. Avoid coloured moisturizers made to act as make-up as well. Next to your skin you should only wear the purest, unadulterated film; the pigments used in coloured moisturizers often irritate sensitive skins. There's nothing wrong with coloured make-up at all, but wear it *over* your moisturizer.

All moisturizers contain oil or grease and any old oil will do as well as any other. So don't feel you're doing yourself any good by paying a lot of money for shark oil, mink or any other exotic oil.

Thinners Use a rough wet face-cloth if your skin is unblemished (and young). The cloth will remove the few excess surface cells that exist. Go over the whole face and the front of the neck using a circular motion for the forehead, chin and cheeks, and a horizontal or vertical motion for nose, sides of the face and neck. Don't rub too hard. Go on for about a minute and do it several times a week. Always cleanse before doing this.

Older skins need heavier thinning but less rough treatment. There are cosmetic products sold for this: sponges, brushes and other specially textured surfaces with all of which you use the face-cloth technique described above. Alternatively you can get almond meal, or a preparation of even-sized plastic particles in a base of cream or soap. Follow the manufacturer's instructions.

Chemical thinners are sometimes called clarifying lotions and should only be used by a professional. If you do want to use a chemical thinner buy one which contains salicylic acid or resorcin. Don't buy a medicated lotion unless the label tells you what's in it.

Gloves One of the most useful preventive measures for hands. But you must use them properly if you are not to do more harm than good. First take all your rings off before you put on working gloves. Don't wear gloves with linings. Linings hold dirt and sweat and can cause more problems than they prevent. The best thing is to wear slightly large rubber or plastic gloves. You can wear light cotton gloves inside them but if you are not that organized turn the gloves inside out, and wash and dry them before you wear them again. You can dry them over a wine or a milk bottle. Rolls of very thin throwaway gloves are useful.

Hand cream Older people often have dry skin, and the skin on the hands and feet is no exception. So rub hand cream into your hands every time you put your hands in water. The same cream will almost certainly do for your feet as well, which you should treat twice (or at least once) a day.

Cresols Derivatives of phenol (carbolic acid) found in coal tar. Powerful disinfectant. Used in lavatory cleaners and general disinfectants. An ingredient in the disinfectant Lysol.

Deodorants Household deodorants were used originally to cover up smells you didn't like with others you minded less. Modern deodorants, however, are often made actually to destroy smells by chemically reacting with them. Obviously these are especially useful in rooms which you can't air easily – for instance the W.C. There are solid deodorants which sit around letting out long-term deodorizing substances, or aerosols for squirting around when you need them and lavatory deodorizers which sit in the cistern or hang below the water line in the lavatory bowl itself, and disinfect and deodorize it every time the lavatory is flushed.

Body deodorants and anti-perspirants Anti-perspirants inhibit the perspiration and prevent clothes being stained and smelly. Deodorants simply stop the perspiration from smelling as it dries. As with most other toilet products, it's probably better to choose one with little or no added smell. After all, you're trying to cover up your own sweaty smell – the deodorant will counteract that chemically and the synthetic smell may clash with your perfume and may irritate the skin.

Descaling fluids For removing 'fur' or scale caused by minerals in hard water. Kettles, hot-water tanks, steam irons and water pipes are all likely to get furred up if you live in a hard-water area. Proprietary descalers are available from hardware stores. Follow the instructions carefully. Some descalers can be used on their own, others have to be used with household ammonia.

It is not necessary to buy a special preparation, though. One tablespoonful of borax to a kettleful of water will do the trick and so will a water softener such as Calgon or sodium sesquicarbonate. Boil the water up. Leave to cool and then rinse. You may have to repeat this.

Methods of preventing scale include putting a marble in the kettle or a piece of loofah or little wire-mesh balls from hardware shops. I have never found these to work satisfactorily.

Detergents The word detergent is used to describe a substance that cleans surfaces or removes dirt. However, for the purposes of this book I am taking the word to mean synthetic detergents as opposed to soap, abrasives, solvents, etc.

Soapless detergents, which I am calling detergents, are synthetic substances available in various versions for cleaning around the house and for laundry and dishwashing. The first ones were made with vegetable oils but since they are valuable as food, most detergents are now made from petroleum by-products such as benzene, naphthalene and alkane gases.

Additives (or builders) of various kinds are included to make the powders clean better and to prevent dirt being redeposited on the fibre. Perfumes and whitening agents are also included.

Liquid detergents are solutions of concentrated detergent diluted with water. Salt is added to make it easier to work with.

An important feature of detergents is their degree of alkalinity. For most cleaning needs, a neutral detergent is used as this does little damage to surfaces or skin but the higher the pH value (see page 223) of a detergent, the better it is at removing dirt. Most household detergents are neutral.

Because of the huge range of materials and methods used to make detergents they can be varied to do any number of household jobs. They dissolve easily in hot or cold water, are effective in hard water without the use of water softeners. They do not create scum and don't leave a film on washed surfaces or in bowls or buckets.

Laundry detergents are in two main types: light duty or heavy duty. Light-duty alkane-free detergents should be used on delicate or brightly coloured fabrics, silks and wools. But they are not strong enough for very dirty articles.

Heavy-duty detergents are the ones with most of the additives. Some produce a lot of suds, some practically none. Suds are not necessary for a good wash. Front-loading washing-machines must have a low-sudsing variety, however, or the suds will interfere with the washing action and will froth all over the room.

Cold-water detergents are available for washing synthetic garments and durable-press finishes.

When using detergent for stain removal use the liquid kind.

Biological (enzyme) detergents can be used to remove protein stains (blood for instance). Very hot water will prevent the enzyme reaction and so will chlorine.

The enzymes need time to work and it's best to use this sort of detergent as a pre-soak treatment. Dissolve the detergent in warm water and leave for twelve hours or so. Then rinse and wash as normal. For immediate laundering, the enzymes won't have time to work and it would be cheaper to use an ordinary detergent. There is a school of thought which believes the benefits from enzyme detergents are small and that soaking in any detergent would be as effective. Do not use them in front-loading or 'suds-sensitive' machines.

All detergents vary in strength, blueness etc. You will just have to experiment until you find the right amount to use of the one you choose. Too much detergent will eventually make white clothes greyish and coloured clothes dull, because most of these detergents have a blue colour (for whitening) and too much of that builds up to being more than white!

Here is a list of things you may expect to have in your washing detergent:

1. Dirt-suspending agent, made from cellulose which helps to stop the dirt settling back on to the fabric. It is included in most detergents and some soaps.

2. Builders (mainly phosphates) help to soften the water and remove dirt. Types and quantities vary between products.
3. Suds stabilizers, ensure that the suds indicate how much washing powder is left in the solution.
4. Metal protector, to prevent corrosion of aluminium.
5. Oxygen bleach (sodium perborate) to remove tea, coffee and fruit juice stains and add whiteness. It won't work at low temperatures so won't affect coloured clothes.
6. Enzymes (see above).
7. Fluorescent whitening agents; these only work properly on thoroughly clean fibres.
8. Colouring.
9. Perfume.

Washing-up liquids Don't use too much. They don't need to froth about all over the place to do their job properly. If you run out of detergent or soap for hand laundering you can use washing-up liquid. They may have ingredients added to 'stabilize lather' and make them 'mild to the hands'.

Obviously you should choose a detergent that is biodegradable, i.e. readily broken down in sewage works and natural waters. Since 1964 all leading soapless detergents (and soaps) in Britain have been biodegradable.

Household detergents include powder ones for floors.

Specialized detergents are available for washing wool in cold water and for washing man-made fibres and foundation garments.

Disinfectants 'Anything that destroys the causes of infection' says my dictionary. Antiseptics, disinfectants and germicides are all produced to kill or check the growth of bacteria and/or moulds. Antiseptics are used in or on the human body; disinfectants are for surfaces not on the body, and a germicide is any material that kills bacteria, mould or yeast.

The first disinfectants used in surgery were carbolic acid solution. Then cresols and phenols were found to be more effective, and in 1930 chloroxylenol was evolved which formed the basis of Dettol. Since then all sorts of new substances have been evolved.

The following are the main types of disinfectants used in houses today.

Chlorine bleaches (q.v.) are also disinfectant and chlorine is used for sterilizing water supplies. Quaternary and chlorine bleaches can be used in hot, warm or cold water. Store carefully in upright position. Wash away any spills with lots of water. If swallowed wash out mouth, give milk and get a doctor. If on skin, wash off and apply an oily ointment. If very bad get a doctor. If in eyes, apply oily eye drops. Get a doctor.

Hexachlorophene Used in toilet products, soaps, etc. but has been discovered to be potentially toxic and is scarcely used in Britain now.

Hydrogen peroxide Oxidizing bleach. Used for cleaning cuts and wounds and as a mouthwash. To be effective the disinfectant must come into direct contact with the organism so any layers of dirt or grease must be removed.

Phenol, cresol, chloroxylenol Used in general disinfectants for cleaning floors, surfaces, drains, W.C.s and for timber preservation. If spilled, wash away with water. If swallowed, get a doctor. If spilled on to skin, wash off with soap and water. Put on oily ointment. Eyes: wash out with water followed by oily eye drops. Get a doctor.

Quaternary ammonium compounds These are bactericides, used in disinfectants. They are non-toxic and can safely be used on clothes, bedclothes, dishes.

Triethylene glycol Used in antiseptic air sprays or purifiers.

Dyes and dye products Dyeing isn't just dyeing. There are a number of different dyes for different purposes and your dyeing will be much more satisfactory if you choose the right one and follow the instructions.

Multi-purpose dyes are for use in hot water. They will dye smallish articles:

dresses, shirts, beads, satin bags and shoes, scarves, tights, lampshades, cushion covers and dried flowers. For natural fabrics and most synthetics.

For large items there is a special dye which washes and dyes at the same time so that you can dye bedspreads, curtains, sheets, etc., in the washing-machine. It's a blend of dye powder and detergent. For use on natural fabrics and most synthetics.

Instant fabric dyes are for use in hot water. Use one bottle to 500 g (one pound) of fabric if you want a deep colour. This dye is good for nylon shirts and blouses, socks and tights, fabric gloves. Boiling is necessary if you want really bright, deep colours.

Cold dyes are for use in cold water. For each dyeing session you will need the cold dye itself plus washing-soda and salt. This dye is good for things you wash often: sheets, tablecloths, towels, T-shirts, cotton pyjamas and nighties.

If you are dyeing a coloured garment you may have to use a colour and stain remover before you dye. Any article that is faded or streaky must be stripped before re-dyeing or you won't get even results. Colour and stain remover will remove most colour unless a fabric is fast-dyed. You can use it on nylon, cotton, linen, wool, viscose and acetate.

Carpet dyes are available for use on wool, nylon, Evlan and mixtures of these and even some mixtures like Courtelle. But don't attempt to dye cotton, acrylic carpets or those with foam rubber backing.

There is a white dye for restoring whiteness to nylon, wool, cotton, linen, silk, acetate, viscose, and a special whitener for net curtain.

Leather dyes or paints are available in gorgeous colours. These are suitable for shoes, bags, belts, watch straps and luggage. You must first treat the leather with a special conditioner. These are available from shoe shops, shoe repair shops and department stores. Suede dyes are available in the same colours, first clean the suede with suede and brushed pigskin cleaner.

For more details, see Chapter 5.

Emery A mixture of aluminium and iron oxides used as an abrasive. Grey granules in varying degrees of fineness used for polishing metals and hard stones. Emery cloth and paper can be bought at hardware stores and D.I.Y. shops.

Enzymes See Detergents.

Ether Solvent. Dissolves animal oils and fats. Not recommended for general use. Highly flammable.

Ethyl alcohol Another name for ethanol. See Alcohols.

Fabric conditioners Sometimes called fabric softeners or fabric retexturizers. They are used in the rinsing water and make textiles soft and fluffy, less likely to crease and help to reduce static electricity. They have to be used each time you wash the article.

Floor polishes There are two kinds of polish for floors. Wax-based polishes and resin-emulsion polishes. Wax is available in cream or liquid form. There are also brick-red wax polishes for tiled floors or steps.

Wash-and-wax emulsions are usually dry bright polishes to which a detergent has been added. There is no build-up of wax, as with some other wax polishes, so the floor won't become dangerously slippery.

Fluorocarbon Wide range of useful synthetic chemicals. Some are used as dry-cleaning solvents which boil at a low temperature and are good for delicate fabrics. P.T.F.E. (q.v.) is another fluorocarbon.

French chalk Soapstone or steatite, a compact kind of talc with a soapy feel. Tailors use it to mark cloth. Powdered French chalk can be used as an absorbent for soaking up fresh grease stains from fabrics. It is quite harmless to all fabrics and will not leave a mark. From chemists.

Fuller's earth A clay mineral used as an absorbent. It is used mainly to remove grease from unwashable fabrics such as coloured art needlework and suede jackets. You can safely use it on old fur coats, hats and fox collars too.

Furniture polishes Blends of waxes, spirit solvents and often silicones, which make the polish easier to apply and give more resistance to heat and moisture. Available in cream, wax, liquid or aerosol form. For polished wood furniture use a good wax polish.

Sealed wood does not need to be polished. Teak can be cleaned with a teak oil or cream which leaves the wood with a matt finish.

Hair shampoos Opinions differ about shampoos as they do about anything in the beauty business. Some experts recommend baby shampoos. Others say baby shampoos are made for babies. The best thing is to try various shampoos until you find one your hair seems to thrive with. Then stick to it. Some experts scoff at herbal shampoos. If the product really is made of herbs and not just synthetically treated to smell like them, they certainly won't do any harm and do seem to have a soothing effect.

Conditioners and hair dressings containing protein attach themselves to the hair surface of each hair which gives the impression that the hair is thicker than it actually is. Obviously these are useful for people with thinning hair. It will also help to protect the hair from the effects of bleaches and colourings which may make your hair more brittle.

Hexachlorophone A disinfectant/ deodorant used until recently in soaps and ointments. It was found to have toxic effects and is now hardly used in British products.

Hydrochloric acid A colourless liquid with a strong smell. A solution of hydrochloric acid in water is called muriatic acid and is used to clean down new bricks and tiles. The solution is dangerous, will damage skin, woodwork and fabrics and should only be used by a professional. Also used to be known as spirits of salts.

Hydrogen peroxide A disinfectant and bleach (see Chapter 4). Used for cuts, wounds and mouthwash. A solution that is too strong or used for too long will attack any organic material, such as clothing fabric or human skin. So use carefully. It is sold at chemists in a dilute solution (usually in twenty times its own volume of water). When used as a laundry bleach on white articles you should dilute it further with water. Use one part peroxide to eight parts water (e.g., 50 ml to 4 litres, or 1 pint per gallon). If you want to use hydrogen peroxide as a stain remover on coloured fabrics, test a small piece first, especially on rayons or nylons.

If you want to remove a stain, rather than bleach the whole garment, apply peroxide with a medicine dropper or a squeezy bottle directly on to the stain, putting a pad of tissue underneath. Keep adding more bleach until the stain disappears. Never pour any peroxide back into the bottle. It is very susceptible to impurities.

Insecticides and pesticides Most household insecticides are made with D.D.T. or malathion. Both are highly toxic. Others, especially those for flying insects, are made with African pyrethrum. This insecticide was discovered by accident in Africa when it was noticed that dogs running through fields of pyrethrum flowers would lose all their fleas and ticks. These insecticides are made from the flowers of pyrethrum or from synthetic pyrethrum. They are not toxic to humans but care should be taken in their use all the same.

Insecticides are available in aerosol cans, for spraying into the air. These are mainly for flying insects. Others are residual sprays for spraying on to surfaces, and there are some in solid blocks. The two latter may stay effective for quite long periods.

All pesticides and insecticides and fly-killers should be used with caution. Never spray where there is uncovered food or drink, nor where pets (or their food) are. (Don't forget fish in the fish-tank.) Don't spray in rooms where there are babies or old people and make sure you get the right product for the particular insect you want to get rid of. Read the label on the can carefully and follow the directions.

Iodine A chemical element used as an antiseptic and to remove silver nitrate stains.

Iron mould See Rust Removers and Inhibitors.

Isopropyl alcohol A solvent sometimes used instead of methylated spirit for dissolving lacquer, varnish, French polish and removing ball-point pen marks.

Javelle water Solution of sodium hypochlorite in water. See Chloride Bleach.

Jeweller's rouge See Rouge.

Lanolin A yellow sticky wax obtained from sheep fleece. It is mainly a mixture of fatty acids, alcohols and cholesterol. It is used for skin creams, certain hair preparations and waterproofing wool. (See also Wax.) It is used as a conditioner for leather.

Laundry soil and stain remover There doesn't seem to be a useful snappy term for this sort of product. It is fairly new and consists of solvent and detergent in an aerosol can. Spray it on to stains about forty-five seconds before washing and it will loosen the dirt, which will then come out quite easily in the wash. It is useful for most foods and for dirty marks round neck and cuffs etc. Also for tar and grease stains. It is sold with rather unhelpful brand names such as Shout and Frend, which don't describe its function at all. But is is an invaluable aid to busy parents.

Lavatory cleaners Powder cleaners are acid, often based on sodium acid sulphate in crystalline form and these should never be used on any surface other than the lavatory pan as they are corrosive. The cleaner should be sprinkled on the sides of the pan and should be left as long as possible before flushing. Bleach is often used as a cheap cleaner and disinfectant for lavatory pans. Bleach can lose its effectiveness if you store it too long. Caustic soda is also used in lavatory cleaners. Never use one type of lavatory cleaner with another. The result may be explosive and/or toxic.

Lemon juice A mild acid which can be used to counteract alkali stains.

Lemon oil This is just paraffin oil (mineral oil) with a little oil of lemon in it (an essential oil from lemon grass).

Linseed oil This oil comes from common flax seeds and has practically no taste or smell. It is used for making oil paints and varnishes and furniture polishes. Boiled linseed oil is obtained by boiling rather than pressing the seeds, is darker in colour, and has a strong characteristic smell. Specify when you buy whether you want 'raw' or 'boiled' linseed oil. Get it from hardware shops or chemists. Highly flammable.

Liquid detergents See Detergents.

Lye Any strong alkali used for making soap and for various cleaning operations.

It is used in many lavatory cleaners and for unblocking drains. Common household lye is usually sodium hydroxide. It is extremely dangerous. It can cause severe external as well as internal poisoning. Never let your skin come into contact with it. It will burn through cloth, enamel surfaces, bristle brushes, rubber gloves and damage some metals including aluminium. Don't use it to unblock the kitchen sink, because it could combine with grease to form a hard soap which will block the drain completely. (Use washing-soda and boiling water or a plunger.)

When cleaning the lavatory with a product containing lye, never use another cleaning agent with it.

Lysol A very strong and poisonous disinfectant which is a solution of cresols in soap. In some countries the word is a trade mark.

Metal polishes Most metals will become corroded or tarnished in oxygen, water, acids, alkalis and certain chemical compounds like hydrogen sulphide. There are numerous proprietary polishes on the market. Make sure you use the right product for the metal.

Aluminium resists most corrosive agents except alkali, caustic soda and washing-soda. It rapidly corrodes if it contains iron as an impurity. A dessert-spoon of vinegar added to the water when you are boiling eggs, or puddings in tin foil, will prevent an aluminium pan from darkening. However, a tarnished aluminium pan can be cleaned by boiling one teaspoon of cream of tartar in a pint of water in the pan for a couple of minutes.

Brass and copper cooking utensils are coated inside with a layer of tin. Use a proprietary metal polish to deal with tarnishing caused by food acids.

Old brass or copper preserving pans should always be cleaned or relined professionally if you want to use them for food. Shops selling catering kitchen equipment or specialist brass and copper shops should be able to help.

Gold Use Goddard's Jewellery Cleaner.

Silver Goddard's Jewellery Cleaner; Goddard's Silver Dip; Long Term Silver Polish and Tarn-i-Shield have a long lasting effect. Keep silver polishes away from other metals. The cheapest silver cleaner is plate powder but you must mix it with meths, alcohol or water. The dip removes tarnish chemically; with the long-lasting polishes you use physical rubbing.

Stainless steel Mista Bright is a glass and metal polish suitable for use on stainless steel. From department stores or car accessory shops.

Methanol (methyl alcohol, wood alcohol) This is one of the things put into ethanol to make it undrinkable (methylated spirit).

Methylated spirit (or denatured spirits) Ethanol with additives including dye and methanol. Dissolves essential oils, castor oil, shellac and certain dyes, ball-point pen ink, iodine, grass stains and some medicines. Useful for cleaning mirrors and glass objects. Highly flammable, poisonous. From chemists and hardware shops.

Milton Bleach and disinfectant used especially for disinfecting nappies and babies' bottles. From chemists.

Mineral oil Name originally given to crude oil (petroleum) and later to a colourless or yellowish-white oil distilled from crude oil. The semi-solid form is Vaseline (petroleum jelly).

Moth-proofers Choose a suitable proprietary insecticide. There are anti-moth bags to hang on coat-hangers, crystals to put in chests and drawers, and aerosols. Sprays usually contain D.D.T. Naphthalene is an ill-smelling hydro-carbon and is used in the traditional moth-balls. They attract moisture and may liquefy. Paradichlorobenzene smells far less strong, can be bought in crystals which act faster and do not liquefy. Moth-proofing products are available from chemists and department stores.

Muriatic Acid See Hydrochloric Acid.

Naphtha Made from coal tar. Used for fuel and lighting, as a rubber solvent and a solvent for certain greasy stains and in some paints, varnishes and wax polishes. It is one of the things added to meths to make it undrinkable. It is available from chemists but don't use or store large quantities at home. If possible use it out of doors. It is highly flammable.

Napisan Specialized detergent for washing nappies. From chemists and domestic stores.

Neat's-foot oil An amber-coloured oil from the feet of cows and similar animals. It is an excellent leather conditioner and protector (but not cleaner). Use saddle soap first then rub the oil in with the finger tips. Don't use neat's-foot oil on shiny surfaces as it leaves a dull finish and is difficult to polish up afterwards. From chemists, shoe shops and hardware shops (and some haberdashery departments).

Neutral detergents See Detergents.

Neutralization Neutralization is used when washing clothes to remove acid or alkaline residues.

Acetic acid (or white vinegar) will rinse away alkaline residues caused by soap or the deposits left by soap reacting with calcium in hard water, which make coloured fabrics look dull. Ammonia rinses remove acidic residues after using sodium hypochlorite bleaches or after using an acid stain remover.

Oven cleaners Some ovens are self-cleaning – they can be heated up to a temperature which will burn off any food splashes. Others should be cleaned while still warm by wiping with a damp cloth, otherwise a caustic cleaner may be necessary. Caustic is very strongly alkaline. Wear gloves and don't let it touch any aluminium pans. You can get it from ironmongers, and general grocers or deparment stores. (See also Caustic Soda.)

Oxalic acid One of the strongest organic acids, found in wood sorrel (*Oxalis*) and in rhubarb leaves. It can be easily synthesized and is used for stain removal and cleaning brassware. It is also used as a bleach and stain remover especially for ink and rust stains. One teaspoon of oxalic crystals should be dissolved in half a pint of warm water. Make up in a glass or china dish as it will damage metal. Test before using on nylon and rayon. Rinse well with water. Wear protective gloves. Poisonous, so label clearly and keep out of children's reach. Available from chemists.

P.T.F.E. (Polytetrafluoroethylene) Used to coat frying-pans and saucepans, baking-tins, etc. with a non-stick surface which makes them easier to clean. Teflon and Fluon are similar products.

Paintbrush cleaners Generally speaking the thinner for a paint will be the best substance for cleaning the brushes. For cellulose paint or lacquers use cellulose cleaners or acetone. For emulsion paint use soap or detergent and water. For rubber paints use petrol. For oil paints, varnishes and enamels, use paraffin or turpentine. For shellac use white spirit.

Paraffins A group of hydrocarbons obtained from petroleum. The more complex paraffins are solids (paraffin wax) used in some furniture polishes, in cold creams and in hair preparations. Liquid paraffins (paraffin oil) are burned in paraffin stoves and can be useful for getting rid of rust from bicycle and motor-car parts, ancient screws, nuts and bolts, etc. Poisonous, flammable. From Ironmongers and some petrol stations.

Perchloroethylene Non-flammable cleaning fluid or solvent. Used by most professional dry-cleaners. The symbol (P) on the care label in a garment means it may be cleaned in perchloroethylene.

Peroxide See Hydrogen Peroxide.

Pesticides See Insecticides.

Petroleum jelly See Vaseline.

Phenol See Carbolic Acid.

Plate powder Contains whiting and jeweller's rouge. For cleaning silver and silver plate. From ironmongers. (See also Rouge.)

Polishes See individual polishes: car, floor, furniture, leather polishes, etc.

Potassium hydrogen oxalate See Salts of Lemon.

Pumice A frothy piece of lava from volcanoes. A pumice stone is grey and full of holes. It is used for smoothing or cleaning. Powdered pumice is also available and used as an abrasive. Many commercial scouring powders have pumice in them. My mother always kept a pumice stone in the bathroom for cleaning elbows and gardener's fingers.

Rainwater See Water.

Rotten-stone A decomposed siliceous limestone that has lost most of its calcareous matter. Used for polishing metals. Mixed with linseed oil it will get rid of white spots on polished wooden furniture. Apply lightly with a soft clean cloth along the grain of the wood.

Rouge Jeweller's rouge is a red powder made of ferric oxide. It is used for cleaning and polishing metals, especially silver, glass, gemstones, etc. Special silver-polishing cloths are often treated with rouge.

Rust removers and inhibitors Rust removers help to remove rust; rust inhibitors help to prevent it forming. Sometimes they are combined in one product.

Rust on clothes and fabrics can be treated with oxalic acid or a proprietary dye remover. Slight stains may come out with lemon juice (half a teaspoon of oxalic acid to half a pint of hot water). Don't use oxalic acid on silk or wool and test rayon or coloured fabrics first.

To get rust off kitchen utensils and pans use wire-wool pads.

For outdoor tools use a proprietary rust remover (available from car accessory shops or hardware shops). Follow directions carefully.

Bathroom rust stains can be removed with similar products. Badly stained baths, basins, lavatory or sinks may have to be treated with a special bath stain remover.

Saddle soap This is a special soap for cleaning leather. You can use it on all polished leathers and buff the leather up afterwards. Follow the instructions on the tin.

Salt Sodium chloride. Neutral. May be used as an absorbent for liquid stains on carpets. May be used as an absorbent, together with olive oil for white ring stains on polished wood furniture. May be used as an abrasive with oil for the legs after bathing.

Salts of lemon (Potassium hydrogen oxalate) Used as an iron stain remover. Poisonous. From chemists.

Scouring pads and powders Be careful when you use these because of course they do scratch. O.K. on already scratched sinks, on fireclay sinks, etc. There are several kinds and some are less rough than others. Always use the least rough you can. There are nylon scourers for enamel pans, glass etc.

Steel wool The soaped ones like Brillo are better because they don't go rusty, but are more expensive. Don't use them on stainless steel. Squares of woven nylon like Golden Fleece are very hard and resistant.

Silicones These are derived from the mineral silica. They resist water, electricity, weathering, chemicals and don't react to heat or cold. They are used in waterproofed clothing, barrier hand creams and in small amounts in many polishes, not just for protection but because they help the product to spread smoothly and easily over the surface. They are also included in metal polishes, on non-stick pans, baby lotions, hair dressing, lipsticks. Silicone cosmetics stay on better in water. You can get silicone sprays for coating oven walls, lids of electric frying-pans and so on.

Silver polish See Metal Polish.

Silver sand Clean, fine sand. Used as an absorbent and an abrasive. From ironmongers or domestic stores for small quantities; nurserymen or garden suppliers for sand-pit or fire-bucket quantities.

Soap Manufactured from animal fats, such as mutton fat or tallow, and olive or palm-kernel vegetable oils. The hot fats and oils are heated with water to produce fatty acids and glycerine. Caustic soda is added to the fatty acid to make soap.

'Builders' are often added to household bar soaps, soap powders and laundry soaps. They include sodium carbonate, borax, water-glass and sodium phosphates. Don't use such soaps for washing the body.

The best soap is the simplest, whitest, least scented.

Perfumes are usually added to toilet soaps and most soap powders and so are dyes. Antiseptics may also be included in certain toilet soaps but these are quite unnecessary for normal skins.

A soap is said to be neutral when there is a correct balance between fat and soda. Too much soap will spoil a wash.

Sodium A large family of compounds of sodium are used in the manufacture of washing products.

Sodium bicarbonate (bicarbonate of soda or baking-powder) White powder. Used as a mild alkali for laundry work. It will remove stains from china, glass, tiles, teeth and the refrigerator. You can wash jewellery in it. Non-poisonous. From chemists or supermarkets.

Sodium carbonate (washing-soda, soda-ash, sal soda) Crystalline powder or crystals. Medium alkali for laundry work. Water softener, varnish remover. Useful for cleaning and clearing drains. Do not use on aluminium, silk, wool, sisal, or vinyl flooring. Wear gloves or use a greasy hand cream. Available as crystals from chemists, ironmongers or supermarkets.

Sodium hydroxide or sodium hydrate (caustic soda or lye) It is a very strong alkali. It is used in the manufacture of soap, as a grease remover from ovens, sinks and drains and as a paint remover. Caustic soda is poisonous and can burn the skin badly. See Caustic Soda.

Sodium Hexametaphosphate (Calgon) A water softener. It is neutral, gentler than washing-soda and disssolves easily. From chemists and department stores. Not often found in supermarkets because it is expensive. (See Calgon.)

Sodium hypochlorite Also called Javelle water or Labarraque solution. Household bleach or chlorine bleach. It's made of washing-soda and chloride of lime with water. See Chlorine Bleach.

Sodium hyposulphite A colour remover useful for bleaching and stain removal.

Sodium perborate A soft bleach for all fabrics but don't use hot solution on heat-sensitive fabrics such as wool or silk or synthetics. When using proprietary sodium perborate preparations, follow the manufacturer's directions. Pure sodium perborate crystals can be bought from chemists. Use china or glass not metal containers to mix the bleach in and always test colours first.

For washable materials dissolve one or two tablespoons of the crystals in one pint of water as hot as the material will stand. Soak the stain for several hours as this bleach works slowly. If a fabric becomes yellowed by the solution sponge it well with acetic acid (white vinegar) and then rinse it.

Cottons and linens which need something more drastic can have sodium perborate sprinkled on the stain and boiling water poured over. This should be effective in a few minutes. Rinse thoroughly and repeat if necessary.

Non-washable materials may be sprinkled with sodium perborate and covered with a cotton-wool pad dampened with water. Use hot water when you can, lukewarm on heat-sensitive fabrics. Keep the pad damp until the stain has disappeared, which will take several hours. Then rinse.

Sodium sesquicarbonate A powdery alkaline water softener, a combination of bicarbonate of soda and washing-soda. Dissolves easily. More effective and milder than washing-soda. Cheaper than Calgon.

Sodium silicate See Water-glass.

Sodium thiosulphate (sodium hyposulphite, known to photographers as 'hypo') Can be used to remove chlorine and iodine stains. Can be used on all fibres. Won't hurt colours. From chemists and photographers' suppliers.

Trisodium phosphate Similar to washing-soda. Sold as T.S.P. in decorating shops for cleaning paint. There are various brand names. Use it to clean glazed and unglazed ceramic tiles and most paints. It will make enamel paint dull.

Solvent A substance used to dissolve another substance. In this book solvent means specifically a liquid which will dissolve the greasy dirt from fabrics. They include perchloroethylene, trichloroethylane and fluorocarbon, used in professional dry-cleaning machines. Also proprietary household spot removers.

Methylated spirit, trichloroethylene, perchloroethylene, acetone, amyl acetate, turpentine, isopropyl alcohol and ether are all solvents. (See under separate headings.)

General instructions for the use of solvents will be found in Chapter 4.

Water is the commonest solvent and should always be used immediately and before trying another. Water will dissolve mineral salts, carbohydrates, and certain proteins from foods forming soups, extracts and cordials.

Starch Usually made from cereals and used to stiffen fabrics and give them body. Starches used in laundry work include powders to be 'cooked' with water and aerosols sprayed on the fabric before ironing.

Stove polish (See also Blacklead.) For use on black metal ranges, woodburning stoves, grates, etc. Available in powder, liquid, paste, cake or stick form. The most convenient are in tubes.

Sunlight Acts as a bleaching agent for fabrics, wicker and ivory.

Surgical spirit Methylated spirit with small amounts of castor oil and oil of wintergreen (methyl salicylate). Used as a solvent. Flammable and toxic. From chemists.

Synthetic detergents See Detergents.

Talc A soft pliable, greasy, silvery white powdery mineral. Used for soothing skin powders and also as an absorbent. (See Absorbent.)

Teak oil A treatment for teak sometimes used instead of polish. From modern furniture shops, decorating shops, ironmongers.

Teepol The basis of many liquid detergents.

Toothpaste and tooth products Toothpastes with fluorine in them are recommended by many dentists as preventing caries better than those without. On the whole it is more important to clean the teeth correctly than to use a toothpaste! Though a paste will help a bit. Plaque revealer is something with a brightly coloured dye which will stick to the plaque on your teeth and give you an

indication where you need to clean your teeth with most care. These are available in liquid or tablet form.

Dental floss is a nylon thread which you use to slip between the teeth once a day to remove plaque an ordinary toothbrush will leave behind. Various brands are available. All from chemists. Denture cleaners are also available from chemists. Check with your dentist which he recommends.

Trichloroethane An excellent solvent, not flammable and not very toxic. Most of the proprietary grease-stain removers are made of this.

Trichloroethylene A non-flammable solvent. Used mainly for industrial metal-degreasing applications.

Tripoli Another name for rotten-stone (q.v.).

Turpentine A balsam made from pine trees. It is used as a solvent in some paints, varnishes and waxes. Always use real turpentine when specified as there is no real substitute. But white spirit will sometimes do and is certainly cheaper. Turpentine is flammable, toxic, dries up the hands. From chemists.

Upholstery shampoos See Detergents.

Vaseline Registered trademark for various products but usually taken to mean a specific petroleum jelly.

Vinegar A dilute, impure acetic acid made from beer, weak wine, etc. Often used in cleaning because it diminishes scum and film from soap. It is also often used in stain removal to counteract alkalis and restore dulled colours or colours altered by alkalis. When removing stains from fabrics use white vinegar.

Vinylan For washing up melamine and similar plastics. Don't use it with aluminium. From department stores or hardware shops.

Washing powders See Detergents.

Washing-soda Sodium carbonate. Also called soda-ash and sal soda. Crystalline powder or crystal. Medium alkali for laundry work. Water softener, varnish remover, drain cleaner and cleanser. Do not use on aluminium, silk, wool, sisal or vinyl. From chemists, ironmongers or some supermarkets.

Water Water is the commonest solvent. It's always worth treating a non-greasy stain with lots of clear water before trying other solvents. If water produces a lather which lasts five minutes when mixed with soap, it is called soft. Hard water won't lather easily with soap because of certain salts it has collected as it ran over rocks. Sixty-five per cent of water in Britain is hard and forth-five per cent is classified as very hard. (See Water-softeners.)

Much of our water has had fluoride

salts added to it to help strengthen teeth and prevent tooth decay.

Rainwater, if it falls through clean country air away from the sea, is very pure and very soft. Town rainwater contains suspended soot, dust and dissolved carbon dioxide, sulphur dioxide and oxides of nitrogen. Rainwater feels smooth to the hands and is good for hair washing and rinsing clothes. If you do live in a clean-air area, it might be worth having a rainwater butt to catch the rain from the gutters off the roof.

There are two sorts of hard water, temporary and permanent. Temporary hardness or alkaline hardness is caused by the soluble salts of calcium and magnesium carbonates which have got into the water by flowing over chalk or limestone. Solutions of bicarbonate are alkaline. Such water may be softened by boiling. A calcium and magnesium carbonate scale is formed which is what you find in your kettle.

Permanent hard or non-alkaline hard water contains calcium and magnesium sulphates dissolved from rocks. This cannot be removed by boiling. If you've got both kinds of hardness your water is totally hard.

Hard water forms a sort of curd with soap, giving a grey look to textiles and damaging the texture. It also appears as a tide line on the bath, and clings to hair and skin. Rinsing won't get rid of it. Vinegar or acetic acid may be used as an acid rinse.

Water-glass Sodium silicate. Well known as an egg preserver. Also used as a paint-stain remover. From ironmongers or chemists.

Water-softeners If your water is hard use soapless detergents rather than soap. Washing-soda, sodium hexametaphosphate (Calgon) or sodium sesquicarbonate are all suitable for softening permanently hard waters and the last two are ingredients in many laundry washing-powders and bath salts. Always make sure the powder is thoroughly dissolved before adding the clothes.

In the ion-exchange water-softening process or zeolite process the hard water is passed through a tank packed with natural or synthetic zeolite ion-exchange materials. The calcium or magnesium ions in the water exchange with sodium ions in the zeolite. The process continues until no more sodium ions remain. Periodically the used-up ion-exchange material is regenerated by flushing the water tank with a solution of sodium chloride which replaces calcium with sodium ions. This sort of water softener is fitted by specialist firms into the main water system where it comes into the house. In the older zeolite systems solutions of salt are added to the tank by hand every two weeks or so. Installing such a system is expensive but in areas with very hard water it may well be worth the expense because it will prevent the hot water cistern and pipes from 'furring up'. If they become very blocked they will work less efficiently and eventually have to be replaced which is expensive too.

Wax Natural waxes are hard non-greasy solids which do not leave grease marks on paper as other fats do. They are obtained from either plant or animal sources. Waxes are used in various ways for polishing and protecting furniture, cars, shoes, floors, etc. Waxes can also be synthetic waxes synthesized for use in polishing and waterproofing.

A wax polish covers a surface with a shiny, hard, transparent coat which will repel water. Wax polishes are available in liquid or paste form and often have silicones added.

Paste waxes are made of wax and white spirit. The spirit evaporates leaving a thin film of wax. Liquid waxes are thin creams of wax with an emulsifying agent and water. Silicones make these polishes spread more easily and help to make them more water-repellent.

Natural waxes include *carnauba*, which is very hard, made from the leaves of a Brazilian palm. It is used for furniture, floors, shoes, cars and for toughening other soft waxes.

Spermaceti A white, crystalline solid

made from sperm oil taken from the head of the sperm whale and not therefore recommended as the whale is an endangered species. It is used in polishes.

Lanolin A yellow sticky wax from sheep fleece. Used for skin creams and waterproofing wool.

White spirit A colourless solvent made from a mixture of mineral oils used as a thinner for paints, a general-purpose grease and stain remover and in the manufacture of polish. It helps the polish to spread but evaporates quickly leaving a hard smooth surface. It is flammable and toxic and will dry out the natural oils from your hands, so put on a greasy hand cream after using it. If you wear rubber gloves, wash them afterwards.

Whiting A very finely ground chalk, free from impurities, used as an abrasive and a colouring in cleaning powder, polishes, in putty and in whitewash. There are various grades: Spanish white; gilder's white used for polishing silver and Paris white which is the finest. From hardware stores.

Window-cleaning products Proprietary window cleaners are made from a water-miscible solvent to which a little synthetic detergent or alkali has been added with, occasionally, a fine abrasive. Cheaper to use is a mixture of equal parts of methylated spirit, paraffin and water or just water and vinegar or water and meths.

Water and detergent are effective too and if the windows are very dirty you can add 25 ml of ammonia per 500 ml (one tablespoon per pint).

Woolite and Adamite These are both proprietary cold-water detergents specially formulated for washing wool. Always follow the directions.

CHAPTER 12

INFORMATION SOURCES

CONSUMER PROTECTION

Consumer Advice Centres Listed in Yellow Pages.

Citizen's Advice Bureaux Local branches listed in telephone directories (but not in Yellow Pages).

Leaflet: *Launderers and Dry-Cleaners* (published by Office of Fair Trading in its 'For Your Protection' series). Available free from Consumer Advice Centres and Citizens Advice Bureaux.

Consumers' Association Publishers of 'Which?' magazine, 14 Buckingham Street, London WC2N 6DS.

GENERAL ADVICE ON LAUNDERING, FABRICS, ETC.

National Association of the Launderette Industry, 77 New Bond Street, London W1.

The Persil Advice Bureau, Lever House, 3 St James's Road, Kingston-upon-Thames, Surrey KT1 2BA. Mrs Mary Holiday will help on laundering problems.

International Wool Secretariat, 6 Carlton Gardens, London SW1. Have information on the care of wool, including carpets, and a list of shops selling woollen upholstery. Brochures on woollen upholstery and carpets, especially 'Caring for You Wool Carpets', free of charge on application.

British Man-Made Fibres Federation, 24 Buckingham Gate, London SW1E 6LB. Publish booklet 'Guide to Man-Made Fibres'. Single copy free of charge from above address. Send S.A.E.

Good Housekeeping Institute, National Magazine House, 72 Broadwick Street,

London WIV 2BP. Have leaflets on various aspects of laundering and cleaning: 'Floors and How To Care for Them', 'Choosing and Using Home Laundry Equipment and Products', 'G.H.I. Answers Questions About Fabrics', 'Out Damned Spot'. Send large S.A.E.

British Standards Institution, 2 Park Street, London WIA 2BS. Information on British Standards for textiles and clothing.

Dylon, Annette Stevens, Consumer Advice Bureau, Dylon International Ltd, Worsley Bridge Road, Lower Sydenham, London SE26 5HD.

Home Laundering Consultative Council, 24 Buckingham Gate, London SWIE 6LB. Advice on the Textile Care Labelling Code.

HOUSEHOLD CLEANING

Good Housekeeping Institute (Address above).

Kleen-E-Ze Ltd, Hanham, Bristol, BS15 3DY. Sell own products door-to-door only.

BODY

Disabled Living Foundation, 346 Kensington High Street, London W14. Will advise on equipment for the incontinent and the bedridden.

Elizabeth Arden, 20 New Bond Street, London W1. Face and beauty treatments for women.

Institute of Dental Surgery, 256 Grays Inn Road, London W1.

Society of Chiropodists, 8 Wimpole Street, London WC1.

SPECIALIST CLEANERS

Blinds

Clean Blinds Ltd, Tower Works, Broughton Street, London SW8. Venetian blinds. Collect, re-tape, re-install or just wash. Seventy-two hours.

Supply most makes of Venetian blinds, and vertical and Dutch blinds.

Lelliotts Ltd, 70 Broadwater Road, Worthing, West Sussex. Clean and repair blinds and awnings. Gale repair service.

Carpets

Carpet Cleaners Association, 97 Knighton Fields Road West, Leicester. Code of Practice. List of Members.

Permaclean (U.K.) Ltd, 103/5 Brighton Road, Coulsdon, Surrey.

Patent Steam Carpet Cleaning Co, Furmage Street, Wandsworth, London SW18 4DF.

Launamay Ltd, Head Office: 7a Lower Northam Road, Hedge End, Southampton, SO3 4FN. (Atherley Cleaners and Campbell Cleaners.) Water extraction or soap and brush methods. Will clean Persian and Oriental rugs for local companies. Silicone stain resistant finish available.

Anglo Persian Carpet Co (London) Ltd, 6 South Kensington Station Arcade, London SW7. Oriental carpet repairs. Cleaning by hand.

Servicemaster (G.B.) Ltd, Head Office: Little Square, Braintree, Essex. Domestic and contract cleaning. Look in Yellow Pages for nearest branch.

Clothes

Jeeves of Belgravia, 10 Pont Street, London SW1. Hand-finished dry-cleaning and valeting; shirt and fine linen service. (Also shoe repair service at the Snob Shop, 7 Pont Street, Belgravia, London SW1.)

Collins Cleaners Ltd, Head Office: 19 Edgware Road, Marble Arch, London W2. Deliveries. Shirts, valeting service. London area.

Curtains

Curtainmaster Ltd, 33 Wates Way, Mitcham, Surrey CR4 3HR. Curtains taken down, cleaned and brought back or cleaned on the spot.

Launamay Ltd, 7a Lower Northam Road, Hedge End, Southampton SO3 4FN. Trading as Atherley Cleaners and Campbell Cleaners. 'Softhold' curtain cleaning. Curtains up to 5 m (15 feet) high. Fluorocarbon solvent. Flame-proofing service.

Starcraft Cleaners Ltd, 394 Finchley Road, London NW2 2HR. Will reglaze cotton. Mail order.

Jeeves of Belgravia, 10 Pont Street, Belgravia, London SW1.

Collins Cleaners Ltd, Head Office: 19 Edgware Road, Marble Arch, London W2. London area.

Coit (U.K.) Ltd, Park Street Works, Latimer Place, Latimer Road, London W10. Curtains, carpets and upholstery cleaned on site. Estimates.

Leather, Suede and Fur

London Suede and Fur Cleaning Co., 402 Green Lanes, London N13. Postal service. Complete packaging service for customers.

Atherley Suede and Leather Cleaners, 74 Shirley High Street, Southampton SO1 3NE. Use Ledermeister process. Members of the A.B.L.C. Postal service.

Jeeves of Belgravia, 10 Pont Street, Belgravia, London SW1. Suede, leather and fur cleaning and restoration.

Upholstery

Collins Cleaners Ltd, Head Office: 19 Edgware Road, London W2. London area. Collected, cleaned and delivered in forty-eight hours or cleaned in place.

Servicemaster (G.B.) Ltd, Head Office: Little Square, Braintree, Essex. Branches throughout Britain.

Index

References in *italics* are to page numbers in the Glossary.